PROUSTIAN PASSIONS

PROUSTIAN PASSIONS

The Uses of Self-Justification for
A la recherche du temps perdu

INGRID WASSENAAR

OXFORD
UNIVERSITY PRESS

OXFORD

UNIVERSITY PRESS

Great Clarendon Street, Oxford OX2 6DP

Oxford University Press is a department of the University of Oxford.
It furthers the University's objective of excellence in research, scholarship,
and education by publishing worldwide in

Oxford New York

Athens Auckland Bangkok Bogotá Buenos Aires Calcutta
Cape Town Chennai Dar es Salaam Delhi Florence Hong Kong Istanbul
Karachi Kuala Lumpur Madrid Melbourne Mexico City Mumbai
Nairobi Paris São Paulo Singapore Taipei Tokyo Toronto Warsaw

with associated companies in Berlin Ibadan

Oxford is a registered trade mark of Oxford University Press
in the UK and in certain other countries

Published in the United States
by Oxford University Press Inc., New York

© Ingrid Wassenaar 2000

The moral rights of the author have been asserted
Database right Oxford University Press (maker)

First published 2000

British Library Cataloguing in Publication Data

Data available

Library of Congress Cataloging in Publication Data

Data available
ISBN-0-19-816004-6

1 3 5 7 9 10 8 6 4 2

Typeset in Baskerville by
Cambrian Typesetters, Frimley, Surrey

Printed in Great Britain
on acid-free paper by
Biddles Ltd,
Guildford and King's Lynn

Preface

Proust was a writer who could never understand exactly how moral metamorphosis takes place: how a good thing becomes a bad thing if taken to excess, taken away, taken apart, or taken off. Certainly, this 'how' is not a question most people would ask in Proust's incredibly wide-ranging, intensely demanding, and self-critical way. This book is a detailed study of what we might term the ethical language of Proust's novel. It aims to point out the ways in which his moral discourse can be seen to connect up with current discussions in moral philosophy, with what is termed virtue ethics, for example.

Much writing on Proust is criticism of such quality as to seem to invalidate further analysis of *A la recherche du temps perdu*. What seemed to me missing from the field was, however, an attention to how Proust strives to thread together self-justification, indifference, and vulnerability in their manifold guises. These are difficult conceptual categories in themselves: hard to recognize, painful to feel or observe, impossible to contain by explanation, hypothesis, experience. We cannot even provide a watertight answer to the question of whether self-justification, indifference, and vulnerability should be parcelled up under moral or psychological areas of enquiry.

It might be tempting to smile indulgently and say immediately that they (whatever 'they' are) lie somewhere in between debates on morality and theories on psychology. But this was not rigorous enough for Proust. Although in our most relaxed moods 'in-betweenness' might serve as the good-natured conclusion to many disputes, under conditions of extreme duress, or threat, that very same *laisser-faire* is likely to undergo an abrupt switch. Our desire to judge by condemnation, or exclusion, if we are threatened, is not simply very strong, it *is* what Hobbes termed 'power'. We are hardly likely to judge our captors as serving our best interests if they are holding guns to our heads. In such a life-threatening situation, where power is being abused, our only available judgement is, precisely, that we have been disempowered. We are, on the other hand, not very likely to think beyond appearances if appearances comfort us. If we are continually reassured by praise, prizes, or pleasure that our actions are viable, we will continue to perform them, and pass few negative judgements about them. Judgement, especially of a negative, punitive sort, is provoked by need.

Weighing up the pros and cons of particular situations, general principles, loves, losses, or investments requires objects to decide upon, even if those objects are our own subjectivity. And here we come to the substance of this book. When the objects we need to judge are wholly internal, when they are characteristics, memories, passions, or abstract reflections which need accounting for, and when we produce that accountancy pre-emptively, without being prompted for it, what we express is termed self-justification. Very often, when we make this kind of vulnerable disclosure in indifferent or hostile contexts, it precipitates either a direct rejection, or a competitive equivalent disclosure. When the observer can see no reason why the speaker is trying to prove herself, reassurance, indifference, or hostility arise as responses to the *observer's* sense of inadequacy. Firm grounds for judgements are hard to find under these sorts of condition.

This, then, is the difficult material which Proust tries to understand, submitting it to various psychological and moral tests. In turn, I have tried to pay close attention to the material workings of *A la recherche du temps perdu*, in all their provocative, and at times bewilderingly contradictory, splendour. Splendour often crumples up into misery, and this odd paradox flourishes everywhere Proust looks. I have tried to keep, for the most part, very low to the ground, and my guerrilla engagement with the text certainly demands patience from my readers. There are extensive discussions about parties, digressions, thin walls, the irritations of similarity, and the dubiousness of mourning. To see how these apparently unconnected subjects interlink, and hook up with far bigger questions about moral purpose, language, sexuality, and identity, I must beg perseverance with far less justification than could Proust. I hope, none the less, that this is a book which will appeal to readers who know *A la recherche* well, together with those who are in the process of getting to grips with Proust's pervasive and formidable brilliance.

At the end of the twentieth century, it is axiomatic to describe our epoch as individualistic, as privileging the subjective experience. There are different bandwagons to be climbed aboard whether one favours or abhors this privilege. Proust, emerging from a strong French tradition of first-person reflection, both philosophical and fictional, flourishing from the seventeenth century onwards, offers the late-twentieth-century reader an important variation on the theme of self-exploration. He has sought to incorporate the pleasures of self-analysis, of intellectual revelry or reverie, of creative self-absorption, into a major account of our existence as creatures with moral desires, in the form of an astonishingly complex narrative experiment. We have recognized Proust the narcissist, Proust the snob, and Proust the critical theorist. We still need to understand Proust the passionate modeller of ethical thought.

I.P.W.

Acknowledgements

I would like to thank the British Academy for funding this research, and St John's College, Oxford, for offering travel grants, together with intellectual stimulation and moral support during the preparation of the project. To the École Normale Supérieure in Paris, which not only offered the opportunity to act as Lectrice, but also hosts the ITEM Proust genetic criticism seminars, a debt of thanks is owed. I would like to thank St Anne's College, Oxford, whose Kathleen Bourne Junior Research Fellowship allowed me to put the finishing touches to the study. Finally, heartfelt thanks are due to Queen Mary and Westfield College. The kind support of colleagues there, during the tenure of a British Academy Postdoctoral Research Fellowship, ensured the safe delivery of this book.

There are no words that adequately express the thanks that are due to Professor Malcolm Bowie. It was an immense privilege to be supervised by him. I am deeply grateful to Terence Cave, Colin Davis, Christina Howells, Edward Hughes, Nicola Luckhurst, Michael Moriarty, and Jonathan Murphy for their commentary at vital moments. Sophie Goldsworthy, Frances Whistler, and Jane Robson provided steadfast, swift, and highly intelligent editorial support at OUP. I thank them profusely.

A great many people deserve my gratitude, for their willingness to discuss; for their patience, love, and support; for the practical help they gave me. I would like especially to thank Béatrice Dulck and Marianne Souchard, *pour Le Perche, qu'elles ont tendu*. I would also like to thank Elizabeth Barry, Jonathan Brown, Jenny Burns, Simon Christmas, Martin Crowley, Steven David, Robert Douglas-Fairhurst, William Fiennes, Daniel Ferrer, Eric Garcetti, Marie-Dominique Garnier, Christopher Gosnell, Elizabeth Guild, Selina Guinness, Gill Howie, Suzanne Keys, Barney Loehnis, Joanna Macleod, Monica

x   *Acknowledgements*

Martinat, Cormac Newark, Tom Parker, Katie Roden, Nigel Saint, Faith Salie, Julie Schneider, Genevieve Shepherd, Robert Smith, Peter Snowdon, Miriam Ticktin, Craig Turk, and Julia Waters.

This study is for Henk, Paula, and Pierre.

Contents

Notes on References and Abbreviations

I have used the Pléiade edition of *A la recherche du temps perdu*, ed. J.-Y. Tadié and others, 4 vols. (Gallimard, Bibliothèque de la Pléiade, 1987–9). References in my text are by volume (roman numerals) and page number (arabic numerals), followed by 'tr.', then volume and page references to *In Search of Lost Time*, 6 vols. (London: Chatto & Windus, 1992), tr. C. K. Scott Moncrieff and Terence Kilmartin, rev. D. J. Enright.

Unless otherwise stated, the place of publication for works in French is Paris.

Corr.   *Correspondance de Marcel Proust (1880–1922)*, ed. P. Kolb, 21 vols. (Plon, 1970–93).

CSB   *Contre Sainte-Beuve* précédé de *Pastiches et mélanges* et suivi de *Essais et articles*, ed. Pierre Clarac and Yves Sandre (Gallimard, Bibliothèque de la Pléiade, 1971).

JS   *Jean Santeuil* précédé de *Les Plaisirs et les jours*, ed. Pierre Clarac and Yves Sandre (Gallimard, Bibliothèque de la Pléiade, 1971).

MLN   *Modern Language Notes*

SE   *The Standard Edition of the Complete Psychological Works of Sigmund Freud*, tr. under the general editorship of James Strachey, 24 vols. (London: The Hogarth Press and the Institute of Psycho-Analysis, 1953–74).

YFS   *Yale French Studies*

Et en effet, comme ils n'assimilent pas ce qui dans l'art est vraiment nourricier, ils ont tout le temps besoin de joies artistiques, en proie à une boulimie qui ne les rassasie jamais.

(iv. 471; tr. vi. 250)

Introduction

Les 'quoique' sont toujours des 'parce que' méconnus.
(i. 430; tr. ii. 9)

I. AN ALLEGORICAL OPENING

The whole of *A la recherche du temps perdu* is a distension in pursuit of intention. When the adult Marcel recollects the impression he had had as a child of Giotto's Vices and Virtues, from the Arena chapel in Padua, he tells us how Envy's fat serpent 'remplit si complètement sa bouche grande ouverte' that 'l'attention de L'Envie—et la nôtre du même coup—tout entière concentrée sur l'action de ses lèvres, n'a guère de temps à donner à d'envieuses pensées' (i, 80; tr. i. 95). Hard to say whether the serpent is moving inwards or outwards, from this description. Hard also to say what Envy *is*. But the work of disgorging or being engorged with envy is surely strenuous and painful, and brings on an involuntary and empathetic imitation in those who look at it. The images of these allegories, among them the figures of Justice and Injustice, do not give the child much pleasure:

Malgré toute l'admiration que M. Swann professait pour ces figures de Giotto, je n'eus longtemps aucun plaisir à considérer dans notre salle d'études, où on avait accroché les copies qu'il m'en avait rapportées, . . . une Justice, dont le visage grisâtre et mesquinement régulier était celui-là même qui, à Combray, caractérisait certaines jolies bourgeoises pieuses et sèches que je voyais à la messe et dont plusieurs étaient enrôlées d'avance dans les milices de réserve de l'Injustice. (i, 80–1; tr. i. 95–6)

Envy has her serpent to contend with and so can be contained within the framework of her allegorical representation. Between Justice and Injustice, however, despite their graphic separation in the Scrovegni chapel, where they are painted opposite one another, there is, for the child Marcel, some kind of dangerous seepage. For, briefly superimposed upon the plan of the Italian chapel (which the narrator of *A la recherche* has not seen at this moment in the narrative) is the church of Saint-Hilaire. In the middle ground between two allegories, two chapels, and two narratorial voices, separated both temporally and spatially, there is the confusing opportunity for an agon. The young Marcel, overwritten by the mature Marcel, sees that tragic contest played out by teams who seem to keep changing sides: 'enrôlées d'avance dans les milices de réserve' are the Just who are rehearsing as understudies for the infinitely divisible role of Injustice.

Judith Shklar, in her brilliant essay *The Faces of Injustice*, describes Giotto's *Ingiustizia* and *La Giustizia*, for the purposes of her liberal political argument in favour of listening to victims. She says 'Injustice does not appear to suffer at all; he seems completely affectless' (p. 48). Of Justice, she tells us: 'Her face is benign. But apart from that it is expressionless, as one might expect of the impartiality appropriate to a personification of justice. We can certainly feel afraid of Injustice, but Justice radiates no emotional appeal' (p. 103). Separated by a chapel floor in Italy, by many pages of Shklar's reasoned argument against complacent models of justice that take the wrong-doer's part over the suffering victim's, Justice looks impassively on and Injustice looks impassively aside, as each performs their allotted role. These are modern allegories, a far cry from the Furies turned to Eumenides by Athena's persuasive words (and her silky-voiced threat of violence: 'No need of that, not here') as retributive revenge was displaced by distributive justice in Aeschylus' *Oresteia*.[1] The balanced opposition of Justice and Injustice is a lateral one, rather than the threatening imposition of a vertical hierarchy: they seem to offer a human rather than an ideal choice of moral actions. Yet their similarity lies in their indifference. And when later in his life the adult narrator of *A la recherche* meets 'des incarnations vraiment saintes de la charité active', he finds that 'elles avaient généralement un air allègre, positif, indifférent et brusque de chirurgien pressé'. The 'visage antipathique et sublime de la vraie bonté' is also indifferent (i, 81; tr. i. 97).

---

[1] Aeschylus, *The Oresteia: The Eumenides*, l. 839.

Justice is aloof, Injustice couldn't care less, and Goodness is a bossy matron. While we, Proust's pampered readers and Giotto's confident viewers, feel sure of being able to tell the difference between these three versions of indifference, we should perhaps remind ourselves that those telling differences only emerge through an act of interpretation. On the face of it, indifference will always look the same. Marcel the child's confusion over which of the *jolies bourgeoises* are batting for which moral team is not only a Combray question, reserved for the innocence of unpolluted, idealized childhood and its revivification in comforting cups of *tisane* (i. 47; tr. i. 55).[2] It is—or rather Proust is arguing it *should* be—a question that preoccupies and pervades the entire field of human experience. The question, and it is the governing question of this study, is how are we to judge self-justification?

2. CRITICS, PHILOSOPHERS, PSYCHOLOGISTS, AND WORDS

The terms in which I will put forward the answer, or the answers, to this question, as Proust experiments with them throughout his novel, rely almost entirely on intimate readings of the text. This book puts forward an important component of the Proustian cognitive and conceptual apparatus, which has not been analysed before, and the consequences of which show *A la recherche du temps perdu* to be an impressive contribution to ethical debate. My study sets out the intensive hermeneutic endeavour undertaken by Proust's narrator to push to its limits the possibilities of self-justification. Proust, we hardly need reminding, has chosen to write a first-person and retrospective fiction. He asks what judgement is, and how we arrive at our judgements, *by way of* the first-person voice. This reminder raises further questions about the approach I have taken to

---

[2] Vital as the *madeleine* moment is, I do not intend to dwell upon it in this study. Too many others have preceded me. Perhaps the most noteworthy of recent times is Serge Doubrovsky's psychoanalytic account, *La Place de la madeleine* (1974), which has done a great deal to direct psychoanalytic literary criticism away from 'psychobiography', and promoted, along with the profoundly important narratological work carried out by Gérard Genette, delicate attention to Proust's use of language.

what I have to say about *A la recherche du temps perdu*, which I will take a few moments to answer now.

The almost overwhelming difficulty facing Proust's account-givers and his readers alike is the sheer volume, not only of his own output, but of studies written about both man and novel, studies *upon* studies of these things. Seventy-five years after the death of a writer who has taken on the stature of a Shakespeare or a Dante as one of European literature's 'greats', so many brilliant novelists and critics have put forward the vital appraisals of *A la recherche* by now embedded as the fixed truths about this text: Wilson, Shattuck, Beckett, Bersani, Poulet . . . the list goes on.[3] To study the critical texts written about *A la recherche* is to realize with humility and amazement how well Proust's novel was read even in the fizz of publishing hype during and just after his lifetime. There is, because of all this interest in the novel, a Proust currency, a set of keywords which *mean* Proust: *madeleine, mère, grand-mère, jeunes filles,* jealousy, Elstir, Bergotte, Vinteuil, *mémoire involontaire,* Time, Swann. A secondary and biographical swathe: snob, social satirist, neurotic, homosexual, Dreyfus Affair, crowd around behind. What more remains to be said? To propose a *new* study of *A la recherche du temps perdu* seems like an act of wilful idiocy.

Yet, while every critic, of course, addresses the issue of Proust's choosing to write in the first person, therefore shifting the focus of his novel with explosive force into the subjective mode, no one seemed to be answering to my satisfaction a very basic question: was this a morally good or bad decision? Proust's novel is a vast, highly textured, minutely wrought exposition of what the world looks like from one point of view, a sophisticated, well-read, jealous, nervous, leisured point of view. That much is perfectly clear. But what of the fear, shuttled constantly between novelist and narrator, of boring a reader by going on at such length about one life? What of the strategies of persuasion by which a writer might try or expect to keep such a reader's interest, or make her believe the account worthwhile, honourable, true? How to make the balance work between

3 Edmund Wilson, *Axel's Castle* (1931); Roger Shattuck, *Proust's Binoculars* (1964); Samuel Beckett, *Proust* (1965); Leo Bersani, *Marcel Proust: The Fictions of Life and of Art* (1965); Georges Poulet, *L'Espace proustien* (2nd edn. 1982).

telling subjective and unverifiable truths, and allowing for counter-critique, contestation, rebuff, rejection? How much mileage might there be in a narrative strategy which sought to *take account* pre-emptively of all such counter-arguments: a supreme effort to work out a foolproof method of ensuring a reader's trust by accommodating all her suspicions, fears, and hostility into the very point of view she might reject?

This series of questions becomes more interesting with every further addition and permutation of it, for it raises difficult theoretical issues about the limits of answering questions about self-justification using the material of self-justification, along the lines of Alan Turing's notorious Halting Problem. If you ask a piece of self-justification such as 'but I didn't mean to hurt you', to justify itself, would you get an answer with a firm foundation, or a further piece of self-justification? One kind of answer would be 'I didn't mean to hurt you, I did x because I love you'. No firm foundation for truth or reliability is on offer, we must take on trust that the 'I' tells the truth, and either accept or reject the answer. The emphasis has been brought to bear upon the credibility of 'I' as a criterion for trustworthiness. Another kind of response, however, might be 'I knew you were going to ask me to justify my self-justification "but I didn't mean to hurt you", and so here, before you say anything else, are x further justifications of that statement'. Here, the emphasis has been shifted onto the *statement*, away from the 'I'. Straightaway we can see that acts of self-justification work hard to attribute and distribute intention, interpretation, and meaning-bearing emphasis to useful-looking parts of verbal utterances, in attempts to escape censure and judgement *through* apparent exposure. Attempts to confront and head off this self-justificatory work of redistribution will themselves cause further evasion, mobility, internal division, and multiplication: like chasing mercury droplets around a petri dish with a knife and fork.[4]

The answer to the moral problem of self-justification, if there

[4] Compare J. L. Austin's 'A Plea for Excuses', *Philosophical Papers* (1961). Austin points out that flaws in linguistic functioning show *how* that functioning takes place: 'the breakdowns signalized by . . . various excuses are of radically different kinds, affecting different parts or stages of the machinery, which the excuses consequently pick out and sort out for us' (p. 128).

is one, then, is clearly not going to come from Proust himself,
nor from his correspondence, nor from the testimony of any of
his friends, because we would not be able to bracket lies and
self-interest out of their 'answers'. Discovering how to judge
whether or not self-talk is justifiable, might, however, yet lie in
listening to the way in which that question itself is treated
within the confines of *A la recherche du temps perdu*, in hearing
how a series of different kinds of linguistic experiment is set up
to monitor either self-justification or its by-products in
language. Figuring the inquiring reader as a listener, of course,
might introduce its own problems, but we will deal with these as
we proceed, and should offer ourselves a dispensation from
worry about them ahead of time.

By the same token, no one ready-made critical methodology,
or interpretative toolkit, seemed to me mobile or dynamic
enough to generate a satisfactory answer about Proustian self-
justification. A feminist reading of *A la recherche*, for example,
while it would prove the undoubted misogyny in the novel,
would not necessarily be able to answer questions about *how*
judgements are made or should be made. In this book, theoretical concepts and methods have been considered and appropriated from a wide range of recent critical thinkers, without
allegiance being sworn to any. Reference has been made to
broadly structuralist and post-structuralist writers, to psycho-
analysis, to narratology, and to writers on Proust whose aims
have seemed, in the course of researching the concept of self-
justification, to offer a springboard to my own. Any single
explicit hermeneutic methodology (even if such an illusory
beast were to exist) applied *onto* the text of *A la recherche du temps
perdu* would sooner or later run up against its own formal
constraints, would, in discovering that which it had sought,
recover merely its own original premises. Self-justification
describes a special area of speech act typified by the attempt to
persuade a listener of the speaker's credibility. But such a definition takes no account of the variety of such speech acts, or
whether there are in fact important differences between them.
It also seems to rule out of account the very *subjectiveness*, the
messiness, of what it is to persuade, the arguments that might
ensue, the pain of neediness, of not being believed, the sheer
hard work that might go into finding watertight justifications

for dubious actions, and just how much self-justification might be going on in the world. So the desire itself (to find out more about the functioning of self-justification inside Proust's novel) is what should encourage us to listen flexibly to the workings of the text, to gather material for assessment, to be prepared to modify, or abandon experiments, or become very interested indeed in *why* certain kinds of experiment seem to throw up repetitious rather than different answers.

W. V. Quine's brilliant four-page essay, 'On Simple Theories of a Complex World', points out some 'causes for supposing that the simpler hypothesis stands the better chance of confirmation'.[5] He notes that if 'we encompass a set of data with a hypothesis involving the fewest possible parameters, and then are constrained by further experiment to add another parameter, we are likely to view the emendation not as a refutation of the first result but as a confirmation plus a refinement' (p. 245). This is not to be interpreted as a licence to produce only simple hypotheses, such as 'if the earth is flat then we might fall off its edge', but it does remind us to avoid putting all our own hypothetical parameters into one pre-emptive basket *before* hearing how Proust conducts his self-justificatory experiments.

The obvious drawback to this kind of adaptive, flexible, and dynamic methodology is its undoubted potential to wander down garden paths, or fall into drowning pools of doubt and curlicues of minute adjustment. Yet experimental research into the linguistic functioning of the *moi*, of the kind that Proust undertakes in *A la recherche du temps perdu*, positively demands this kind of scientific protocol, and we should not be afraid to work with the problems it will cause us.

I will be reading with an awareness that a first-person retrospective narrative implicitly seeks, in reconstructing a teleology which has already unfolded, to remember it, both in the sense of recalling a process, and that of putting a process back together. Blanchot reads this as Proust's search to experience a quasi-mystical simultaneity of different temporalities: 'certains épisodes ... semblent-ils vécus, à la fois, à des âges fort différents, vécus et revécus dans la simultanéité intermittente de toute une vie, non comme de purs moments, mais dans la

---

[5] See *The Ways of Paradox and Other Essays* (1966), 245.

densité mouvante du temps sphérique.'[6] This is the kind of
vision of Proust's writing which, to my mind, most unfortunately reinforces the oft-touted idea that Proustian subjectivity
is all about being bound up in a nostalgic contemplation of
personal past. It also runs the risk of nudging *A la recherche* into
the category of book in which other subjectivities count only for
the material they might offer an experience-hoarding introspective first-person consciousness. *A la recherche du temps perdu*
responds only partially to such a description. Nostalgia and
introspection have their part to play in the Proustian psyche.
But Proust himself does so much work with these aspects of
human cognitive functioning that, unless we are very careful,
even loving descriptions of his writing can come to sound like
apologies for it.

As commentators have been at pains to analyse, the
Proustian narratorial voice is itself composed of many, sometimes ambiguously differentiated, even conflicting agencies.[7] I
do not intend to repeat the work of that important analysis
here. Once we have seen and understood the elasticity and
mobility built into Proust's use of the narratorial convention, it
is enough to carry it with us as we read, and to be prepared at
times to signal instances of special relevance to points in hand
about self-justificatory activity. No work on Proust can entirely
avoid the question of who is speaking and when, but it should
not be allowed to take over all forms of argument about *A la
recherche*.

Sartre, in 1943, offered the following analysis of what is meant
by *caractère*, and used as an exemplary literary text Proust's *A la
recherche du temps perdu*. Sartre's brief comments brilliantly
summarize and orchestrate one of the central questions that
Proust experiments with in his work. I will quote Sartre's points
in full:

le caractère n'a d'existence distincte qu'à titre d'objet de connaissance pour autrui. La conscience ne connaît point son caractère—à
moins de se déterminer réflexivement à partir du point de vue de
l'autre—elle l'existe [*sic*] en pure indistinction, non thématiquement

---

[6] Maurice Blanchot, *Le Livre à venir* (1959), 32–3.
[7] See principally Marcel Muller, *Les Voix narratives dans la recherche du temps
perdu* (1983).

et non thétiquement, dans l'épreuve qu'elle fait de sa propre contin-
gence et dans la néantisation par quoi elle reconnaît et dépasse sa
facticité. C'est pourquoi la pure description introspective de soi ne
livre aucun caractère: le héros de Proust 'n'a pas' de caractère directe-
ment saisissable; il se livre d'abord, en tant qu'il est conscient de lui-
même, comme un ensemble de réactions générales et communes à
tous les hommes ('mécanismes' de la passion, des émotions, ordre
d'apparition des souvenirs, etc.), où chacun peut se reconnaître: c'est
que ces réactions appartiennent à la 'nature' générale du psychique.
Si nous arrivons (comme l'a tenté Abraham dans son livre sur Proust)
à déterminer le caractère du héros proustien (à propos par exemple
de sa faiblesse, de sa passivité, de la liaison singulière chez lui de
l'amour et de l'argent) c'est que nous interprétons les données
brutes: nous prenons sur elles un point de vue extérieur, nous les
comparons et nous tentons d'en dégager des relations permanentes et
objectives. Mais ceci nécessite un recul: tant que le lecteur, suivant
l'optique générale de la lecture, s'identifie au héros de roman, le
caractère de 'Marcel' lui échappe; mieux, il n'existe pas à ce niveau. Il
n'apparaît que si je brise la complicité qui m'unit à l'écrivain, que si je
considère le livre non plus comme un confident, mais comme une
confidence, mieux encore: comme un *document*. Ce caractère n'existe
donc que sur le plan du pour-autrui et c'est la raison pour laquelle les
maximes et les descriptions des 'moralistes', c'est-à-dire des auteurs
français qui ont entrepris une psychologie objective et sociale, ne se
recouvrent jamais avec l'expérience vécue du sujet.[8]

Marcel Muller quotes this passage, but his criticism of it, that
Sartre's comments are applicable to any first-person narrative,
and therefore miss the specificity of 'le véritable secret du *je*
proustien', itself misses Sartre's point.[9] What has been so corus-
catingly pinpointed is the agonizing fulcrum across which the
Proustian narrator—in all of his temporal manifestations,
moods, and agencies—and the reader of first-person confessional texts are delicately poised and interlocked. Character
appears only when complicity is broken, when reader–narrator
identificatory patterns and cycles and compulsions are undone,
when the narrator is seen no longer as everyman, but as a
particular, neurasthenic, possibly hysterical, would-be novelist.
Grateful as we must be to Muller for offering Proust criticism a
multipartite taxonomy formalizing the interconnections

[8] Jean-Paul Sartre, *L'Être et le néant* (1943), 398–9.
[9] *Les Voix narratives*, 15–16.

between, and independent statuses of, the narratorial selves
(*Héros, Narrateur, Sujet Intermédiaire, Protagoniste, Romancier,
Écrivain, Auteur, Homme, Signataire*), these terms seem to deprive
the first-person narrative of its relationships to external objects
and selves, whether in or beyond the confines of the text, and
it is upon these relationships and the kinds of processes they
inaugurate that my study focuses.

A retrospective first-person novel, as the narratologist Gérard
Genette so convincingly demonstrates, will both manipulate
and suffer from periodic attacks of prolepsis and paralepsis.[10]
Genette's tough-minded and careful attention to the workings
of Proust's narrative offer a sound methodological principle
informing the way in which I read, but my argument, in showing how self-justification works and is put to work, does not
attempt to construct a new narratology of *A la recherche*. The
main point I take from Genette's work is that great attention
must be paid, when studying works of confessional fiction, to
what we might term a rhetoric of reliability. A temptation is
automatically built into the reconstructive narrative enterprise
to produce an improved and stylized version of the lost original
(experience, or *histoire*). Like the genre of autobiography, first-
person retrospective fiction strives to tell the truth of subjective
experience, but yearns for the wider claim that such truth
should be a universal truth. Augustine's *Confessions*, Rousseau's
similarly titled *Les Confessions*, Constant's *Adolphe*, Fromentin's
Dominique, Gide's *récits*: all are characterized by, and to be
included in an intertextual history of, first person retrospective
fiction, confession narratives, and autobiography.[11] I deliber-

---

[10] See Gérard Genette, *Figures III* (1972). For 'prolepsis' (anticipation), see p.
82; for 'paralepsis' (here the narrator knowing too much for the formal, temporal,
and epistemological constraints within which he seems to be functioning),
Genette's own neologism, see pp. 211–12. For more of Genette's narratological work
on Proust, see 'Métonymie chez Proust', *Figures III*, 41–63, and of course the much
more detailed 'Discours du récit' in the same book, pp. 65–273; but also other
essays, such as 'Proust palimpseste', *Figures I* (1966), 39–67; and 'Proust et le langage
indirect', *Figures II* (1969), 223–94.

[11] Augustine's *Confessions*, c. 397; Rousseau's monumental *Les Confessions*,
composed between 1764 and 1770, appeared posthumously from 1782; and his *Les
Rêveries du promeneur solitaire* and three dialogues, *Rousseau juge de Jean-Jacques*
supplemented this vast autobiographical exercise; Benjamin Constant's *Adolphe* was
published in 1816; Fromentin's *Dominique* was first published in serial form in *La
Revue des Deux Mondes* (April–May 1862); André Gide published *L'Immoraliste* in 1902,
La Porte étroite in 1909, and *La Symphonie pastorale* in 1919.

ately blur the distinction between the three genres here, because it is the confessional *mode*, and not its generic history or histories, which detains me: my focus is the human speaking subject in the movement and moment of offering a justification for his or her actions, thoughts, intentions, or motives—or indeed the attempts he or she might make to conceal them.[12]

Dennis Foster reads the act of confession by focusing on the aspect of complicity between confessing subject and listener: for Foster, confessional narrative takes place 'between two substantial, unsettled subjects'. He goes on: 'By "subject" I do not mean an autonomous, centred being that founds the individual, but that representation of the self, particularly as it is objectified through language. The subject is that aspect of the self available to understanding.'[13] This is a useful working definition of the speaking subject, which I want to retain, although Foster's emphasis, in other parts of his introduction, on guilt as prime motivation for confession is not part of my definition of self-justification. I define self-justification as an act of speech seeking pre-emptively to ward off attack which the subject fears might take the form of exclusion, rejection, deprivation, abandonment. The main prompting for an act of self-justification, then, is the desire to avoid pain, rather than the desire to confess guilt, although, of course, some kinds of self-justification might very well *take the form of* a confession of guilt. It would hardly constitute a discovery to announce that Proust wrote about guilt at ambivalence felt towards parents, particularly the mother. Nor would there be much of an argument in the assertion that *A la recherche* is a justification of Marcel Proust's life to his mother. I will attempt to avoid that particularly well-trodden significatory matrix, but we should take a moment to see why

[12] See, however, for more detailed analysis of the genre of autobiography in France and Europe than I can give here: Philippe Lejeune, *Le Pacte autobiographique* (1975) and his *Je est un autre* (1980); John Sturrock, *The Language of Autobiography* (1993); Michael Sheringham, *French Autobiography* (1993); Paul Jay, *Being in the Text* (1984). This is an ever more fully theorized (and circumscribed) critical field, drawing its methodologies particularly from speech act theory, psychoanalysis and deconstruction. Autobiography has fascinating siblings in witness or testament narrative, particularly of the Holocaust; see e.g., Elie Wiesel, *La Nuit* (1958). Michel Foucault is the obligatory starting-point for critique of confession, see *Histoire de la sexualité*, i, *La Volonté de savoir* (1976).
[13] Dennis A. Foster, *Confession and Complicity in Narrative* (1987), 3.

the answer to self-justification does not, as it were, lie with the mother.

It is, undeniably, psychoanalytic criticism of *A la recherche* that has been most concerned with the novel's questions of morality, but these have tended to stay at the level of the subjective or individual quest for 'self-discovery', such as Lejeune's disturbingly smug essay on narcissism, masturbation, and creativity, Doubrovsky's *La Place de la madeleine*, or Baudry's work.[14] Their other main manifestation is as readings of castration/artistic sterility complexes, such as Riffaterre's work on the 'Med-' tag:

Add to this linguistic mechanism the diegesis of the myth; add the interplay of Andromeda and the monster, the strand as the stage of a plight common to her and to the jellyfish turned monstrous woman, top it with the homophony of Andromeda's last syllables and Medusa's first, and we understand how easy it is for the -med- morpheme to stand for woman and for the monstrous or negative component in the sign system designating a woman. Hence the displacement of *androgyne*, within which man and woman were united but equal, by *Andromeda* that opposes desirability in man and terror in woman, a terror suffered or a terror inflicted. Hence, a valorization of the mediating last syllables (meda) made into an egregious symbol of unhappy or dangerous femininity.[15]

Riffaterre's work, which seeks to demonstrate 'how fantasies and repressed drives are born of a lexical coincidence rationalized into semantic identity', can quickly seem less like analysis than meddling, or worse, misogynistic muddling.

Too many psychoanalytic readings of *A la recherche* concentrate on such maternally directed, guilt-riddled early nuggets of the Proustian textual palimpsest as 'La Confession d'une jeune fille', 'Avant la nuit', and 'Sentiments filiaux d'un parricide', reading these in combination with the Montjouvain scene (i. 157–63; tr. i. 190–7).[16] These kinds of readings see enormous

[14] Philippe Lejeune, 'Écriture et sexualité', *Europe* (1971); Jean-Louis Baudry, *Proust, Freud et l'autre* (1984).

[15] Michael Riffaterre, 'Compelling Reader Responses', in A. Bennet (ed.), *Reading Reading* (1993), 100.

[16] To be found, respectively, in *JS* 85–96 (written between 1892 and 1895, for *Les Plaisirs et les jours*); *JS* 167–70 (1893); *CSB* 150–9 (based on the van Blarenberghe matricide in 1907). Compare also 'Violante ou la mondanité' (1892), *JS* 29–37. A novella suppressed from *Les Plaisirs et les jours* was *L'Indifférent* (1896), ed. Philip

significance in the 1906 *idée de pièce* given to René Peter, a friend of Debussy's, during a visit to Versailles, a play project also mentioned in a letter to Reynaldo Hahn.[17] As Painter notes in his biography, with a typically bluff yet apologetic tone, this sketch for a play has: 'a preposterous but significant plot, about a sadistic husband who, though in love with his wife, consorted with prostitutes, said infamous things about her to them, encouraged them to answer in kind, and was caught in the act by the injured lady, who left him, whereupon he committed suicide.'[18] The list of ghostly *avant-textes* which might be (and are) triumphantly held aloft as proof of Marcel Proust's ambivalence towards his mother goes on and on.[19] These early texts are basically seized upon to license psychoanalytic readings informing us that Proust's 'œuvre faisait de lui sa propre mère'.[20] But apart from telling us little about the way Proust's *writing* behaves, the underlying misogyny at work in this kind of criticism risks reducing literary critical psychoanalytic discourse itself to a dubious grudge against what might be termed a Gestalt ready-made of the obstinately absent, love-denying Mother.

If psychoanalytic readings of *A la recherche* do not tempt me as a methodological approach, then perhaps another critical discourse to step inside, this time one which certainly does not run the risk of leaving figural stones unturned, might be deconstructive literary criticism. It is precisely the foundationalist aspiration written into any first-person fiction or autobiography, for subjective truth to *be* apodictic or universal truth, which deconstructive literary criticism is at pains to expose and question. For

Kolb (Gallimard, 1978), which has received renewed interest recently. See Julia Kristeva, *Le Temps sensible* (1994), 21–3. Kristeva's interest is in the name of its heroine, who suffers from a man's indifference (because of his secret obsession with brothels and prostitutes): it is, naturally, Madeleine.

[17] 18 or 19 Sept., 1906 (*Corr.* vi. 127). See Baudry, *Proust, Freud*, 29.
[18] George D. Painter, *Marcel Proust* (1990), ii. 64.
[19] Here is Proust's comment on the reversible transmission of characteristics between mother and son in *Jean Santeuil*: 'Peu à peu, ce fils dont elle avait voulu former l'intelligence, les mœurs, la vie, avait insinué en elle son intelligence, ses mœurs, sa vie même et avait altéré celles de sa mère' (*JS* 871).
[20] Baudry, *Proust, Freud*, 41. Antoine Compagnon demonstrates how casually ingrained this maternal guilt topos has become in readings of Proust's work, with uncritical commentary on Proust's so-called Baudelairean fascination with the love–hate maternal relationship (see *Proust entre deux siècles* (1989), 160–5).

Proust, some of the best deconstructive criticism remains Paul de Man's demonstration (again, using the Giotto allegories) that Proust inscribes his text with its own unreadability.[21] The careful attention de Man pays to rhetorical tropes in the genre of autobiographical confession, in 'Excuses (*Confessions*)', which looks at key childhood incidents in Rousseau's autobiography, is part of a welcome return to the study of rhetoric in literary criticism generally.[22]

While the careful textual analysis of these thinkers attracts me, however, the aporia in which they sometimes find their endings, or the unwarranted hostility with which they sometimes treat literary texts, do not. Autobiography criticism, especially deconstructive criticism of autobiography, tends to pounce triumphantly on evidence *of* self-justification. Self-justificatory moments are, in general for this type of criticism, held to offer proof that the subject of autobiography has acknowledged, however fleetingly, the impossibility of telling the truth about the self, or of constituting selfhood as some whole and totalizable entity or quantity in writing. Self-justificatory moments can tend to function for deconstructive criticism as proof *that* autobiographers do not know themselves, or do not know that they will always fail to know themselves; that autobiographers are to be sternly told off for thus dallying with their readers' sympathies, and that it is the task of deconstruction to unmask and reprimand this underhand connivance.

This, however, begs the whole fascinating question of *why* acts of self-justification attract such scapegoating, such a moral high tone, even if it is couched in the terms of seemingly objective or neutral criticism. After all, in *A la recherche*, Marcel is perfectly open about both the sources which might inspire him to write a novel, and the difficulties of maintaining personal self-belief and public credibility when those sources are revealed as being entirely subjective:

Grave incertitude, toutes les fois que l'esprit se sent dépassé par lui-même; quand lui, le chercheur, est tout ensemble le pays obscur où il

---

[21] In 'Reading (Proust)', *Allegories of Reading* (1979), 57–78. See also 'Autobiography as De-Facement', *MLN* 94 (1979), 919–30, on prosopopoeia as the trope of autobiography. Jonathan Culler has also written brilliantly on individual rhetorical devices. See among other writings, his essay, 'Apostrophe', *diacritics*, 7 (1977), 59–69. [22] De Man, *Allegories of Reading*, 278–301.

doit chercher et où tout son bagage ne lui sera de rien. Chercher? pas seulement: créer. Il est en face de quelque chose qui n'est pas encore et que seul il peut réaliser, puis faire entrer dans sa lumière. (i. 45; tr. i. 52)

Deconstruction is certainly not a nihilistic or sceptical enterprise. Indeed in recent years, much thought has gone into its potential as an ethical discourse.[23] The triumph of textual blind spots and their location can, however, without some willingness in the critic to be confused and moved by literary texts, lead to a type of complexity in critical writing which has not arisen in the texts themselves. There is complexity enough in Proust's *A la recherche du temps perdu*, together with vast tracts of it that are never read critically, and the sense of these two important points is another part of what motivates my study. Blanchot strays perhaps too near a repetition of the early understanding of *A la recherche*, which decided the novel was a celebration of interiority, solitary withdrawal, and wistfulness.[24] Deconstructive analyses of *A la recherche*, on the other hand, too often repeat the problem, also that of much psychoanalytic writing on this text, of focusing too narrowly on only a handful of incidents in the text, rather than seeking to read across its span. Deconstruction has its own blind spot, which is a failure to allow the texts it reads to speak and be heard.

Having spoken at such length about what I will *not* be doing, it is perhaps time to return to what will be included. This is certainly a study about psychological processes but it is also a phenomenological study that considers very closely the relations dramatized and given signification between speaking subjects and a variety of object-types. With that in mind, I will bring some of Freud's metapsychological thinking into what I argue about self-justification, sometimes for comparative and sometimes for analytical purposes. Freud's willingness as a thinker to undertake speculative forays into the wilder hinterlands of mental functioning, with all the risks of experimental

[23] See, for an example of this trend, Simon Critchley, *The Ethics of Deconstruction* (1992).
[24] For a good overview of early responses to Proust's writing, see Leighton Hodson (ed.), *Marcel Proust: The Critical Heritage* (1989). For responses by contemporary writers, see Jean-Yves Tadié, *Proust* (1983), 153–231.

failure that such a venture entails, offers sometimes astonishing points of purchase on Proust's narrative experimentation.[25]

I will also have occasion to look at genetic material, earlier rough drafts so usefully published in the most recent Pléiade edition of *A la recherche* in the form of *Esquisses*. I am in general, however, suspicious of genetic criticism, since the task of sifting through variants sometimes results in readings which cannot move easily between early drafts and an interpretation of the 'final' state of a given text. But as a text-handling theory of some rigour, generated as an adjunct to the vast editorial operation of producing a variorum edition such as the new Pléiade Proust, it forces readers of *A la recherche* to bear in mind the fragility of any idea that texts are 'finished'.[26]

3. A SHORT HISTORY OF SELF-JUSTIFICATION

Self-justification finds its definition, in French as in English, subsumed under the definitions given of *justification*. *Le Grand Robert* tells us that the noun *justification* comes from the medieval theological Latin *justificatio*, with appearances of *Justificaciun* around 1120. It denotes the 'action de justifier quelqu'un, de se justifier'. Its synonyms include *décharge, défense, excuse, compte, explication, argument, raison, apologie, preuve*. Its theological usage is as the 'rétablissement du pécheur en l'état d'innocence, par la grâce'. *Justification* also signifies, in the world of book-printing, the 'action de donner aux lignes la longueur requise'; 'longueur d'une ligne d'impression, définie par le nombre de caractères'. From around 1521, the expression *justifier une ligne* means 'la mettre à la longueur requise au moyen de blancs'. *Justifier*, the transitive verb, signifies 'rendre juste, conforme à la justice' (rare, 1564); 'innocenter (quelqu'un) en expliquant sa conduite'; 'rendre (quelque

---

[25] See Malcolm Bowie, *Freud, Proust and Lacan* (1987), for excellent analysis of these points of theoretical crossover, fusion, and complementarity.

[26] See the journal series *Bulletin d'informations proustiennes. Genesis* is the organ of the Institut des Textes et Manuscrits Modernes (ITEM/CNRS). A measure of the recent interest in the critical and theoretical possibilities offered by genetic criticism can be seen in the publication of an issue of *Yale French Studies*, 89 (1996), devoted to the subject.

chose) légitime' (towards 1585); 'faire admettre, ou s'efforcer de faire reconnaître comme juste' (seventeenth century); 'confirmer (un jugement, un sentiment)'; and 'montrer comme vrai, juste, réel, par des arguments' (1368, *Ordonnances des Roys de France*). *Autojustification*, 'le fait de se justifier soi-même', makes its lexicographical début only in the mid-twentieth century.

In English, the noun *justification* stands generally for the 'action of justifying or showing something to be just, right, or proper; vindication of oneself or another; exculpation; verification'.[27] It also has specific theological connotations ('the action whereby man is justified, or freed from the penalty of sin, and accounted or made righteous by God'); a judicial sense ('the showing or maintaining in court that one had sufficient reason for doing that which he is called to answer; a circumstance affording grounds for such a plea'; and the same use in printing (1672) as its translation has in French. The *OED* tells us that 'Protestant theologians regard justification as an act of grace . . . through *imputation* of Christ's righteousness', while Roman Catholic theologians 'hold that it consists in man's being made really righteous by *infusion* of grace, such justification being a work continuous and progressive from its initiation' (my emphasis).

Self-justification is thus neatly contained, for lexicographers, by the definition of *justification*, as just one among many of the forms the latter might take. The 'self' is treated as one more unit to be shifted from a minus to a plus rating by the activity of justification.

We should bear in mind, however, that self-justification is a term with an active philosophical as well as a psychological history, albeit a fragmentary one. André Lalande's 1926 *Vocabulaire technique et critique de la philosophie* tells us that the primitive use of *justification* was to 'rendre ou de se rendre juste'. His definition goes on: 'Puis, par affaiblissement du sens primitif, se dit de tout acte par lequel on réfute une imputation ou même par lequel on la devance, en montrant qu'on est dans

---

[27] It comes from late Latin, *justification -em*, in Augustine, etc.; comparable with the 12th-cent. French *justification* (in Godefroy, *Dictionnaire de l'ancienne langue française*, perhaps the immediate source).

son droit (soit moral, soit logique), qu'on avait raison de dire ce qu'on a dit, ou de faire ce qu'on a fait' (i. 552). Justification, then, has apparently lost its medieval emphasis on justice, and seems to have come to be used for a situation in which self-defence, refutation, or pre-emptive assertion of any kind take place in language. Lalande gives as his examples two thinkers. Nicolas Malebranche, theologian, scientist, and philosopher (1638–1715), considers justification in *De la recherche de la vérité*.[28] Théodule Ribot (1839–1916), the influential experimental psychologist, subsequently refers to Malebranche's writing when discussing justification in *La Logique des sentiments*.[29] Understanding their views is crucial to discovering how Proust deals with this slippery concept, since it serves to emphasize how revolutionary Proust's treatment of self-justification is. The limitations and exclusions which comfortably shield Malebranche and Ribot are essentially Proust's starting-point. They have no equipment to deal with the rigours of self-justification—Proust effortlessly goes on building it.

Both Malebranche and Ribot examine justification from the perspective, not of its linguistic manifestations, but of its connection to the workings of *reason*. Malebranche is interested in how we make reasons for ourselves to support feelings; in other words, of how we construct a mental foundation to suit our underlying desires. Ribot, writing two centuries later, is keen to delineate a strict compartmentalization of the reasoning produced by different kinds of affect, in order to classify (but in the process, distribute moral worth to) psychological functioning.

Malebranche did not make a distinction between faith and reason. Although an admirer of Descartes, he held that God was the sole cause and source of divine reason, surpassing our own imperfect reason; and that God was the operator of some kind of correspondence between external objects and human ideas. But he also held, to a certain degree, that the human will is free. In 'Que toutes les passions se justifient', he starts with

---

[28] Nicolas Malebranche, 'Que toutes les passions se justifient, et des jugements qu'elles [nous] font [faire] pour leur justification', *De la recherche de la vérité* (1674–5), 3 vols. (Vrin, 1962), ii. 146–51.

[29] Théodule Ribot, 'Le Raisonnement de justification', *La Logique des sentiments* (1906; 5th edn. Alcan, 1920), 111–15 (p. 111).

the assumption that human desire, once ignited, seeks justification from reason, in order to achieve its ends (those of pleasure) in human actions. His introduction enacts a mini-allegory: 'L'esprit est tellement esclave de l'imagination, qu'il lui obéit toujours lorsqu'elle est échauffée. Il n'ose lui répondre lorsqu'elle est en fureur, parce qu'elle le maltraite s'il résiste, et qu'il se trouve toujours récompensé [de quelque plaisir], lorsqu'il s'accommode à ses desseins' (p. 146).

In fact, Malebranche's seemingly general introduction relies on exclusion. The difference between *esprit* and *imagination* turns out to have, not a universal, but an ideological bent: the self-effacing, humorous introductory allegory neatly shifts its author out of the line of fire, into alignment with the audience to whom the ensuing discussion is addressed, by allowing the gender of *esprit* to signify a personality-type: that of the henpecked man. The discussion seems to proceed from the assumption that *no one* is exempt from justification's effects, when actually a split has been introduced into the conception of 'one' that relies on the French grammatical tradition of gendering nouns: that part of 'one' which is *esprit* is implicitly also 'masculine', while that which is *imagination* is implicitly feminized. His categories of mental functioning are thus also implicitly anthropomorphized and thrust into a narrative context of the amorous relation. But let us not be too concerned for the moment with the difficulties of finding a neutral language in which to speak about mental functioning. There is still Malebranche's argument to follow.

Building upon his model of the cringing *esprit*, his aim is apparently to expose the dependencies that exist, but that are disguised, between the promptings of *désir*, and the judgements that are passed in order that *désir* may be satisfied and also securely justified: 'le désir nous doit porter par lui-même à juger avantageusement de son objet, si c'est un désir d'amour; et désavantageusement, si c'est un désir d'aversion. Le désir d'amour est un mouvement de l'âme excité par les esprits, qui la disposent à vouloir jouir ou user des choses qui ne sont point en sa puissance' (p. 146). A continuous circuit must be set up, in which it is desire's responsibility to act as dynamic current, in order that supporting moral judgement may continue to prompt the step between impulse and action in the world. In this triangular structure, the *âme*, having fallen a prey to *les esprits*, first of all creates and then disowns *désir*, or the dynamic of justification. The justificatory circuit must operate independently once it has been set up.

Positive moral judgements thus become a function of the *plaisir* that the 'objet de nos passions' affords us, since *l'esprit* can form no judgements by itself: 'l'esprit ne peut concevoir que la chaleur et la saveur soient des manières d'être d'un corps' (p. 147). Yet by the same token, 'il est très facile de reconnaître par la raison, quels peuvent être les jugements que les passions qui nous agitent forment en nous' (p. 147). Precisely because *raison*, in opposition to the *esprits*, is unable to make a *subjective* link between an object and its inherent moral worth, it is simultaneously, Malebranche asserts, the perfect instrument for recognizing a situation in which desire has initiated the judgement-forming circuit, and for calculating the *étendue* (p. 147) of the judgements and thus the violence of the desire. Desire takes over responsibility from the *esprits* and even from *passion*, for instigating moral judgements. Reason, on the other hand, is still supposed to be able to judge in a detached manner the justificatory judgements it *has itself offered desire*. *Désir* finds itself helplessly in the middle. It is judged by *raison*, from which it is simultaneously deriving justifications to support the actions of the *âme*. Yet the *âme*, which has been *excité par les esprits*, refuses to declare itself the real initiator of the justificatory loop.

Malebranche tries to make this complex and highly allusive model work by turning to empirical examples: 'L'expérience prouve assez ces choses, et en cela elle s'accommode parfaitement avec la raison' (p. 147). A discursive switch shifts the argument from the erotic to an apparently neutral epistemological domain: 'le désir de savoir, tout juste et tout raisonnable qu'il est en lui-même, devient souvent un vice très dangereux par les faux jugements qui l'accompagnent' (p. 147). 'Le désir de savoir' is another name for *curiosité*, and Malebranche adopts the position of the *moraliste* to condemn its falsifying dangers. *Every* form of knowledge, he maintains, has 'quelque endroit qui brille à l'imagination, et qui éblouit facilement l'esprit par l'éclat que la passion y attache' (p. 149), but the light of truth only appears when passion subsides. This would seem clear enough, but his most important point is yet to come.

The most serious impediment to detached reasoning, for Malebranche, is when an animating passion 'se sent mourir', because it seems to contract 'une espèce d'alliance avec toutes les autres passions qui peuvent la secourir dans sa faiblesse':

Car les passions ne sont point indifférentes les unes pour les autres. Toutes celles qui se peuvent souffrir contribuent fidèlement à leur *mutuelle conservation.* Ainsi, les jugements qui justifient le désir qu'on a pour les langues ou pour telle autre chose qu'il vous plaira, sont incessamment sollicités et pleinement confirmés par toutes les passions qui ne lui sont pas contraires. (p. 149; my emphasis)

It is this *mutuelle conservation* of passions which is the real source of danger to reason. If the passion of desire operated on its own, he argues, the only judgement it would be able to obtain from reason would be one agreeing that possession of the desired object was a real possibility; in other words, passion would only be able to slip the most basic feasibility study past reason:

Mais le désir est animé par l'amour; il est fortifié par l'espérance; il est augmenté par la joie; il est renouvelé par la crainte; il est accompagné de courage, d'émulation, de colère et de plusieurs autres passions qui forment à leur tour des jugements dans une variété infinie, lesquels se succèdent les uns aux autres et soutiennent ce désir qui les a fait naître. (p. 150)

Stylistically the most impressive sentence in Malebranche's text, it also complexifies the dynamic looping it has described desire as performing, by splitting *désir* into a fully interconnecting set of moving passion parts. But the very impressiveness and dynamism of this textual demonstration do much to undermine his careful progression towards rejecting justification as a corrupting influence on reasoning.

In Malebranche's justification model, desire is expected to keep a circuit going between the *âme* and *raison*, which was supplying the *âme* with justificatory reasoning for the pursuit of its goal. The responsibility for the functioning and maintenance of this circuit can then be disowned by both the *âme* and *raison*, the former by pretending to be passive, the latter by pretending to be detached. Reason benefits, by being released from the pestering by desire *for* justificatory reasoning, and the *âme* benefits *from* that justificatory reasoning.

If the desiring circuit were to suffer some kind of intermittent fault, a kind of desiring short-circuit, or power failure, however, reason and the *âme* would suddenly be deprived of their mutually beneficial but unacknowledged relationship. The two components of mental functioning would be linked, paradoxically, only by *indifference*. And we might speculate that, however short this period of linkage of *âme* and *raison* by indifference, it is too closely imitative of a state of inertia, or death, to be borne, which is why other types of link, not always justificatory, are imported as soon as possible to replace it. Malebranche represents *mutuelle conservation* as an irritating side-effect introduced by the passions, since to approve it would sound too much like approving justification over reason. Yet this mutual conservation practised by the passions might have much more to tell us about human survival than moralizing disapproval can allow into its modelling.

The final section of Malebranche's discussion of justification is at once uncannily astute and highly suspect. He uses a physiological model of how sense impressions travel to the brain, 'd'une manière propre à former des traces profondes qui représentent cet objet' (p. 150):

[Ils plient] et rompent même quelquefois par leur cours impétueux les fibres du cerveau, et l'imagination en demeure [longtemps] salie et corrompue; car [les plaies du cerveau ne se reprennent pas aisément, ses traces ne se ferment pas à cause que les esprits y passent sans cesse]. . . . Ainsi les passions agissent sur l'imagination, et l'imagination corrompue fait effort contre la raison en lui représentant à toute heure les choses, non selon ce qu'elles sont en elles-mêmes afin que l'esprit prononce un jugement de vérité, mais selon ce qu'elles sont par rapport à la passion présente afin qu'il porte un jugement qui la favorise. (p. 150)

This fascinating model of interconnection between a neurological and a moral vision of the human mind remains inextricably involved in the rhetorical and metaphoric signifying systems by which it is represented. No firm purchase seems possible upon either a purely material explanation of the workings of the brain, or upon the explanatory metaphors by which names for these workings also escape back into theological and moral interpretative traditions. Explanation is suspended between spirit, flesh, and language. And when Malebranche, whose text so successfully enacts the interdependence of explanatory metaphor with what it seeks to explain, tries to leap clear of his own language, in order to propose a kind of empirical socio-logical study which would divide people into different kinds of justifying groups, we find his text meshed up in what it had seemed merely to be describing from an external perspective:

> Si [l']on considère maintenant quelle peut être la constitution des fibres du cerveau, l'agitation et l'abondance des esprits et du sang dans les différents sexes et dans les différents âges, il sera assez facile de connaître à peu près à quelles passions certaines personnes sont plus sujettes, et, par conséquent, quels sont les jugements qu'elles forment des objets. (p. 151)

In wanting justification to be read off from physiology, Malebranche suddenly seems to deny the sophisticated inter-connective cognitive modelling he has just been attempting. Malebranche has been caught in his own self-justificatory noose. His starting-point had been empirical: 'Il n'est pas nécessaire de faire de grands raisonnements pour démontrer que toutes les passions se justifient; ce principe est assez évident par le sentiment intérieur que nous avons de nous-mêmes, et par la conduite de ceux que l'on voit agités de quelque passion: il suffit de l'exposer afin qu'on y fasse réflexion' (p. 146). His conclusion tries to rejoin a supposedly empirical science, that of physiology. Yet his exposition, or his exposure, of how the passions justify themseves, has required speculative leaps of investigative imagination, and brave conclusions about cogni-tive modelling. His argument implodes when he tries to make cognitive models fit with the physical brain, because there is no flexibility in his model which would allow in *subjectivity*. Malebranche's exposition of justification fails by screening out the writer and intended readership.

Théodule Ribot, philosopher and experimental psycholo-gist, who later concentrated on psychopathology, writing in Proust's lifetime, profers a very different reading of justifica-tion. In *La Logique des sentiments*, he seeks to divide affective modes of reasoning into five distinct groups: 'passionnel, inconscient, imaginatif, justificatif, mixte ou composite'.[30] 'Le

---

[30] André Lalande, *Vocabulaire technique et critique de la philosophie* (1993), i. 552.

raisonnement de justification' opens with a categorical and unambiguous denigration of this kind of affective reasoning: it is, Ribot sneers, 'la plus simple, la plus enfantine, la plus banale de toutes' (p. III). For Ribot, justification is: 'engendrée par une croyance ferme et sincère qui se refuse à être troublée et aspire au repos. Le raisonnement de justification est nettement téléologique. Malgré quelques apparences de rationalisme, il appartient au type affectif pur se manifestant dans sa plus grande pauvreté' (p. III). For Malebranche, the act of justification had been an animating, if corrupting, influence connecting, however inappropriately, the *âme* to reason. But for Ribot, exactly the opposite is true: justification appears to be an agent of death and destruction in human reasoning. The *croyance aveugle* which causes the justificatory act, he says, is itself prompted by a need for 'l'affirmation de l'individu dans son désir et son sentir les plus intimes' (p. III). He calls justification's tenacity '*une manifestation partielle de l'instinct de la conservation*' (p. III; Ribot's emphasis): 'Mais si inébranlable qu'elle paraisse, le doute la traverse au moins par moments. Il s'ensuit une rupture d'équilibre mental qui appelle un remède. C'est le raisonnement de justification' (p. 112).

Justification, he asserts, is what happens when our instinct for self-preservation is overcome, or interfered with by doubt. Justification, instead of functioning *as* the connective circuitry between two kinds of mental functioning, desire and reason, as it did for Malebranche, is here the name *given only to what causes ruptures and intermittences* in mental circuitry.

Ribot takes as examples political fervour, theoretical moralizing, and religious faith. He argues that moral thinkers rely on 'une tendance maîtresse, une préférence individuelle, une subjectivité qui, dissimulée sous cet appareil logique, guide vers une fin posée d'avance' (p. 112). They wish to found their thought on a priori concepts that do not need empirical justification, and yet smuggle in subjective and teleological material along the way of their reasoning. 'Les vrais croyants', on the other hand, take the events thrown at the world by God, and interpret them according to a fixed pattern: 'Sans s'inquiéter d'un double illogisme, ils déclarent que les voies de la Providence sont impénétrables, mais ils essaient de les justifier' (p. 113). They try to work backwards, justifying disaster after the event, so that they can continue to cling to their belief systems.

A sudden shift takes place in Ribot's argument here, from the relatively safe ground of people he calls *normal* (but justificatory), to the quicksands of reasoning among *aliénés*, people with persecution complexes. For them, apparently, 'le raisonnement de justification est sans cesse en action' (p. 113). He refuses, however, to go further into this subject, although he is willing to assert that justificatory reasoning operates at the same pitch in both the sane and the mad, an assertion which would seem to require more qualification: is justificatory reasoning, then, a function of insanity? Might the states of madness and health be linked through justificatory reasoning?

He next asserts that, because his study is 'consacré au raisonnement affectif' (p. 113), he does not intend to pursue a line of reasoning which would take him into an examination of the unconscious prejudice affecting all so-called pretence at scientific objectivity: historians, theologians, and philosophers, he says, are all prey to this. He accuses, for example, Nietzsche of falling into the same dialectic trap which the latter accuses Kant of doing:

Dans tous les cas de ce genre, la forme est celle de la logique rationnelle. La structure du raisonnement est ferme, sans lacunes, irréprochable; mais c'est un état d'âme extra-rationnel qui a l'initiative et la haute direction. Ce qui paraît démonstration n'est que *justification*. La logique de la raison semble maîtresse; en réalité, elle est servante. On s'y trompe, parce que l'édifice logique, bâti par des ouvriers habiles et subtils, n'a pas les apparences naïves du raisonnement affectif où le dénouement est connu d'avance. (p. 114)

His final section is a grudging afterthought on *raisonnement de consolation*, which is 'né du besoin de trouver un remède à la douleur morale' (p. 114): 'un effort pour restituer, par des moyens artificiels, la quantité de vie et d'énergie perdues', in order to combat the effects of 'les malheurs de l'existence' (p. 115). It consists in 'la *mise en valeur* d'états passés ou futurs propres à compenser le présent' (p. 115). The genre of compensatory writing, the 'Consolation', he attributes to Seneca and other rhetoricians, but 'le simulacre de raisonnement qui le constitue reste vivace dans toutes les formes de condoléance journalière' (p. 115). Casually, Ribot dispenses with an entire area of human activity, our everyday dealings with pain, sorrow, and misery. Justificatory reasoning, even if it helps soothe pain? Away with it, 'tis false.

Ribot has no hesitation in using an accusatory language which hopes to place justification well outside his own position as arbiter and judge. But beginning with unequivocal rejection of the concept, and a description of it as parasitic on the poorest kind of rationality, he proceeds to undermine his own statement with every succeeding example brought in. The more categories he includes as using justificatory procedures to obtain their ends, the more complex and multi-jointed the concept becomes, and the more its separable but interconnected forms and parts rebound on Ribot's text. His own logic relies explicitly on separation: his very attempt at divisive categories of affective reasoning demonstrates his belief that language consists in neutral semantic units, whose combination does not result in a self-reflexive flow, which starts to mean more than its producer intended. In Ribot's short essay, the whole of philosophy, indeed the activity of thought attempts of any kind, seems to disappear into an underworld of impossibility. No one, no one at all, knows how to think. Except perhaps the one man left standing, the exclusive omniscient, Ribot himself? This is wildness of a totalitarian kind, disturbingly persuasive in its scathing sweeps, yet reduced to a precarious foothold in serious danger of undermining itself so completely that it too disappears into the gulf left by the implosion of philosophy.

There is a good reason for having examined so deeply two bad analyses of self-justification. As part of Proust's exposure to and immersion in a long history of philosophy and psychology, these two close commentators on my governing concept are also part of the overall history of ideas soundlessly informing *A la recherche du temps perdu* and against which the novel project slowly took shape.[31] Malebranche the philosopher who tolerates but gently mocks a conceptual category of reasoning, and

---

[31] See Kristeva, *Le Temps sensible*, 307–37, for an excellent summary and analysis of Proust's exposure to contemporary philosophy and psychology through his school and university education, an exposure which took in a range of approaches from the idealism of Schopenhauer's concentration on Will, to Gabriel Tarde's resolutely cultural interpretation of society.

Ribot the psychologist who strives to hold at bay a threatening component of mental functioning, may be seen as two kinds of hook holding up the intellectual backdrop upon which Proust's experimentation in subjectivity is conducted. Their analysis contributes a set of thoughts, attitudes, and terminologies which will recur as the study proceeds, and to which the main missing ingredient supplied by Proust's rigorous investigation of justification is, very precisely, self.

4. AN INTRODUCTORY OVERVIEW OF THE STUDY

I need to make just two more points before going on to summarize my book's argument. The first is a kind of bookmark, to tell us how far we have already come in getting to grips with the concept of self-justification. 'A work that aspires, however humbly, to the condition of art should carry its justification in every line.'[32] Conrad's injunction to the artist seems to refer to a perfectionism which is also bound up in the relation between the art-maker and the art-receiver, or reader, or consumer, or viewer. Proust, sometime in the murky *Contre Sainte-Beuve* gestation period of 1908–9, has a similar note, but it is a self-directed one, a goad and a goal. 'Au fond', he says, 'toute ma philosophie revient, comme toute philosophie vraie, à justifier, à reconstruire ce qui est.'[33] Proust's emphasis, at this melting-pot period out of which emerges a first-person narrator, is vitally different from Conrad's: for Proust, it is an ontological drive which spurs him to completion; for Conrad, completion is arrived at by satisfactorily arranging the presentation of the artwork. The perfectionism injected into the whole course of the Proustian narrator's experience, and his concurrent or retrospective writing about it, is massive, general, total; Conrad's is local, measured, focused. Among the plethora of other lustrous subjects Proust inspects: the functioning of Time, the workings of Memory, the needs met and dispatched by Habit, the language of flowers, the Dreyfus Affair, monocles,

---

[32] Joseph Conrad, *The Nigger of the 'Narcissus'* (1897; preface, 1914), 3.
[33] Cahier 29. N. a. fr. 16669, publ. in *CSB* as part of 'Notes sur la littérature et la critique', p. 309.

manacles, the Pompeian Métro, the *calle* of Venice, he has rigorously analysed, articulated and then run to ground the multiform modes of a very particular set of cognitive functions and relations. Proust, of course, though it is a very felicitous 'of course', and my second point, has thus built into his narrator's perfectionism *its own greatest blind spot*. Wittgenstein puts it this way: 'Justification by experience comes to an end. If it did not it would not be justification.'[34] For Marcel, ontological considerations are inextricably meshed with empirical methods of analysis, which translates, as we will hear, into a powerful capacity to split open apparently stable justifications into their component self-justificatory parts.

How then am I going to show you self-justification in action? Making use of the new Pléiade edition of *A la recherche du temps perdu*, Brunet's concordance of the novel, *Le Vocabulaire de Proust*, and the electronic concordancing capacities of FRANTEXT (both of which are based on the previous 1954 Pléiade edition of the text), it is the purpose of this study to show the contents of various Proustian textual laboratories, each conducting separate, but ultimately interconnected, linguistic, psychological and moral experiments upon the possibilities offered by self-justification.[35]

The book divides into three parts. The first section examines the workings of three of the set-piece salon and *soirée* scenes. Party-going, that most unlikely of domains for research purposes, yields up some strange self-justificatory performances which are almost always passed over or giggled at without their vital significance as notes on acceptability being analysed.

---

[34] Ludwig Wittgenstein, *Philosophical Investigations*, tr. G. E. M. Anscombe (1953), 136, §485.

[35] Étienne Brunet, *Le Vocabulaire de Proust*, 3 vols. (1983); Marcel Proust, *A la recherche du temps perdu*, 3 vols. (Gallimard, 1954), Online, FRANTEXT Base de données textuelles du français (http://www.ciril.fr/~mastina/FRANTEXT), Internet. FRANTEXT has an extremely useful concordancing programme. Its use as a labour- and time-saving device cannot be over-estimated. The concordancing programme can search not only for single-word instances, but also for word clusters, verb declensions, and collocations. Lists of pertinent quotations may then be conveniently downloaded and studied. At this time, the only difficulty is the subsequent page-referencing work required in order to locate the word-pattern discoveries in the 1987–9 edn. of *A la recherche*, but this will be resolved when the first CD-ROM hypertext edition of the text is put together, with *esquisses*, a publishing event that cannot be far off.

If self-justification towards an external world perceived as intolerant and indifferent is clearly important in *A la recherche*, occupying large swathes of *Le Côté de Guermantes* and *Sodome et Gomorrhe*, other questions arise from its study. The second part of the book divides into three subsections. They look, in bald terms, at rhetoric, metaphor, and characterization.

Digression is the subject of Chapter 2. One of the most beloved of Proustian stylistic features, digression is a trope which builds a seductive play into rhetorical organization. Alarmingly, however, it is not far from seductive play to defensive strategy of avoidance or evasion. Stopping in the middle of digressions, rather than announcing triumphantly that there *are* digressions in the novel, enables us to pursue a surprising, and painful line of argument from parties to people, in other words, between group functioning and relationships with individuals.

This line of argument that moves via the bulges of digression in *A la recherche* resolves itself in the third chapter into a model for self-justification. My model shows how self-justification works in two directions in *A la recherche*. Vulnerability and doubt might be said to facilitate a dynamic engagement with the outside world, to the extent that admission to inadequacy opens a channel for the admission of alterity. They are also, clearly, mental states prone to blockage. The figure of the *cloison* is suggested as a focus of narratorial engagement with an intimate external reality, which demonstrates Marcel's investigative skills but also the site of their potential failure. The *cloison* is a semi-permeable partition, a temporary screen which divides spaces internally, and enables the transmission of sound but not of light. It is used in the text both figurally and literally. Chapter 3 shows how, while justifying himself to the outside world can be seen as a learnable skill, even a necessary defence mechanism, based on imitation and disguise, self-justification in relation to the discovery of homosexuality at the beginning of *Sodome et Gomorrhe*, or the narrator's realization that he has lost a source of unconditional love with the death of his grandmother, hints at its potential to mutate into wilful self-protection.

We now have a great deal of evidence about self-justification going on, so to speak, *outside* the narrator: mindstuff he can see or hear, and only very occasionally feel. So far, self-justification has been safely contained as something that happens to other people. The final subsection, however, continues work begun in the *cloison* chapter, to question the safety of that detached spectacle. It investigates a particular difficulty apparent in the matter of Proust's characterization. Characters in the text who seem at first sight straightforwardly comic, or one-dimensional, turn out to represent a potential threat to the narratorial self, and we will need to spend some time considering what Marcel does about this.

The first two sections of the study, then, show how Marcel justifies himself in relation to external criteria. But when all of these external means of measurement are removed, self-justification takes on an entirely new aspect. In the final section of the argument, an investigation of the processes of mourning is undertaken. Marcel mourns Albertine throughout *Albertine disparue* in a solitary narrative of distress. It is a section of the text rarely analysed, and reveals how Proust allows the different aspects of self-justification to fuse, with devastating results.

This is a very new vision of how *A la recherche du temps perdu* works, an epistemological and hermeneutic dilemma on active duty in the novel. And, in due course, the claims that Proust makes about the uses of self-justification, as they are presented in the text, will themselves suggest some deeply troubling and painful conclusions. These will be conclusions first about what Proust has written. In the second place, my conclusions are about how literature makes an impact upon the world only and precisely to the extent that it arises from intimacy with the world.

I

Outwards

I

Doing the Right Thing: A Study of Proustian Parties

> Nous travaillons à tout moment à donner sa forme à notre vie, mais en copiant malgré nous comme un dessin les traits de la personne que nous sommes et non de celle qu'il nous serait agréable d'être.
>
> (ii. 485; tr. iii. 212)

I. THE FAUBOURG SAINT-GERMAIN

The opening chapter of my study takes us to the parties of the Faubourg Saint-Germain. Occupying hundreds of pages in *Le Côté de Guermantes*, *Sodome et Gomorrhe*, and the last hundred or so pages of *Le Temps retrouvé*, they are famously rumbustious, chaotic, nonsensical, full of local humour, and packed with chatter. Their frippery and detail slip easily from the reading mind; they merge into indistinguishable wholes. There are by and large two exceptions to this seemingly inexorable slide into homogeneous mass. One is the so-called 'Bal de têtes' sequence with its climactic moment of narratorial comprehension, time's passage embodied in the form of Gilberte's daughter (iv. 609; tr. vi. 430).[1] The other is Charlus's frightfully prolonged expulsion at the hands of Mme Verdurin, after the performance of Vinteuil's Septet.[2]

Proust's parties are among those parts of his novel which remain most severely underread. There are two main ways of approaching them. Commentators tend on the one hand to

---

[1] At the *matinée* held by the princesse de Guermantes (iv. 496–609; tr. vi. 285–430). The princesse is, of course, none other than the erstwhile *Patronne* (i. 203; tr. i. 247) of the *petit clan des Verdurin* (i. 184; tr. i. 225).

[2] iii. 777–830; tr. v. 300–72.

subsume their content to their form, and see them as a series of
symbolic initiations to a social élite found to be empty once
conquered.[3] On the other hand, they summarize party-going as
Proust's comic or economic critique of a class-based society.[4]
But if we take a moment to consider a table showing the distribution of party scenes across the novel, and the sheer proportion of it they occupy, we can see at a glance that simply
accounting for formal characteristics will not do.[5] Something
apart from aimless socializing must be going on to warrant the
presence in *A la recherche* of all that chat.[6]

Something else *is* going on. For ignoring the whimsy and
endlessness of party scenes in the novel rather conveniently
avoids all the complexities of reading Marcel as hermeneut of
his own experience—as first-person accountant of his own past.
Why would the narrator, that conscientious objector to and

[3] Serge Gaubert calls each successive one an *étape*. By searching for an idea of
progress, he effectively closes off other valuable readings of the scenes which attend
to their inner workings. Michel Raimond has written extensively about the party
scenes, and treats them as a series of initiations. His logic repeats exactly Gaubert's
idea of progress. Both models reduce rather than show what is there already. René
Girard, in *Mensonge romantique et vérité romanesque* (1961), draws on structuralist and
anthropological thinking to put forward a compelling thesis on the idea of external and internal mediation of desire. For Girard, Proust's analysis of snobbery as
the fine art of desiring nothing explodes Romantic assertions that desire be defined
as dignified yearning for an unattainable object, and exposes it instead as the
ambivalent and strangulated impetus to *be* the other who has what we think we
want. Fascinating though Girard's reading is, it tends to avoid moment-by-moment
encounters with Proust's text.

[4] Michael Sprinker tells us that the narrator of *A la recherche du temps perdu* does
not question the nature of a tripartite class-based social structure. The narrator
himself clearly emerges from a *haute bourgeoisie* background. Theodor Adorno
summarizes in one sentence what Girard subsequently takes as his main theme in
Mensonge romantique: 'Le snobisme, en tant que concept dominant dans la *Recherche*
de Proust, est l'investissement érotique de faits sociaux', *Notes sur la littérature*,
(1984), 147. Walter Benjamin's brilliant essay, 'The Image of Proust', in *Illuminations*
(1968), contains another excoriating analysis of the class system that Proust tells us
about: 'everywhere pledged to camouflage its material basis and for this very reason
. . . attached to a feudalism which has no intrinsic economic significance but is all
the more serviceable as a mask of the upper middle class' (p. 212).

[5] The table may be found in Appendix I.

[6] Even commentators who have looked *at* the scenes themselves have avoided
reading them closely. Ross Chambers none the less makes a fascinating link
between gossip and the case-study. Maxine G. Cutler only lists the obvious puns or
calembours. Jonathan E. Marks approaches the scenes as though they were directly
biographical, their reproduction in the novel a kind of revenge on the world, but
this again avoids the real complexities of the text.

updater of all the daily debris he encounters, take parties so
seriously, both as he goes to them, and as he comes to write
about them? After all, from the very beginning of his social
career the narrator is highly critical of, not naïve and innocent
about, the kind of people who go to Faubourg Saint-Germain
parties, but this does not prevent him attending such events. At
the *soirée* given by Mme de Villeparisis he tells us:

J'avais beau savoir que le salon Guermantes ne pouvait pas présenter
les particularités que j'avais extraites de ce nom, le fait qu'il m'avait
été interdit d'y pénétrer, en m'obligeant à lui donner le même genre
d'existence qu'aux salons dont nous avons lu la description dans un
roman ou vu l'image dans un rêve, me le faisait, même quand j'étais
certain qu'il était pareil à tous les autres, imaginer tout différent;
entre moi et lui il y avait la barrière où finit le réel. (ii. 670; tr. iii. 433)

Another set of factors might be motivating party-going, then,
troublesome hermeneutic questions being posed about how to
pass judgement in situations in which one is oneself under
scrutiny, in a combative and harshly critical arena. Marcel
perceives the structures of the Faubourg's exclusivity as
founded doubly, first on inherited status, but secondly on
hostile judgement, and in taking his chances among the
Frobervilles, the Cambremers, the Iénas, he posits himself as
besieged protector of his own identity, undertaking reconnais-
sance missions to deliver himself vital information which will
save him from expulsion. Vincent Descombes asserts in his
excellent and careful study that: 'La rhétorique du monde,
celle que comprennent les gens du monde, est la façon dont on
se justifie dans le monde'.[7] Right. That self-justification organizes the rhetorical frameworks governing parties is quite clear.
One-upmanship always flourishes exactly where nothing is at
stake. Nothing could be more straightforward than to point this
out. What is much more difficult and important about self-justification, the aspect of it that will go on producing questions and
posing problems right the way through this book, is that self-
justification constantly mutates. It is Marcel's ongoing doubts
about and attempts to produce stable definitions of *what self-
justification is*, which throw out, almost as a side-effect, his

---

[7] *Proust: Philosophie du roman* (1987), 213.

tremendously careful manœuvring between a moral and a psychological explanation of parties and party-going.

This chapter will follow the movements Marcel makes in the Faubourg, as he pays close attention to the babble of its direct speech. It is one of the major observation sites for watching the powerful self-justificatory reflex action in *A la recherche* at work: in the syntax of assimilation. Marcel's analysis, as we will hear, generates odd and sometimes frankly contradictory models for self-justification, but we should not let ourselves be daunted by his intense close-up focus, and his apparently insatiable appetite for minute variation. Once we have accumulated and sorted for ourselves a wide range of samples and local moments of the self-justification he monitors, we will be in a better position to home in on particular problems in the way it works, and also to see how these local moments are anything but isolated malfunctions in the Proustian narrative machinery.

2. ASPECTS OF ASSIMILATION: THE SCAPEGOAT AND THE EAVESDROPPER

The event held in Mme de Villeparisis's salon constitutes the narrator's first entrance into the higher echelons of Faubourg Saint-Germain society, and Marcel's first major analysis of assimilation concerns Bloch, erstwhile Combray friend of the narrator, now bombastic 'jeune auteur dramatique', 'le menton ponctué d'un "bouc" ' (ii. 487; tr. iii. 214). As a character with a past already identified in the novel, and with a career as writer akin to the narrator's own ambitions, Bloch's significance is scrutinized with attention, its focus, curiously, his beard. The meaning of his *bouc*, as both an indication of an oriental origin, but also as mere fashionable facial hair, is immediately projected by the narrator from the particular to the general. Bloch's Jewishness is seized upon by the narrator, and worked up into an intense, accelerated digression into Semitic origins, and the status and acceptability of Jews in French society at this early stage of the Dreyfus Affair. The narrator's childhood friend cannot simply exist, he must be turned into material that can be judged.

The analysis runs thus:

Les Roumains, les Égyptiens et les Turcs peuvent détester les Juifs. Mais dans un salon français les différences entre ces peuples ne sont pas si perceptibles et un Israélite faisant son entrée comme s'il sortait du fond du désert, le corps penché comme une hyène, la nuque obliquement inclinée et se répandant en grands 'salams', contente parfaitement un goût d'orientalisme. Seulement il faut pour cela que le Juif n'appartienne pas au 'monde', sans quoi il prend facilement l'aspect d'un lord, et ses façons sont tellement francisées que chez lui un nez rebelle, poussant, comme les capucines, dans des directions imprévues, fait penser au nez de Mascarille plutôt qu'à celui de Salomon. (ii. 487–8; tr. iii. 214–15)[8]

On the one hand, the French image of the Jew is said to be so caricatural that simple imitation of its outline will grant access to a French salon; on the other, high-class Jews are being chastised here for losing their Semitic signatures, and for letting themselves be *francisés*. Bloch's *bouc* is the ambiguous punctuation mark which could mean either of these situations: he is either to be stigmatized by the French community as not being French enough, or scapegoated by the Jewish community as trying to be something he is not.[9]

[8] Edward W. Said makes the point in his acclaimed book, *Orientalism* (1995), that Semites, in *A la recherche* and elsewhere, do not represent themselves, but are made to be represented for a Western audience (p. 293). The faint filigree of the Jew figured as desert animal is uncannily echoed by Charlus, when he fantasizes about parental desecration and Bloch: 'frapper cette créature extra-européenne [Bloch's mother], ce serait donner une correction méritée à un vieux chameau' (ii. 585; tr. iii. 331). At another point the narrator has been told something shocking about what Norpois remembers of him. In situations like these, he says, we have the same 'soupçon d'une erreur que le visiteur d'une exposition qui devant un portrait de jeune femme lit dans le catalogue: Dromadaire couché' (ii. 569; tr. iii. 312). His comment is itself so surprising that we do indeed suspect something, but it is the return of a repressed anxiety about homosexuality and Jewishness in the text, rather than a sense that other people's opinions of us are wrong. Edward Hughes, in 'The Mapping of Homosexuality in Proust's *Recherche*', *Paragraph*, 18 (1995), 148–62, writes about 'the strains of European colonialism', that 'colour the depiction of sexuality which Proust's narrator offers' (p. 148).

[9] Jacques Derrida's seminal essay 'La Pharmacie de Platon', in *La Dissémination* (1972), is by now the obligatory critical intertext that will not allow us to forget the double-edgedness of signifiers. René Girard picks up the point that the Greek term for scapegoat is *pharmakon*, both poison and cure, in *Le Bouc émissaire* (1982). Girard's contention is that after the crucifixion of Christ, scapegoating loses its capacity to validate the finding of a victim whose sacrifice will solve a social problem, since the crucifixion turns sacrifice into the *ultimate* social problem, and introduces guilt and shame into the very process of victim-hunting. Bloch's *bouc* can be seen within this paradigm as signifying the cusp of Judaeo-Christian belief systems: it is both guilty and innocent.

Fascinated with Bloch's Jewishness, the narrator returns to it via another enabling mechanism, that of photography: 'si j'avais dans la lumière du salon de Mme de Villeparisis pris des clichés d'après Bloch, ils eussent donné d'Israël cette même image, si troublante parce qu'elle ne paraît pas émaner de l'humanité, si décevante parce que tout de même elle ressemble trop à l'humanité, que nous montrent les photographies spirites' (ii. 489; tr. iii. 216). The reference to *photographies spirites* dematerializes Bloch's presence even more successfully than did orientalizing it. A *goût d'orientalisme* was an imported fashion, or a fashion for importing, while *photographies spirites* were a European interest.[10] If integration into a social group depends on that group's taste for the East, the essential molecules of the body to be integrated are still preserved, but if Bloch is turned into a trick snapshot, then he is dematerialized in the glare not of 'la lumière du salon de Mme de Villeparisis', but of the narrator's focus. Bloch can only be restituted to the text through humour and direct speech:

Il n'est pas, d'une façon plus générale, jusqu'à la nullité des propos tenus par les personnes au milieu desquelles nous vivons qui ne nous donne l'impression du surnaturel, dans notre pauvre monde de tous les jours où même un homme de génie de qui nous attendons, rassemblés comme autour d'une table tournante, le secret de l'infini, prononce seulement ces paroles—les mêmes qui venaient de sortir des lèvres de Bloch: 'Qu'on fasse attention à mon chapeau haute forme.' (ii. 489; tr. iii. 216)

It is the very pragmatic nature of Bloch's utterance that confirms what is *surnaturel* about his presence to the narrator. The curiously heightened attempt to perceive Bloch's Semitic essence through his French accoutrements is exploded by the very words uttered by the character under examination. Direct speech saves him from complete etherealization: bracketed into a world of Bloch's own, and only reportable rather than manipulable, as Bloch's physical presence is manipulated by

[10] As Julie Eisenbuch reminds us, in *The World of Ted Serios* (1989), 180. 'Psychic images' on photographic plates were reported notably in the 1860s and 1870s. The concept was in disrepute by the early 1930s. The link between the photographic image and mortality has been movingly commented upon by Roland Barthes, in his autobiographical *La Chambre claire* (1980). See Ch. 3, which looks at how Proust writes about the *cloison*, or permeable partition.

the writing, these words of direct speech afford the impression of being imported wholesale into the text. Anything can be done with Bloch, his body can be entirely 'transvertebrated', but unlike Golo, projecting forth from a magic lantern, Bloch can speak.[11] His corporeal physicality and his Semitic origins are infinitely malleable and depictable. His direct speech, however, as evidence of presence, testimony of event, is not, or needs to seem as though it were not. The corporeal can be punished and the verbal cannot. While bodily transformations may be effected on characters through the agency of narratorial perception, direct speech uttered by these characters is demarcated as untouchable, because it is the closest approximation to a pure selfhood that characters who are not the narrator may possess.

This delicate mimetic boundary, by which textual definition may be given to characters, and by which a first-person narrator may be situated at once inside a fiction and outside it, seems a relatively straightforward narrative convention. But Proust makes strange and subtle inroads into it, which draw out its underlying moral significance. Later at the salon the narrator talks to Bloch: 'craignant . . . qu'il n'enviât ma vie, je lui dis que la sienne devait être plus heureuse. Ces paroles étaient de ma part un simple effet de l'amabilité. Mais elle persuade aisément de leur bonne chance ceux qui ont beaucoup d'amour-propre, ou leur donne le désir d'en persuader les autres' (ii. 498; tr. iii. 227). Fear's words, 'craignant . . . qu'il n'enviât ma vie', are deemed the side-effect of wishing Bloch well. But the authenticity of the narrator's goodwill is called into question by the rather less *simple effet* of the acidic sentence which follows. Here sarcasm rebounds on the narrator, turning on *mais*, for *mais* should be an unnecessary supplement if *amabilité* is genuine: no afterword should be required. Its presence betrays a further need, one which is implosive and which sucks at the otherwise

---

[11] Golo's impervious will to adapt terrifies the narrator when a child. He sees in it a supernatural ability to coat all the surfaces of his world with evil intention: 'Le corps de Golo lui-même, d'une essence aussi surnaturelle qui celui de sa monture, s'arrangeait de tout obstacle matériel, de tout objet gênant qu'il rencontrait en le prenant comme ossature et en se le rendant intérieur, fût-ce le bouton de la porte sur lequel s'adaptait aussitôt et surnageait invinciblement sa robe rouge ou sa figure pâle toujours aussi noble et aussi mélancolique, mais qui ne laissait paraître aucun trouble de cette transvertébration' (i. 10; tr. i. 9).

wholesome sincerity of *amabilité* by drawing forth that unpleasant side of it: friendliness which is self-interested. The need that *mais* speaks about is the need to judge. Characterizing Bloch opens up, beside itself and despite itself, an abyss in which the narrator confronts his own activities as characterizer, and this confrontation occurs as a pre-emptive bid to account for all the possible interpretations engendered by one of his own utterances. When Bloch assesses his quotient of happiness, in answer to Marcel's question, by saying: 'Rare est le mortel à qui le père Zeus accorde tant de félicités' (ii. 498; tr. iii. 227), the narrator explains: 'Je crois qu'il cherchait surtout à se louer et à me faire envie. Peut-être aussi y avait-il quelque désir d'originalité dans son optimisme. Il fut visible qu'il ne voulait pas répondre les mêmes banalités que tout le monde. . . .' (ii. 498; tr. iii. 227). The wilfully innocent *je crois* is again superfluous. Qualifying Bloch's desire to be original with *quelque désir* is downright provocative: Bloch's desire for originality is agonizingly palpable, not vague but specific and defining of him. We already know about Bloch's history, his Parnassian sensibility, and artistic ambition.[12] A moment of mastery becomes available to the narrator: the suppression of a past already recounted in the novel calls forth an undecidable presentation of Bloch. A smokescreen of confusion about intention and decipherability is thrown up, which enables the narrator to sidestep what might otherwise be a painfully proximate issue: banality in his own behaviour, either at parties or in writing.

In conversation with the narrator, then, Bloch's excessive language finds an attentive and negatively critical ear. Marcel fears, however, that attentiveness is no match for discrimination. More important for the narrator than being a good listener is to obtain an objective measure by which he can know how speech like Bloch's, crammed as it is with literary reference, hyperbole, self-conscious irony, and heightened response to stimuli, is received in the context of party-going.

Marcel takes an opportunity by eavesdropping on a conversation: he is thus still listening, but does not need to contribute to the dialogue. Bloch has managed to attend several days of the Zola trial, and is drunk with the headiness and fatigue of

---

[12] See i. 89; tr. i. 106.

it.[13] He buttonholes Norpois, eager for information about the Dreyfus Affair, and the following narratorial aside occurs to account for this: 'L'homme jouant perpétuellement entre les deux plans de l'expérience et de l'imagination voudrait approfondir la vie idéale des gens qu'il connaît et connaître les êtres dont il a eu à imaginer la vie' (ii. 531; tr. iii. 267). Bloch's alleged reason for talking to Norpois sounds very like the narrator's desire to find out more about the context in which he finds himself. When Norpois begins to answer questions about lieutenant-colonels Henry and Picquart, Bloch interrupts him:

'Mais,' s'écria Bloch, 'la divine Athénè, fille de Zeus, a mis dans l'esprit de chacun le contraire de ce qui est dans l'esprit de l'autre. Et ils luttent l'un contre l'autre, tels deux lions. Le colonel Picquart avait une grande situation dans l'armée, mais sa Moire l'a conduit du côté qui n'était pas le sien. L'épée des nationalistes tranchera son corps délicat et il servira de pâture aux animaux carnassiers et aux oiseaux qui se nourrissent de la graisse des morts.'

M. de Norpois ne répondit pas. (ii. 531; tr. iii. 267)[14]

Listening in on Bloch's excessive speech, the narrator notes that the lack of response here functions like a judgement: for Norpois's silence cauterizes the dialogue. Bloch is presented as a scapegoat to the extent that his speech is sacrificed to silence. He makes himself vulnerable by expressing his thoughts in a language whose relationship to the truth of the Dreyfus Affair does not imitate Norpois's own use of language, and this language is then rejected, along with any of its claims to be a representation of the truth. Bloch's presentation shows the narrator that he is incapable of doing the right thing, not in absolute terms, but in terms of a set of conventions about which

[13] Zola was brought to trial at the Assises de la Seine by the ministre de la Guerre following the publication of a letter in *L'Aurore* (13 Jan. 1898), famously entitled 'J'accuse!' and addressed to the president of the Republic. The trial took place between 7 and 23 Feb. 1898. Proust attended several days of the hearing, here attributed to the dreyfusard Bloch. Mention is made of his emotional response to it in *JS* 619–59: 'le soir quand il revenait dans Paris au milieu de gens qui n'étaient pas dans cet état physique, si doux, de ceux dont la vie est brusquement modifiée par une excitation spéciale, il éprouvait bien de la tristesse et de l'isolement à sentir cette vie excitante tout à coup finie' (p. 620).

[14] For valuable detail about the journalistic context surrounding the Dreyfus Affair, see Stephen Wilson's *Ideology and Experience* (1982).

the narrator is learning through his own silent appraisal of the agents performing within its strictures.

If Bloch is seen to be rejected, because of his excessive language, at the hands of Norpois, then Norpois seems to have become the agent of judgement at this salon, and we find that the narrator himself is not exempted from Norpois's opinions. Bloch's excessive linguistic performance calls forth a memory of the young narrator's own excessive performance in front of Norpois, when the latter had promised to speak to Odette on the narrator's behalf.[15] Marcel had barely managed to restrain his delight: 'j'eus peine à me retenir de ne pas embrasser ses douces mains blanches et fripées, qui avaient l'air d'être restées trop longtemps dans l'eau. *J'en ébauchai presque le geste que je me crus seul à avoir remarqué*' (i. 468; tr. ii. 64, my emphasis). The gleeful revelation of the near-miss, however, finds itself start-lingly reactivated, and worse, conveyed back to its own point of origin by Odette herself: 'M. de Norpois leur aurait dit—c'est inepte, n'allez pas vous mettre martel en tête pour cela, personne n'y a attaché d'importance, on savait trop de quelle bouche cela tombait—que vous étiez un flatteur à moitié hystérique.' (ii. 568; tr. iii. 311)

The narrator's surprise at being thus remembered redrama-tizes the urgency of discovering what people think and how and why they think it. Here his reaction is to formulate a general law at some length, moving instantaneously from his particular circumstance to the universal, in an attempt to encompass his shock at being given away. He begins his formulation in the language of sketching, but a curious change of medium is surreptitiously introduced:

Ce que nous nous rappelons de notre conduite reste ignoré de notre plus proche voisin; ce que nous avons oublié avoir dit, ou même ce que nous n'avons jamais dit, va provoquer l'hilarité jusque dans une autre planète, et l'image que les autres se font de nos faits et gestes ne ressemble pas plus à celle que nous nous en faisons nous-même qu'à un dessin quelque décalque raté où tantôt au trait noir correspondrait un espace vide, et à un blanc un contour inexplicable. Il peut du reste arriver que ce qui n'a pas été transcrit soit quelque trait irréel que nous ne voyons que par complaisance, et que ce qui nous semble ajouté

---

[15] At 'Le dîner avec le marquis de Norpois' (i. 443–68; tr. ii. 25–64).

nous appartienne au contraire, mais si essentiellement que cela nous échappe. De sorte que *cette étrange épreuve qui nous semble si peu ressemblante a quelquefois le genre de vérité, peu flatteur certes mais profond et utile, d'une photographie par les rayons X.* (ii. 568–9; tr. iii. 311–12; my emphasis)

The *épreuve* is an overdetermined term, sweeping from the heroic test to the publisher's proof and, from the mid-nineteenth century, to the photographic contact-sheet.[16] Here, it is a kind of photographic exposure that gossip and short-circuited report takes of us, which can stand for truth without looking like our own impressions of ourselves, in the same way that X-rays show us in an unflattering but scientifically useful light.[17] A past action has been unexpectedly retrieved, and transformed into a judgement Norpois has seen fit to pass on the narrator and pass on to other people. As ordeal is transformed into exposure by *épreuve*, a word with a double meaning, the narrator has a veritable proof of his own failure to judge himself correctly, for his actions may be spirited away from him and magically transformed into simulacra of himself, which will satisfy other people's need to judge. The narrator feels helpless in relation to judgement when it behaves like an X-ray, when judgement, in other words, looks straight through him indifferently. He abandons himself to its superior truthfulness: his pre-emptive strategies for dealing with criticism have not worked in this instance. Apparently, he cannot afford to stop listening to the verbal performances of those who seem at all like him (Bloch, for example), because it is only by hearing their mistakes that he will be able to disguise himself as an acceptable Faubourg guest, and fit in.

Anxious listening to other people's speech and gestures might be the way forward to the defeat of externally imposed judgement, yet eavesdropping turns out to have unexpected side-effects, which have direct links with rivalry, but rivalry that is only partially or indirectly expressed.

[16] Roland Barthes in *La Chambre claire* asserts that the earliest photographs must have been seen as paintings and not as themselves (p. 55). Perhaps this explains why *épreuve* does not enter the photographic lexicon until around 1857. The word has been in use since the 12th cent. to mean 'action d'éprouver', 'ce qui permet de juger la valeur', 'danger qui éprouve le courage, la résistance'; and since the 16th cent. in the sense of publisher's 'proof'.

[17] X-rays were discovered by Wilhelm Röntgen in 1895.

When the narrator tries to talk to Norpois, the latter launches into a long disquisition comprising various reasons why he should not support the election of Marcel's father to the *Académie*, culminating in the triumphant, 'Donc lui donner ma voix serait de ma part une sorte de palinodie' (ii. 523; tr. iii. 257). The narrator is silenced at that moment, but later, having listened to Bloch trying to extract Norpois's true opinion of the Dreyfus Affair from a welter of inconclusive generalizations about it, Marcel gives vent to a *palinodie* of his own:

Peut-être la raison pour laquelle M. de Norpois parlait ainsi à Bloch comme s'ils eussent été d'accord venait-elle de ce qu'il était tellement antidreyfusard que, trouvant que le gouvernement ne l'était pas assez, il en était l'ennemi tout autant qu'étaient les dreyfusards. Peut-être parce que l'objet auquel il s'attachait en politique était quelque chose de plus profond, situé dans un autre plan, et d'où le dreyfusisme apparaissait comme une modalité sans importance et qui ne mérite pas de retenir un patriote soucieux des grandes questions extérieures. Peut-être, plutôt, parce que les maximes de sa sagesse politique ne s'appliquant qu'à des questions de forme, de procédé, d'opportunité, elles étaient aussi impuissantes à résoudre les questions de fond qu'en philosophie la pure logique l'est à trancher les questions d'existence, ou que cette sagesse même lui fît trouver dangereux de traiter de ces sujets et que, par prudence, il ne voulût parler que de circonstances secondaires. (ii. 538; tr. iii. 274–5)

Elegant as this tripartite undercutting of Norpois and his manner is, with its crescendo of parts each opened by *peut-être*, it is wide of the mark. For its final phrase, 'par prudence, il ne voulût parler que de circonstances secondaires', applies equally well to the narrator's choice of interlocutor. He is avoiding a confrontation with the object of his attack and complaining to a substitute, the reader. The narrator's attack imitates Norpois's own evasiveness. His judgement of Norpois may well be accurate, but does no more than announce itself, without being put to work. It looks very much like plaintiveness. We as readers are the recipients of a self-justificatory outburst, which is not converted into action.

The significance of this needs to be drawn out. There is another side to complaint, and it centres, as I suggested earlier, on the imperatives of rivalry. Norpois, like Bloch, can be considered the narrator's rival. Yet there is something strange about this: why should 'flat' characters, only present in the text to afford comic relief, threaten the narrator's far more complex textual existence as a self?[18] Rivalry there is, however, and unmistakably. When in conversation with Bloch, Norpois's changing tack on the Dreyfus Affair finds a subtle witness in the narrator. Bloch takes Norpois literally, and is thus easily outwitted by diplomatic language: 'Bloch pensait que la vérité politique peut être approximativement reconstituée par les cerveaux les plus lucides' (ii. 538; tr. iii. 275). The narrator knows better, and has not just an attack to offer the reader on Norpois, but a lesson in diplomacy and knowledge to offer on Bloch. This lesson is based on an understanding of medical diagnostic method:

> Or, même quand la vérité politique comporte des documents, il est rare que ceux-ci aient plus que la valeur d'un cliché radioscopique où le vulgaire croit que la maladie du patient s'inscrit en toutes lettres, tandis qu'en fait, ce cliché fournit un simple élément d'appréciation qui se joindra à beaucoup d'autres sur lesquels s'appliquera le raisonnement du médecin. . . . (ii. 538; tr. iii. 275)

X-rays here are evidence that the narrator knows how to read: 'un simple élément d'appréciation' must be combined 'à beaucoup d'autres', so that X-rays are only useful as *part* of an analysis. Yet we have seen how in another situation which involved Norpois, Marcel was rendered helpless by the idea that in fact X-rays might, of themselves, be able to reveal an absolute truth. Here, the narrator knowingly tells the reader what he could be telling Bloch about knowledge and smugly puts Bloch in his place. A rival is defeated although he is not aware of his defeat. Even more troublingly, the narrator's cleverness constitutes an *appeal* for us to ignore, or compensate him for, a previous moment of weakness, his own defeat at the hands of Norpois's X-ray memory.

This kind of displaced self-justification, passing in a circuit via the silent reader, but avoiding its real object within the text, has further ramifications. The narrator is presented with a very different type of 'rival' in the prince de Faffenheim-Munsterburg-Weinigen, Norpois's diplomatic equal, and

---

[18] See Ch. 4 on the tricky problem of character and characterization.

himself as hopeful as is Marcel's father for Norpois's support in an election to the *Académie des sciences morales et politiques*. The narrator of *A la recherche* starts his rendition of the conversation between Norpois and the prince Von by *ventriloquizing* the latter's thoughts on his chances of support. He makes the prince speak as though he were 'un naïf, un docteur Cottard' (ii. 554; tr. iii. 295):

les mots ont tout de même un sens, que diable! sans doute s'il ne me propose pas de voter pour moi, c'est qu'il n'y pense pas. Il parle trop de mon grand pouvoir, il doit croire que les alouettes me tombent toutes rôties, que j'ai autant de voix que j'en veux, et c'est pour cela qu'il ne m'offre pas la sienne, mais je n'ai qu'à le mettre au pied du mur, là, entre nous deux, et à lui dire: Hé bien! votez pour moi, et il sera obligé de le faire. (ii. 555; tr. iii. 295)

The narrator is thus rendering one fictional character *through* another already fictional character. This *naïf* sounds like a Cottard, the bumbling Verdurin acolyte, but also like a Bloch, because they both run the risk of taking language literally, taking the letter at face value, and thereby missing its essentially coded nature. The pastiche points to the gap between one person's understanding of another's intention by piling up a series of dead metaphors which the naïve speaker uses as clumsy meaning-building tools, instead of as codes which substitute for quite different meanings.

The pastiche fails to colonize the prince's language, however. He is no such *naïf*, and is used to 'ces conversations où on sait d'avance jusqu'où on veut aller et ce qu'on ne vous fera pas dire. Il n'ignorait pas que dans le langage diplomatique causer signifie offrir' (ii. 555; tr. iii. 295). The performance of pastiche will not do away with diplomatic conversation. In the world of diplomacy the art of conversation wears a helpless expression of indifference that breathes the desire to fulfil a request, without the commitment that concrete allusion to the request might bring. Here, the narrator can enjoy a display of private desire (the prince's desire for a 'présentation à l'Institut') which relies on the same 'méthode de lecture à travers des symboles superposés' (ii. 557; tr. iii. 297) that in affairs of state would signify war or peace. Such labour-intensive methodology, in which the 'possibilité que l'adversaire a, s'il est assez fort, ou n'a pas, de contenter, par moyen d'échange, un désir' (ii. 556; tr. iii. 296) is a sophisticated substitute for direct negotiation.

Yet the narrator's enjoyment is tempered with disquiet. In the prince Von, the narrator is faced not with a rival whom he can better by prating to the reader about technical deficiency, but one who by showing the hermetic closure of the diplomatic world and in relying on its means for all his needs, is a danger to the possibility of other kinds of interpretation not reliant on a *moyen d'échange*, in other words, a danger to the possibility of unmediated communication. The diplomatic *méthode de lecture* defines itself by means of fixed symbols, and judgements based on those symbols, excluding all that does not fit, appointing itself supreme judge of all action and intention. Denial of diplomacy's self-appointed status as arbiter will only restitute the importance of that status, by acknowledging it dialectically in order to deny it. So, the narrator tries another tack, and simply *desanctifies* the method by wilfully reapplying it to an unexpected context:

Il faut souvent descendre jusqu'aux êtres entretenus, hommes ou femmes, pour avoir à chercher le mobile de l'action ou les paroles en apparence les plus innocentes, dans l'intérêt, dans la nécessité de vivre. Quel homme ne sait que, quand une femme qu'il va payer lui dit: 'Ne parlons pas d'argent', cette parole doit être comptée, ainsi qu'on dit en musique, comme 'une mesure pour rien', et que si plus tard, elle lui déclare: 'Tu m'as fait trop de peine, tu m'as souvent caché la vérité, je suis à bout', il doit interpréter: 'Un autre protecteur lui offre davantage'? (ii. 557; tr. iii. 298)

Showing that the supremacy of the diplomatic method is only as sacred as the strength of the illusion its practitioners can maintain about it, diplomatic *symboles superposés* are here inverted to become the underpinning of all sexual negotiation.

The narrator seems, in the violence of his wilful reapplication, to have triumphed over both his rivals. Yet his flourish is not enough, it would seem:

Mais M. de Norpois et le prince allemand, . . . avaient accoutumé de vivre sur le même plan que les nations, lesquelles sont aussi, malgré leur grandeur, des êtres, d'égoïsme et de ruse, . . . qui peut les pousser jusqu'au meurtre, un *meurtre symbolique* souvent lui aussi, la simple hésitation à se battre ou le refus de se battre pouvant signifier pour une nation: 'périr'. Mais comme tout cela n'est pas dit dans les divers

Livres jaunes et autres, le peuple est volontiers pacifiste; s'il est guer-
rier, c'est instinctivement, par haine, par rancune, non par les raisons
qui ont décidé les chefs d'État avertis par les Norpois. (ii. 557; tr. iii.
298; my emphasis)

Diplomats think they are nations, and construct an idea of what
nationhood is on the basis of a grandeur which in reality merely
accommodates the grandeur of diplomatic egotism; nations,
the narrator asserts, are but humble bodies, composed of
smaller bodies, and they act on the basic imperatives of instinct
and will, hatred and resentment, in absolute ignorance of decisions taken by a Norpois. Diplomatic language, whose connotations must be implicit and never explicit in order to function
and maintain itself as a closed system, is judged by the narrator
by means of violent exposure. This collapsing of the uses of
diplomacy is a final kick aimed by the narrator, but it is a
perilous kick which signals its own desire for a *meurtre symbolique*, a kick of frustration which fears itself powerless in the face
of a closed system of judgements.[19] If the narrator has
triumphed over a set of rivals, it is to the reader and in a private
sphere. There is no direct confrontation with Bloch, Norpois,
or the prince in any of these encounters.

3. DESIRE AND INDIFFERENCE

When a *desired* object enters the frame, however, and more
importantly, one indifferent to the narrator (both sexually and
socially), Marcel's close attention produces not the indirection
of displaced self-justification, but a protective weave of textual
effects around attentiveness. Here is how, for example, the
duchesse de Guermantes mocking both the absent Mme de
Cambremer and her aunt Mme de Villeparisis is written, 'pour
avoir la satisfaction de montrer qu'elle était savante autant que

---

[19] The *meurtre symbolique* in another theoretical language is a hypothesis for the
establishment of power relations and a hierarchized social structure: we are one
step away from Freud's *Totem and Taboo*. The narrator attacks the prince again,
much later in the text, by revealing to the duc de Guermantes at the prince de
Guermantes's *soirée* that, 'A propos de dreyfusards . . . il paraît que le prince Von
l'est' (iii. 77; tr. iv. 90). It should be noted that this is one of the very few times that
the narrator speaks directly at a party.

puriste': ' "Mais si," dit-elle avec un demi-rire que les restes de la mauvaise humeur jouée réprimaient' (ii. 500; tr. iii. 230). The duchesse is *savante* and *puriste*, in a good mood and a bad mood, all simultaneously. Or rather, her being all of those things depends on the writing's capacity for showing that she wants to show all of these states. There is something strange about this narratorial refusal to judge. The narrator writes up indiscriminately what he sees of the duchesse, catching into his writing embryonic or fully formed components of critical judgements without sifting and sorting them into a definite stance, a final character delineation. Let us look at more examples of this catch-all contradiction. The duchesse is a virtuoso exponent of how the state of indifference can benefit those who wish to seem different, and different because superior:

cette attention indifférente qui commence par ôter tout point de contact entre ce que l'on considère et soi-même, son regard fixait tour à tour chacun de nous, puis inspectait les canapés et les fauteuils mais en s'adoucissant alors de cette sympathie humaine qu'éveille la présence même insignifiante d'une chose que l'on connaît, d'une chose qui est presque une personne. (ii. 503; tr. iii. 233)

The duchesse's manipulation of indifference is infectious and the narrator feels constrained to use the Guermantes name as nonchalantly as everyone around him: 'Mais ce devait être une affectation de leur part comme quand les poètes classiques ne nous avertissent pas des intentions profondes qu'ils ont cependant eues, affectation que moi aussi je m'efforçais d'imiter en disant sur le ton le plus naturel: la duchesse de Guermantes, comme un nom qui eût ressemblé à d'autres' (ii. 506–7; tr. iii. 237–8).

Yet not two pages on, his besotted reverence appears to have been forgotten: the duchesse becomes a woman 'en qui on pouvait toujours, comme au moment d'une marée spirituelle, voir le flux d'une curiosité à l'égard des intellectuels célèbres croiser en route le reflux du snobisme aristocratique' (ii. 508; tr. iii. 240). Then again, the duchesse is capable of expressing surprising opinions, and her approval of Bergotte, for example, falls into this category. 'C'est la seule personne que j'aie envie de connaître,' she says, and enjoys Bergotte's unconventionality: 'Il ne lui a pas dit une fois "Monseigneur" '(ii. 508 and 509;

tr. iii. 240). Flimsy though the actual content of her view might seem, the narrator chooses to read into it a harbinger of future public opinion: 'Ces jugements subversifs, isolés et malgré tout justes, sont ainsi portés dans le monde par de rares personnes supérieures aux autres. Et ils y dessinent les premiers linéa-ments de la hiérarchie des valeurs telle que l'établira la généra-tion suivante au lieu de s'en tenir éternellement à l'ancienne' (ii. 509; tr. iii. 240). An extraordinarily complex fascination is playing itself out here: the narratorial dramatization of the duchesse's indifference to animate objects is itself undertaken using a mode of indiscriminate inclusiveness. The semantic switchover through which Guermantes disdain is rendered *by way of* narratorial enthusiasm shows us self-justification working to quite a new aim: the desire to please through faithfulness. This unfiltered, uncensored desiring response to indifference comes clad about with material a non-desiring eye might judge negatively. We are not dealing here with the fantastic mobility of desire's gaze as it plots the movements of the *jeunes filles*, but the self-justificatory desire to get everything into the picture, regardless of utility or even pleasure to the narratorial *moi*.

Perhaps we are coming up against nothing more unusual than an authorial wish (even if shuffled off under the guise of a narratorial voice) to be surprised by his own characters, rem-iniscent of Freud's observation of a child's 'Fort-da' game?[20] Admiration, however, breeds other kinds of interpretation: self-justifications which grant temporary dispensation from admira-tion, to compensate for indifference and rejection. An aristocratic maverick opinion is not always authorized. During a discussion of *Les Sept Princesses*,[21] the narrator sneers mentally at the duchesse:

'Quelle buse!' pensais-je, irrité de l'accueil glacial qu'elle m'avait fait. Je trouvais une sorte d'âpre satisfaction à constater sa complète

---

[20] *Beyond the Pleasure Principle, SE* xviii. 14–17. By pretending to lose an object the child knows she can retrieve, she can experience all the pleasure of control over the object, as well as simulate the surprise of its return. But since the object's autonomy is simulated, the child is only demonstrating the more profoundly her dependence on it.

[21] By Maurice Maeterlinck (1891). One-act Symbolist play: the action is almost completely static, with the eponymous princesses asleep for the most part on a marble flight of steps, totally silent throughout, and one of them dying of her long wait.

incompréhension de Maeterlinck. 'C'est pour une pareille femme que tous les matins je fais tant de kilomètres, vraiment j'ai de la bonté! Maintenant c'est moi qui ne voudrais pas d'elle.' Tels étaient les mots que je me disais; ils étaient le contraire de ma pensée; c'étaient *de purs mots de conversation*, comme nous nous en disons dans ces moments où trop agités pour rester seuls avec nous-mêmes nous éprouvons le besoin, à défaut d'autre interlocuteur, de causer avec nous, sans sincérité, comme avec un étranger. (ii. 526–7; tr. iii. 261; my emphasis)

Compressed into these few lines are further informing patterns about self-justificatory activity. Overriding all other memories internal to the novel which return as the narrator silently mocks the duchesse, in order to compensate himself for her *accueil glacial*, is the memory of Swann's cry of self-disgust:

Et avec cette muflerie intermittente qui reparaissait chez lui dès qu'il n'était plus malheureux et que baissait du même coup le niveau de sa moralité, il s'écria en lui-même: 'Dire que j'ai gâché des années de ma vie, que j'ai voulu mourir, que j'ai eu mon plus grand amour, pour une femme qui ne me plaisait pas, qui n'était pas mon genre!' (i. 375; tr. i. 459)

Talking to ourselves defuses tension, and plays out scenarios in which our liberty from certain all-embracing mental states like love or jealousy may be reclaimed. *Purs mots de conversation*, however, or talking to a stranger, are a relief only when the interlocutor is a true stranger. When Swann cries out within himself, his crassness, the *muflerie*, marks knowledge that he is telling himself a monolithic truth about his own life. The textual repetition that is activated by the narrator's internal conversation with himself here is both a stronger and a weaker echo of Swann's point-blank truthfulness, for the knowledge that the narrator consoles himself with here is theoretical knowledge about a play, hence about an extraneous object. For Swann, the playing out of theoretical revenge scenarios by talking to himself comes too late to extricate him from the real scenario he has played into. The narrator's heavy-handed reapplication of the same self-justificatory technique to an unimportant item is a move whose very excessiveness might yet screen him from Swann-type errors, by forestalling a situation in which self-justification might be crucial and not just playful.

4. THE IMPLICATIONS OF SYMPATHY

All the encounters so far analysed have, as it were, had a happy ending: the narrator has been able to wriggle out of implicatedness in other people's lives through various strategies of rejection and compensation. Far more difficult to negotiate, however, is the kind of self-justification involved when a face-to-face encounter enmeshes him with another self, and I want now to look in some detail at two kinds of implicatedness that take place while the narrator is at Mme de Villeparisis's salon.

The first concerns that other Combray throwback, Legrandin. He cannot contain his astonishment on seeing the narrator at the same salon as himself: 'Il s'arrêta net en m'apercevant' (ii. 498; tr. iii. 227). The narrator strikes up conversation, and makes a gaffe, 'sans songer combien j'allais à la fois le blesser et lui faire croire à l'intention de le blesser'. He says, 'Eh bien, Monsieur, je suis presque excusé d'être dans un salon puisque je vous y trouve' (ii. 501; tr. iii. 230). Legrandin's response, or rather the way it emerges from him runs thus: 'une voix rageuse et vulgaire que je ne lui soupçonnais pas et qui, nullement en rapport rationnel avec ce qu'il disait d'habitude, en avait un autre plus immédiat et plus saisissant avec quelque chose qu'il éprouvait' (ii. 501; tr. iii. 231). This *voix rageuse* giving utterance to Legrandin's unconscious thought processes also gives them away, and marks them with an unmistakable signature. Legrandin's reaction is out of all proportion to the narrator's unintended insult. The narrator seizes upon this evidence of a private self only tremulously separated from the public manifestation of selfhood, and rushes straight to a general rule:

C'est que, ce que nous éprouvons, comme nous sommes décidés à toujours le cacher, nous n'avons jamais pensé à la façon dont nous l'exprimerions. Et tout d'un coup, c'est en nous une bête immonde et inconnue qui se fait entendre et dont l'accent parfois peut aller jusqu'à faire aussi peur à qui reçoit cette confidence involontaire, elliptique et presque irrésistible de votre défaut ou de votre vice, que ferait l'aveu soudain indirectement et bizarrement proféré par un criminel ne pouvant s'empêcher de confesser un meurtre dont vous ne le saviez pas coupable. (ii. 501; tr. iii. 231)

The passage begins from an empathetic, inclusive position, in which any of us might unexpectedly give away a perceived defect we had chosen to hide, precisely because of having no voice on tap in which to dilute it. At first his generalization about public self-exposure is written in the first-person plural. Mid-sentence, however, the general ownership of a *bête immonde* is handed over to a *vous*, mysteriously becoming 'votre défaut ou . . . votre vice'. The subject of the passage splits, pushing responsibility for both revealing and receiving a guilty secret onto another.[22] Moreover, such a shift of personal pronoun exempts the first-person singular. The narratorial *je* tries three methods of self-exculpation: first of all he explicitly says that he did not mean to insult Legrandin; then he transforms Legrandin into the object of a general examination of actions that give us away; and thirdly, he gives away the responsibility for revelation altogether. The *bête immonde* he has noticed in somebody else suddenly puts him in Norpois's place: other people's messy revelations about themselves seem to call for some kind of response. The narrator glimpses that self-exposure and any subsequent condemnation or endorsement of that exposure is an infinitely mobile hinge between the self and the world, but for the time being, at least, he treats exposure merely as a giveaway that must be passed on as soon as possible. If rivalry at parties consists in attack and defeat of a perceived enemy, Legrandin has literally given the game away, and no attack is called for. The narrator not only sees Legrandin's mistake, but, importantly, fears that it calls for some kind of compensation from himself. As though the narrator's thoughts have led him too close to another truth he wishes to avoid, he retreats to a safer tack: 'Mais vraiment Legrandin n'avait pas besoin de rappeler si souvent qu'il appartenait à une autre planète quand tous ses mouvements convulsifs de colère ou d'amabilité étaient gouvernés par le désir d'avoir une bonne position dans celle-ci' (ii. 501; tr. iii. 231).

If there is nothing to pre-empt, the narrator's method of dealing with the rigours of fitting in has nothing to jostle

---

[22] Julia Kristeva has shown the importance of paying close attention to the use of personal pronouns as evidence of unconscious desires. See particularly *La Révolution du langage poétique* (1974).

against, and he is left only with his own irritation, struggling for a response. When resistance is withdrawn, self-justification has nothing to work against.

Our second opportunity to listen to the workings of implicatedness takes place when the narrator talks to the mother of Saint-Loup. Mme de Marsantes behaves towards the narrator with 'un empressement qui me faisait presque de la peine parce que je le sentais dicté par la crainte qu'elle avait d'être fâchée par moi avec ce fils qu'elle n'avait pas encore vu aujourd'hui' (ii. 573; tr. iii. 316). The narrator intuits that Mme de Marsantes has a hidden reason for her *empressement*. From a simple perception that other people's actions are ambiguously motivated, something which at first, as we have seen, is a source merely of curiosity, the narrator's analysis is forced to shift to a complex empathy which implicates him. The unnecessary zeal that he notices in Mme de Marsantes leaves the narrator unable not to include himself in what he notices. Furthermore, he perceives his place in this *empressement* to be transformative *of* himself, not in the way that Norpois's gossip had redistributed his parts, but by turning him into a conduit for an anger which should by rights be directed at her son. Her zeal, which makes such an impression on the narrator, is produced out of fear, but this fear, he realizes, finds its source in his presence. The *peine* that he feels is both psychological and an undeserved sanction for someone else's misdemeanour. The narrator has been turned into a scapegoat: helpless and innocent. But something is peculiar about this process of transformation: he has been turned into a scapegoat by his own powers of observation.

Saint-Loup's response to maternal demands being imposed on him to break with Rachel, his mistress, in turn evinces elements of the guilty frustration demonstrated by his mother towards the narrator:

il fit à sa mère les reproches que sans doute il se sentait peut-être mériter; c'est ainsi que les égoïstes ont toujours le dernier mot; ayant posé d'abord que leur résolution est inébranlable, plus le sentiment auquel on fait appel en eux pour qu'ils y renoncent est touchant, plus ils trouvent condamnables, non pas eux qui y résistent, mais ceux qui les mettent dans la nécessité d'y résister, de sorte que leur propre dureté peut aller jusqu'à la plus extrême cruauté sans que cela fasse à leurs yeux qu'aggraver d'autant la culpabilité de l'être assez indélicat pour souffrir, pour avoir raison, et leur causer ainsi lâchement la douleur d'agir contre leur propre pitié. (ii. 577; tr. iii. 321–2)

Saint-Loup tries to blame his mother for the guilt he feels, as Mme de Marsantes ended up blaming the narrator for not being Saint-Loup. The dynamic of this dyadic structure, with its false triangulation due to the narrator's inclusion as a Saint-Loup substitute, takes on an internal logic when the narrator wants to compensate Mme de Marsantes: 'J'aurais voulu trouver quelque excuse à la conduite de son fils' (ii. 577; tr. iii. 322). He is forestalled by Mme de Marsantes herself: 'Voyez-vous, monsieur, les mères sont très égoïstes' (ii. 577; tr. iii. 322). She repeats and displaces the accusation of egoism she would like to direct at her son onto herself, and in so doing repeats and displaces guilt onto the narrator, by pre-empting his attempt to placate her. Far from excusing the conduct of the son, the narrator finds himself even more the conductor of the mother's misdirected resentment:

Maintenant je me serais aussi volontiers chargé d'une mission pour faire rompre Robert et sa maîtresse qu'il y a quelques heures pour qu'il partît vivre tout à fait avec elle. Dans un cas Saint-Loup m'eût jugé un ami traître, dans l'autre cas sa famille m'eût appelé son mauvais génie. J'étais pourtant le même homme à quelques heures de distance. (ii. 577; tr. iii. 322)

Immediately after their awkward conversation, the narrator and Mme de Marsantes return to the salon from a pursuit of Saint-Loup, and Mme de Marsantes takes her leave of the narrator: 'Mme de Marsantes me dit au revoir avec anxiété. Ces sentiments se rapportaient à Robert, elle était sincère. Mais elle cessa de l'être pour redevenir grande dame: "J'ai été *intéressée, si heureuse, flattée,* de causer un peu avec vous. Merci! Merci!" ' (ii. 579; tr. iii. 325). What might before have stood as a piece of social satire, a mockery of the manners of the *grande dame,* is altered by the way in which the narrator has become involved with Mme de Marsantes. Instead, she seems to mock him. Watching other people and mocking them from a safe distance has unnerving repercussions when the narrator's desire to compensate for Saint-Loup's *conduite* has instead transformed him into a conduit for a mother's frustration.

The outcome of this party, then, is a realization for the narrator that other people's judgements are not simply passed, nor

can they always simply be pre-empted. They can actively transform the person they are passed on. Contradictory judgements
made about the same person, rather than working to cancel
each other out, might instead cancel out the autonomy of that
person.

What we have heard thus far about Marcel's experiments in self-
justification directed externally at a potentially dangerous
social situation shows us that it can offer multiple resources for
disguise, observation, and indirect aggression in terms of
action in the narrative, but also startling possibilities for the
transformative modelling of alterity, in the textures of the writing. And where self-justification is directed either aggressively
or vulnerably *back* at the narrator, he has seen opportunities for
mastery or for tolerance of others come his way. Self-justification has been functioning for the purposes of party-going as
epistemological toe-dipping in dangerous waters, but also as a
powerful hermeneutic and cognitive modelling tool.

The dinner with the duc and duchesse de Guermantes, and
the *soirée* with the prince de Guermantes, however, show self-
justification to be functioning, beyond narratorial performances of it, as a method of preserving a particular social
order, and its key manifestation, which we must spend some
time examining, is through the workings of *politesse*.

Early on at the Guermantes *dîner*, a suspension is put in place
which opens up a mode of assessment enabling observation, but
also tolerance of what is seen. The narrator starts to focus on the
nature of *politesse*, and makes the following comment about the
fact that the duc and duchesse de Guermantes only address the
princesse de Parme in the third person: 'par un reste hérité de
la vie des cours qui s'appelle la politesse mondaine et qui n'est
pas superficiel, mais où, par un retournement du dehors au
dedans, c'est la superficie qui devient essentielle et profonde'
(ii. 719; tr. iii. 492). This 'retournement du dehors au dedans'
rests on the assumption that the *dedans* should be 'essentielle et
profonde'. The movement implies turning outside in; but if
dehors moves *dedans*, whatever was originally inside seems to

vanish. The reversal is incomplete, and the nature of superficiality is thereby suspended, since it is treated both as an *opposite* to profundity (which is being promoted as more valuable), and simultaneously as *replacing* profundity entirely. Superficiality is being both judged and aesthetically appreciated. But as the party scene proceeds, we see more and more of the devastating side-effects of such a suspension.

The workings of *politesse mondaine* are most clearly to be analysed in direct speech. Ever the eavesdropper, Marcel has a keen ear for an aristocratic emphasis on saying 'les choses qui pouvaient faire le plus de plaisir à l'interlocuteur' (ii. 721; tr. iii. 495). There is something deeply troubling for the narrator about this dispensation of pleasure, which seems to stem from the unverifiability of its origins. No fixable starting-point, whether socially or genetically engineered, can account for *politesse*, and yet its performance generates a powerful ideological context, which grips its participants, both binding them within the group to one another, and excluding dissenting criticism:

Dans une partie importante de l'aristocratie, . . . ce trait de caractère a cessé d'être individuel; cultivé par l'éducation, entretenu par l'idée d'une grandeur propre qui ne peut craindre de s'humilier, qui ne connaît pas de rivales, . . . il est devenu le caractère générique d'une classe. Et même ceux que des défauts personnels trop opposés empêchent de le garder dans leur cœur, en portent la trace inconsciente dans leur vocabulaire ou leur gesticulation. (ii. 722; tr. iii. 495)

For the aristocratic class, compliments are more than complements to their general behaviour; generosity 'par des paroles qui n'engagent à rien' (ii. 721; tr. iii. 495) has been internalized, and is practically a phylogenetic consideration, one which distinguishes the aristocracy from the bourgeoisie: 'On y rencontre cette disposition bienveillante, à titre de qualité individuelle compensatrice d'un défaut, non pas, hélas, chez les amis les plus sûrs, mais du moins chez les plus agréables compagnes. Elle fleurit en tout cas tout isolément' (ii. 722; tr. iii. 495).

Amongst the bourgeoisie, giving pleasure to others is merely a gesture compensating for another fault, a defective sincerity, at most an ontogenetic oddity; amongst the aristocracy, it seems to be an ineluctable necessity, a predetermination. The aristocracy has a monopoly on *snobisme évangélique* (ii. 720; tr.

iii. 493). Its widespread currency within the aristocracy, put
another way, designates it as an economy, but which operates
only one way: 'la duchesse de Guermantes, qui m'avait fait tant
de bonjours avec la main à l'Opéra, avait eu l'air furieux que
je la saluasse dans la rue, comme les gens qui, ayant une fois
donné un louis à quelqu'un, pensent qu'avec celui-là ils sont
en règle pour toujours' (ii. 718; tr. iii. 491). Charity may leave
the aristocratic home, but dispensing one's generosity is
expected to grant a dispensation from incoming opportunists.
Inherited status, where the means to sustain that status are not
in question, manifests itself in the Faubourg in indifference,
and turns matters of scruple into matters only of form. The
formalism of *politesse mondaine*, as Benjamin, Girard, Adorno,
Descombes, and many others have so clearly seen, seems, on
one level, to be readable as the purest kind of self-justification:
any kind of system that is self-reproducing must theoretically
be justifying its continued existence solely upon that perfect
replication.[23]

What Marcel wants to know more about, however, is not *that*
but *how* self-justification functions in public language as a
highly sophisticated dynamic of affective engagement and
manipulation, which risks at any moment being transformed
into a hostile means of rejection, judgement, or expulsion. If
what he has feared until this point in the development of the
narrative has been his own expulsion from the Faubourg, but
what he has encountered has instead been group indifference,
what he wants above all to understand are the intricate interconnections that seem to run between self-justification and
indifference, whether his own or the aristocracy's, the different
articulations of themselves that these two categories of human
behaviour provoke in each other, and whether a link may be
drawn between social offhandedness, whose underlying motivation is self-preservative, and asocial evil.

---

[23] The British naturalist, Philip Henry Gosse (1810–88), tried in 1857 (two years
before Darwin's *The Origin of Species*) to prove a link between genetic inheritance
and God in the now entirely ridiculed *Omphalos: An Attempt to Untie the Geological
Knot*. He asserted that evidence of evolution was in fact evidence of God: evolution
was simply a perfect palimpsest, and all the possible evolutionary changes had
already been accounted for by the Creation. This spectacularly circular argument
in favour of navel-gazing is an excellent analogy for the Guermantes's self-sufficient
politesse.

Critics of *A la recherche* tend to avoid the acutely painful question of the limits of tolerance in favour of delighting at the play of subjectivity, and narratorial largesse of interpretation. Leo Bersani and Jean-Pierre Richard have both brilliantly analysed the psychological and phenomenological aspects of the Proustian relation to *having*, in all its modes: taking, ingesting, possessing.[24] But the questions raised by Marcel's presence at parties of what is and is not *tolerable*, of *how much can be taken*, how much is enough, and how much is justifiable, are, above all, a set of moral questions, and it is with the negotiation of these in a public sphere that the rest of this chapter concerns itself.

Historicizing the Guermantes family, for instance, or injecting his own vision of them with time past, does little to justify or root the formalism of *politesse* for Marcel. When he reaches back into French history to the example of Louis XIV, and to Saint-Simon's *Mémoires* for a justificatory explanation of aristocratic identity, the very intactness of the aristocracy over two centuries exerts an unexpected pressure upon Marcel's capacity and inclination to judge the whole of the Faubourg:

dans les manières de M. de Guermantes, homme attendrissant de gentillesse et révoltant de dureté, esclave des plus petites obligations et délié des pactes les plus sacrés, je retrouvais encore intacte après plus de deux siècles écoulés cette déviation particulière à la vie de cour sous Louis XIV et qui transporte les scrupules de conscience du domaine des affections et de la moralité aux questions de pure forme. (ii. 729; tr. iii. 504)

Built into the continuity of the Guermantes descent are unjustifiable, mutually exclusive contradictions which can do nothing to reassure the narrator that *politesse* is available as sincerity, truth, or reliability. And worse, Marcel's own continued presence as observer of people he tells us at length are so despicable bears within it the uneasy potential to lose its footing in several directions: if he stays, and adopts Saint-Simon's mantle as purveyor of the Faubourg's *compte rendu*, he will be justifying

---

[24] See Leo Bersani, *Marcel Proust* (1965). The analysis of the phenomenological language of contagion, assimilation, contamination, and reciprocity in *A la recherche* has come from Jean-Pierre Richard, *Proust et le monde sensible* (1974) and still underpins the best studies of Proustian stylistics.

his own position by means of flattering commentary. If he leaves, exiting the arena, he effectively thereby also preserves it intact. Acts of ironic guerilla sabotage will leave him biting the hand feeding him. There is a very real moral dilemma to be faced here: Marcel must negotiate the configuration of his own presence inside the narrative, and make moral choices, each of which has a distinct drawback in the form of compromise, about which identificatory narratorial position to adopt: revolutionary, apologist, memorialist, or arch critic. Adopting a position will always entail abandoning the privilege of ambiguity and multiple, pre-emptive interpretations, and will introduce the hard contours of binary oppositions, and the possibility of attack.

Yet the temptation is to persevere with inclusive model-building, and its main textual manifestation, we find, takes the form of digression. A digression from the account of the Guermantes *dîner* takes place, lasting a full forty-three pages (ii. 730–73; tr. iii. 505–58). The identity and utility of digressiveness raises a vital question that Chapter 2 will pursue. This long excursus from the direct narration of the events at the *dîner* accounts in convoluted detail for Guermantes wit, for the exclusive importance of the Guermantes within the Faubourg Saint-Germain, for other members of this exclusive set, and their reasons for belonging to it. It begins:

les Guermantes étaient assez différents du reste de la société aristocratique; ils étaient plus précieux et plus rares. Ils m'avaient donné au premier aspect l'impression contraire, je les avais trouvés vulgaires, pareils à tous les hommes et à toutes les femmes, mais parce que préalablement j'avais vu en eux, comme en Balbec, en Florence, en Parme, des noms. (ii. 730; tr. iii. 505)

Reliant on the split Proustian narratorial voice with its extraordinarily elastic capacity for introducing revision, this long digression facilitates, and can hold in play, the very contradictions that might otherwise force the narrator to abandon partygoing and party-goers. He does not formulate one position in relation to the Faubourg which would either hold him at a protective distance from it, or engrain him within it, but which in both identificatory conceptions would posit him as a particle within or outside a leviathan. Marcel's strategy instead is to assimilate its moral discrepancies as so much unsorted and unjudged verbal matter. Having sought in the first instance to be himself assimilated through imitation of that verbal matter, as narrator *inside* the plot action of the narrative, this digression reverses such a movement, and accommodates inside the body of the text inconclusive commentary, analysis, and observation by the narrator *of* the text. To be able to include is the same as not having to conclude.

The narrator makes a false textual separation between an ongoing narrative in which he is a protagonist, and a reflective account of characters, in order to sustain incommensurable expectations, namely, that the famous Guermantes arrogance both is and is not morally worthless: 'Pour un Guermantes (fût-il bête), être intelligent, c'était avoir la dent dure, être capable de dire des méchancetés, d'emporter le morceau, c'était aussi pouvoir vous tenir tête aussi bien sur la peinture, sur la musique, sur l'architecture, parler anglais' (ii. 734; tr. iii. 510). This summary of a competitive, commodified intelligence, pre-packaged into subjects, functions as a maxim about the Guermantes and the way they identify themselves. It points to the aristocratic reliance on a fixed frame of reference into which a rotating stock of new subject-matter is inserted and preyed upon, and we might expect to find the narrator drawing out the significance of this.

Having noticed the way in which the narrator has shuffled parts of his account of the Guermantes *dîner*, so that all his opinions have been stacked into a textual moment out of party time, however, we make another discovery. When it comes to the straightforward narration of the party itself, in the prolonged conversations we witness about art, and contemporary French cultural events, the narrator remains silent. Just as there is no food on offer at this dinner party, the narrator is also withdrawn as a participating entity in the group he describes.[25] Let me give some examples of this odd narratorial self-efface-ment. When the duc gives an opinion on the subject of music, his wife is quick to respond:

[25] There is very little food at this succession of parties. Only soup, *petits fours*, and orangeade make an appearance—a strange irony that one of the received ideas about Proust is his obsession with cuisine.

'Vous ne me croiriez peut-être pas, mais le soir, si ma femme se met au piano, il m'arrive de lui demander un vieil air d'Auber, de Boieldieu, même de Beethoven! Voilà ce que j'aime. En revanche, pour Wagner, cela m'endort immédiatement.'

'Vous avez tort,' dit Mme de Guermantes, 'avec des longueurs insupportables Wagner avait du génie. *Lohengrin* est un chef-d'œuvre. Même dans *Tristan* il y a çà et là une page curieuse. Et le Chœur des fileuses du *Vaisseau fantôme* est une pure merveille.' (ii. 781; tr. iii. 567)

Oriane is at her ease in the galleries, libraries, and concert halls of high culture, but the nonchalant disdain with which she reels off edited highlights of Wagner, taken together with Marcel's silence, create a gap of interpretation: we have seen the narrator justify *himself* in relation to one of her literary opinions, but here we do not know how he would justify Wagnerian opera: his thoughts are not given.

The comtesse d'Arpajon possesses a collection of literary letters,[26] and posits her theories about literary genius on the basis of this ownership: 'Avez-vous remarqué que souvent les lettres d'un écrivain sont supérieures au reste de son œuvre? Comment s'appelle donc cet auteur qui a écrit *Salammbô*?' (ii. 779; tr. iii. 565).[27] Flaubert, which she mishears as Paul Bert or Fulbert, must, according to her logic, be a poor writer, since his correspondence is 'curieuse et supérieure à ses livres' (ii. 780; tr. iii. 566): 'Elle l'explique du reste, car on voit par tout ce qu'on dit de la peine qu'il a à à faire un livre, que ce n'était pas un véritable écrivain, un homme doué' (ii. 780; tr. iii. 566). We are detained at the level of textual rendition of conversation, and our attention is drawn to what lies between the quotation marks. Satire or not, within those quotation marks lie theories about art and literature: Wagner may be reduced to *une page curieuse*, Flaubert's difficulties with writing show that he cannot be a good writer, and the narrator's silence about these theories produces an undecidability about the status of judgement.

The duc announces his boredom at Bornier's *La Fille de Roland*: 'Mon Dieu, c'était bougrement embêtant'.[28] When the

---

[26] By vicomte Henri de Bornier (1825–1901).

[27] Gustave Flaubert, *Salammbô* (1862).

[28] Bornier's *La Fille de Roland*, a historic drama first staged at the Théâtre-Français (1875). It stages characters from *La Chanson de Roland*. Here the duc seems to be referring to a play as though it were the latest craze, while according to the

narrator insinuates that he too has no time for the playwright, the duc immediately assumes that 'un ressentiment personnel' must be at the root of the narrator's distaste: 'Je vois que vous avez une dent contre lui . . . Racontez-nous ça! Mais si, vous devez avoir quelque cadavre entre vous, puisque vous le dénigrez. C'est long, *La Fille de Roland*, mais c'est assez senti' (ii. 780; tr. iii. 566). He changes his opinion in an attempt to draw out the narrator conversationally. The narrator is saved from having to reply by the duchesse's interruption: ' "Senti" est très juste pour un auteur aussi odorant' (ii. 780; tr. iii. 566). Collapsing the possibility of a serious discussion by a narrative diversion, the narrator's integrity remains intact: he does not criticize Bornier's play, or the duc's taste, but by the same token, he offers no resistance to the way in which the duc confuses Bornier with his work, either to the duc or to the reader, although the implications of such a collapse are so famously crucial to *A la recherche*, to its author, and to its bivocal narratorial agency.

The duc also announces what music pleases him, mixing Mozart indiscriminately with comic operas by Auber, and associating with the same negligence *Le Bal de Sceaux* and *Les Mohicans de Paris* (ii. 781; tr. iii. 567).[29] The duc's indiscriminate inclusiveness goes uncommented. We might be tempted to explain all this silence away as a compliment to a discerning Proustian readership, able to work out the appropriate 'value' of each artwork without needing to be told; and as a joke at the expense of the aristocracy, unable to sort 'true worth' from triviality.

Yet this is a hypothesis that does not work satisfactorily: the duchesse, at least, is a character whose critical capacities complicate such a straightforward thesis. She cites from 'A un voyageur', 'avec un sentiment juste, faisant sortir la triste pensée de toutes les forces de son intonation, la posant au-delà de sa voix'.[30] The duchesse's recitation is met with a burst of

chronology of the text, a play from 1875 should have been showing about twenty-three years previously, at the time of Swann's story. Proust's somewhat *ad hoc* treatment of straightforward chronological time is famous.

[29] Auber's comic operas are *Fra Diavolo* (1830), and *Les Diamants de la Couronne* (1841). *Le Bal de Sceaux* (1830) is by Balzac (one of the novellas from *Scènes de la vie privée*), and *Les Mohicans de Paris* (1854) by Alexandre Dumas père.

[30] The full quotation is 'Les morts durent bien peu. Laissons-les sous la pierre! | Hélas, dans le cercueil ils tombent en poussière, | Moins vite qu'en nos cœurs!', Victor Hugo, 6 July 1829, *Les Feuilles d'automne*.

narratorial activity. He sets about transforming her quotation by focusing on its effects on *his* memory, ignoring its present context, and turns the duchesse, rather than her quotation, into a side-effect of what he hears. She is endowed, all of a sudden, with 'un désir de prosaïsme par où elle atteignait à la poésie et un esprit purement de société qui ressuscitait devant moi des paysages' (ii. 785; tr. iii. 572): 'Et quand on était fatigué du composite et bigarré langage moderne, c'était, tout en sachant qu'elle exprimait bien moins de choses, un grand repos d'écouter la causerie de Mme de Guermantes' (ii. 785; tr. iii. 572). As though threatened by the possibility of an authentic pleasure from her knowledge and appropriation of literary work, he makes it inappropriate to her, but useful for his own purposes, withdrawing to pore over her offering until he can produce it again in terms that suit him, exercising in this way a control over the duchesse's trespass onto literary terrain: 'Comme ce goût était à l'opposé du mien, elle four-nissait à mon esprit de la littérature quand elle me parlait du faubourg Saint-Germain, et ne me paraissait jamais si stupide-ment faubourg Saint-Germain que quand elle me parlait littérature' (ii. 786; tr. iii. 572–3). When the aristocracy, far from displaying its own stupidity in its own words, manifests literary sensitivity akin to the narrator's own, then he reworks what might seem like discrimination of a useful kind into a condemnation.

This transformative work, however, does not fully resolve the dilemma of the way literature is used in the Faubourg. When Mme d'Arpajon quotes Musset back to the duchesse, thinking it to be a line from Hugo, and wishing it could be inscribed on a fan that would be presented to her by her former lover, the duc, Mme de Guermantes summarizes her idiocy cogently: 'elle croit qu'elle l'aime comme elle croit en ce moment qu'elle cite du Victor Hugo parce qu'elle dit un vers de Musset' (ii. 786; tr. iii. 573).[31] The duchesse herself is at moments perfectly capable of putting a literary text to work and using it to comment on her own situation with startlingly accurate irony. For all the narrator's transformative and fragmenting manipulation of her

---

[31] The *vers* is, 'Ces reliques du cœur ont aussi leur poussière!', *La Nuit d'octobre* (1837), Alfred de Musset, *Œuvres complètes* (1963), 156.

representation, there are still moments where the duchesse can return intact, and her direct speech displays a capacity to make connections far too like the narrator's own for comfort. Strange perceptiveness indeed for the character so often written off as an allegory of cruelty by commentators because of the 'souliers rouges' incident.[32]

Beyond opinions, critiques, and quotations from or about literature and other kinds of artwork, the duchesse in particular is, furthermore, capable of appealing directly to the narrator in order to try to please him: ' "Vous devez me trouver bien démodée," reprit-elle en s'adressant à moi, "je sais qu'aujourd'hui c'est considéré comme une faiblesse d'aimer les idées en poésie" ' (ii. 787; tr. iii. 574). Self-reflexive enough to understand where her ideas stand in relation to an overall view of poetry, she capitalizes on her knowledge to reassert her *politesse*, and this brings to our attention a crucial gesture on the part of the narrator.

If the duchesse can appeal directly to the narrator's intellect, out of, but therefore, of course, within, the strictures of *politesse*, Marcel is elsewhere himself not above asking for reassurance from her which would placate and justify him, and the subject of his appeal dredges up, once again, Norpois's opinion of him:

Me rappelant que M. de Norpois avait dit que j'avais eu l'air de vouloir lui baiser la main, pensant qu'il avait sans doute raconté cette histoire à Mme de Guermantes et, en tout cas, n'avait pu lui parler de moi que méchamment, puisque, malgré son amitié avec mon père, il n'avait pas hésité à me rendre si ridicule, *je ne fis pas ce qu'eût fait un homme du monde*. Il aurait dit qu'il détestait M. de Norpois et le lui avait fait sentir; il l'aurait dit pour avoir l'air d'être la cause volontaire des médisances de l'ambassadeur, qui n'eussent plus été que des représailles mensongères et intéressées. Je dis, au contraire, qu'à mon grand regret, je croyais que M. de Norpois ne m'aimait pas. 'Vous vous trompez bien,' me répondit Mme de Guermantes. 'Il vous aime beaucoup.' (ii. 817–18; tr. iii. 611; my emphasis)

By the very act of castigating himself for not being a man of the world, he derives solace from the duchesse's desire to express

---

[32] When Swann tells her he is dying, she and the duc are more concerned about the appropriateness of her footwear, since he has arrived just as they are leaving for a party (ii. 884; tr. iii. 689).

opinions that will please, obeying her basic economy of giving pleasure where no demands are imposed upon her. In a further ironic obeisance, however, he is also imitating the duchesse's eye for the cultural and critical main chance, by introducing a variation on the theme of the man of the world, and displaying his (perfectly real) vulnerability in the form of a self-deprecating moment of seductive neediness, instead of competitively asserting his independence from and indifference to mere opinion.[33] The duchesse's capacity for breaking with convention, in order the better to keep convention in place by putting it in relief against what exceeds it, enables her to impress the Faubourg and the narrator. By imitating the duchesse's rule-breaking, the narrator's risk brings him a return, in terms of reassurance.

That reassurance, however, cannot be trusted, because it relies on a truth supposedly inherent in *politesse*. Judgement-forming under the sway of *politesse* is turned into a suspension of truth, because truth has become a commodity that may be exchanged but never measured against a fixed point of reference. Truth may only circulate as opinion and never come to rest as fact. Her words actually force the narrator to reassess his opinion of Norpois: 'Ces médisances étaient assez fréquentes chez lui. Mais cela ne l'empêchait pas d'avoir des sympathies' (ii. 818; tr. iii. 612). By participating in the kind of rule-breaking *which actually upholds convention*, the narrator forfeits the satisfaction of a definitive judgement, both about Norpois, and hence about Norpois's real opinion of him.

6. DETACHED HEARING: SWANN'S LAST JUDGEMENT

This question of an appeal reminds us of Legrandin's *bête immonde*, and Mme de Marsantes's *empressement*; of Swann's *muflerie intermittente* and Marcel's *purs mots de conversation*; and it redirects our attention to the underground grumbling of our original curiosity about why the narrator goes to so many parties and describes them at such length. The narrator is concerned at all times with small talk which gives away a great

---

[33] Ch. 5 will look closely at vulnerability in *A la recherche*.

deal of information, manipulating it in order to disguise his own vulnerabilities, and astonished when he hears moments of vulnerability break through the indifferent veneer offered by others. He learns to imitate indifference as a self-preservative form of justification that allows him to fit into a hostile social group. But one final experiment in the public functioning of self-justification remains, and it takes place at the apogee of the series of Faubourg Saint-Germain parties, a *soirée* held by the princesse de Guermantes. The account of the party circles around Swann, his mortal illness, and the mysterious conversation he has had with the anti-dreyfusard prince de Guermantes. When Marcel sees Swann, ambiguous reactions result:

Plaisir mêlé de tristesse, d'une tristesse que n'éprouvaient peut-être pas les autres invités, mais qui chez eux consistait dans cette espèce de fascination qu'exercent les formes inattendues et singulières d'une mort prochaine ... Et c'est avec une stupéfaction presque désobligeante, où il entrait de la curiosité indiscrète, de la cruauté, un retour à la fois quiet et soucieux sur soi-même (mélange à la fois de *suave mari magno* et de *memento quia pulvis*, eût dit Robert), que tous les regards s'attachèrent à ce visage duquel la maladie avait si bien rongé les joues. (iii. 88–89; tr. iv. 104)

The *tristesse* about Swann's impending death that the narrator thinks no one else feels is not so far from their *fascination*. It had been the narrator, not Saint-Loup, who had quoted from Lucretius, but again attributing it to somebody else: when the duc de Guermantes had complained about Bornier's play, *La Fille de Roland*, the narrator's use of the quotation had referred to the duc's complacency, 'par le *suave mari magno* que nous éprouvons, au milieu d'un bon dîner, à nous souvenir d'aussi terribles soirées' (ii. 780; tr. iii. 566).[34] Projecting complacency and prurient attention onto other onlookers shields the narrator from admitting to its manifestation in himself. But later, he cannot resist focusing on Swann's marked skin: 'Sa figure se marquait de petits points bleu de Prusse, qui avaient l'air de ne pas appartenir au monde vivant, et dégageait ce genre d'odeur

---

34 'Suave, mari magno turbantibus aequora ventis, | e terra magnum alterius spectare laborem' (Pleasant it is, when over a great sea the winds trouble the waters, to gaze from shore upon another's great tribulation), Lucretius, *De rerum natura*, 2. 1–2.

qui, au lycée, après les "expériences", rend si désagréable de rester dans une classe de "Sciences" ' (iii. 98; tr. iv. 115). Having set up distaste about Swann's physical degeneration as other people's negative judgement, the narrator can himself enjoy chemicalizing the illness and drawing an analogy with a scientific experiment. Marcel's specular relation to Swann is that of fascinated revulsion. The aural relation postponed throughout the party is an account of Swann's conversation with the prince de Guermantes, which takes the form of a confession. Swann's intimate confession has also effectively been postponed throughout the novel, and the pressure of its delay increases its cathartic potential to extreme proportions. Swann begins:

'Les gens sont bien curieux. Moi, je n'ai jamais été curieux, sauf quand j'ai été amoureux et quand j'ai été jaloux. Et pour ce que cela m'a appris! Êtes-vous jaloux?' Je dis à Swann que je n'avais jamais éprouvé de jalousie, que je ne savais même pas ce que c'était. 'Hé bien! je vous en félicite. Quand on l'est peu, cela n'est pas tout à fait désagréable à deux points de vue. D'une part, parce que cela permet aux gens qui ne sont pas curieux de s'intéresser à la vie des autres personnes, ou au moins d'une autre. Et puis, parce que cela fait assez bien sentir la douceur de posséder.' (iii. 101; tr. iv. 119)

His words are an attempt to justify by reconciliation various factors in his life, and they constitute a warning to the young narrator. Swann implies that he did not even benefit from the advantages of jealousy, 'par la faute de ma nature qui n'est pas capable de réflexions très prolongées' and 'par la faute de la femme, je veux dire des femmes, dont j'ai été jaloux' (iii. 101; tr. iv. 119). Here telling the truth masks an appeal for sympathetic reassurance. But his self-castigation really is a truth about himself, and not an exaggeration needing a corrective reassurance. The honesty of his truth-telling is called into question by his parapraxis immediately afterwards: for the depth of his jealousy extended only to *one* rather than to *many* women. His mistake demonstrates his sense that jealousy might be worthwhile if multiply experienced. Jealousy over just one, rather worthless, woman, however, is not good enough. His Don Juanism stops short at 'dont j'ai . . .'. He attempts self-critique: 'Même quand on ne tient plus aux choses, il n'est pas absolument indifférent d'y avoir tenu, parce que c'était toujours pour des raisons qui échappaient aux autres. Le souvenir de ces sentiments-là, nous sentons qu'il n'est qu'en nous; c'est en nous qu'il faut rentrer pour le regarder' (iii. 101; tr. iv. 119).

While the conclusions are no different from those that the narrator will eventually formulate and turn into laws of the self, Swann misjudges and plays down his own discovery, calling his maxim-making a 'jargon idéaliste' (iii. 101; tr. iv. 119). Having misjudged, in Proustian terms, his own best attempt to formulate a law of the self, he withdraws from a universal statement to his personal experience, hoping it will speak for itself, but deliberately articulating it as understatement: 'ce que je veux dire, c'est que j'ai beaucoup aimé la vie et que j'ai beaucoup aimé les arts' (iii. 101; tr. iv. 119). He tries to raise love to the status of sole criterion of importance in life, but he gives away the emptiness of his words: 'maintenant que je suis un peu trop fatigué pour vivre avec les autres, ces anciens sentiments si personnels à moi que j'ai eus, me semblent, *ce qui est la manie de tous les collectionneurs*, très précieux' (iii. 101–2; tr. iv. 119; my emphasis). By identifying himself as a collector, Swann's words point up the devastating effects that indifference has had. Instead of investing himself in love as he says he has done, he has invested himself in investment, because the safer risk of collecting up *anciens sentiments*, instead of acquiescing in the instability and fragility of emotions, has allowed him to maintain an indifferent control over those feelings. Swann's self-appraisal is an arthritic articulation, since his past and present are mentioned in the span of a single sentence, but are no longer of any use to him. We have, of course, seen his elegant talent for division, which actually spells out useless confusion, in other parts of the novel. Compare this passage from *Un amour de Swann*, in which he is neatly distinguishing between the functions of the artist and the critic:

Et quand il était tenté de regretter que depuis des mois il ne fît plus que voir Odette, il se disait qu'il était raisonnable de donner beaucoup de son temps à un chef-d'œuvre inestimable, coulé pour une fois dans une matière différente et particulièrement savoureuse, en un exemplaire rarissime qu'il contemplait tantôt avec l'humilité, la spiritualité et le désintéressement d'un artiste, tantôt avec l'orgueil, l'égoïsme et la sensualité d'un collectionneur. (i. 221; tr. i. 270)

The formal perfection of the binary rhetorical structure at the end, each half divided into three parts, is designed to seem coherent, flowing from an immanent logic of what artists and collectors are. It is the third term of each half of the pair which attracts attention. The third term in a classic triple construction emphasizes and summarizes the preceding items. *Désintéressement* and *sensualité*, however, do not form natural compounds with their intended partners. They are only attached to their respective sides of the equation by force of rhetoric, and could just as easily be transposed. Each term thus undermines the triple in which it has been located, *désintéressement* by its potentially negative connotation of a detachment that amounts to cold indifference, *sensualité* by the connotation it has of being proper to the senses, and therefore a vital attribute for an artist, as well as simply applicable to someone who seeks gratification of the senses. *Désintéressement*, furthermore, signifies both disinterestedness and the reparation of a debt. The uneasy suspension and separation of the triples into an apparent binary opposition works against Swann. Rather than generating a satisfactory poignancy, in which his thwarted status as artist is set off by an ironic identification with something less valuable (the status of collector), the opposition constantly threatens to collapse. Misjudgement is marked by the violation of a rhetorical structure.

Un amour de Swann, however, relies on the illusion of completion and distance afforded by its third-person voice. It is far more disconcerting to feel the urgency and compression of Swann's first-person speech, injected right into the ambit of another's first-person sampling of party-prattle, as the dying man reports the content of a conversation he has just had with the prince de Guermantes. Swann performs it, even introducing another character, the abbé Poiré. The following quotation, which is practically impossible to represent within the conventions of English typography, demonstrates graphically how too many voices spoil the plot. Swann is here speaking to the narrator, but *quoting* the prince de Guermantes, *in the act of quoting l'abbé*: ' " ' "Non," me répondit l'abbé,' (je vous dis *me*," me dit Swann, "parce que c'est le prince qui me parle, vous comprenez?) " ' (iii. 109; tr. iv. 128).

The story narrates the previously staunchly anti-dreyfusard prince's realization of Dreyfus's innocence and the army's corruption. In his eagerness to relate this *palinodie*, this retraction, to the narrator, and to maximize its dramatic effect, Swann selects the mode of direct speech, reporting a conversation which reports another conversation, each retold as though in present time. The effect of this is to implicate Swann completely in a particularly complex process of narration. His own illness and impending death are displaced: 'Seulement, j'avoue que ce serait bien agaçant de mourir avant la fin de l'affaire Dreyfus' (iii. 112; tr. iv. 131). Displacing his own mortality into another apparently unrelated issue, itself indifferent to his interest in it, is simultaneously objective and ridiculous. He is adopting the indifference shown by the Guermantes towards the idea of his death as his own attitude. Appropriating a political event as a substitute for his own importance in the world is as empty of significance as ignoring the world to concentrate on a round of parties.

Indifference has ruined Swann's life, and here is his deathbed account of it, presented to the narrator, who has sought out Swann with determination to hear it. Yet the narrator fails to respond. He does not allow the dying man the credit of his report: 'Swann oubliait que dans l'après-midi, il m'avait dit au contraire que les opinions en cette affaire Dreyfus étaient commandées par l'atavisme. Tout au plus avait-il fait exception pour l'intelligence . . . C'était donc maintenant à la droiture du cœur qu'il donnait le rôle dévolu tantôt à l'intelligence' (iii. 110; tr. iv. 129). The narrator's critical appraisal of Swann's political integrity shows no mercy, and no interest in Swann's motivation. It is as though the indifference displayed by the people who currently surround the narrator has been imported as a ready-made solution to a difficult encounter: like Swann, the narrator is also imitating the Guermantes. Swann's indifference to his own life means that he cannot draw conclusions about it, but only have it conclude, while the narrator's artificially imported indifference to the promptings of his self-justificatory consciousness leave him deaf to the potential for judgement about his own future actions that Swann offers.

7. CONCLUSION

We have already learnt a great deal about the functioning of self-justification in *A la recherche*, of an outwardly directed, integrationist kind. The narrator, that would-be writer, does not just go to parties. He actively seeks an entrance into what he perceives as the highest echelons of Parisian society, and tests a wide variety of linguistic strategies on other party-goers in a pre-emptive bid to avoid expulsion.

Yet his feints, asides, displaced commentaries to a reader enlisted as silent companion, his silences, imitation, and eaves-dropping, are not alternatives to passing critical judgements on the parties as he goes to them. He passes judgement and finds them wanting, but continues to go to them. Content for a while to work out the delineations of a social topology, he is success-ful in making himself fit into that topology.[35]

Having and maintaining a face and manner that fit entails other consequences. Identifying indifference as a possible indi-cator of final and stable judgement, he sets about emulating it, and indeed realizes the full potential that his search has to offer him, indifferent as he becomes to Swann's final confession. He successfully learns to justify himself in the terms laid down by the Faubourg, and discovers in the process of assimilating those terms that the limit to judgement offered by them is merely limited.

Listening to the dramatization of pre-emptive criticism, of wilful ignorance, of self-conscious withdrawal in amongst the debris of party babble draws to our attention a further, and much bigger, set of epistemological difficulties which build both play and strain into the workings of Proust's narrative, and which formulate themselves into the three major questions of the central part of my study. How does the rhetoric of self-justi-fication work? How does narratorial self-justification work when what is at stake is not assimilation outwards, but acceptance inwards? And how does it work if what is required is not fitting in, or taking in, but keeping at arm's length?

---

[35] Gk. *topos*, place; topography: a detailed delineation of locality. Topology (1850): the scientific study of where plants are found, or of a particular locality; (1905): the science by which, from consideration of geographical facts about a local-ity, one can draw deductions as to its history.

II

Encounters

Digressions and Self-Justification:
Making the Perfect Fit

> There lives no man who at some period has not been
> tormented, for example, by an earnest desire to tantalize a
> listener by circumlocution. The speaker is aware that he
> displeases: he has every intention to please: he is usually
> curt, precise, and clear; the most laconic and luminous
> language is struggling for utterance upon his tongue; it is
> only with difficulty that he restrains himself from giving it
> flow; he dreads and deprecates the anger of him whom he
> addresses; yet, the thought strikes him, that by certain
> involutions and parentheses, this anger may be engen-
> dered. That single thought is enough. The impulse
> increases to a wish, the wish to a desire, the desire to an
> uncontrollable longing, and the longing, (to the deep
> regret and mortification of the speaker, and in defiance of
> all consequences,) is indulged.
>
> (Edgar Allen Poe, *The Imp of the Perverse*)

I. INTRODUCTION

The uses of self-justification in *A la recherche* begin in what we
might term its outside world, that of party-going, with its
conversational acumen, ritualized humiliation as spectator
sport, and the trickiness of resupplying similitude as difference,
in other words, of being witty. Listening to the direct speech
enacted, reported, and overheard by the narrator has shown
itself to be a focus for moments of his speculation about intention, prejudice, and blindness in utterances conveyed by
language. Such local moments draw attention to another level
of Proust's investigation into the self-justificatory use of
language, by encouraging us to find out more about how his

narrative has been packaged into particular rhetorical features. If Proust has offered us a semiotics of social censure, the uses of self-justification in the service of protective disguise, he has also offered us large-scale experimentation in narrative play with self-justificatory evasion and excess, taking the form of the trope of digression.

Digressiveness in *A la recherche* might seem a redundant subject of study. And Proust himself was certainly anxious, if not about the redundancy of digressiveness, at least about its obfuscatory supplementation to his ever-burgeoning text: 'Quant à ce livre-ci, c'est au contraire un tout très composé, quoique d'une composition si complexe que je crains que personne ne le perçoive et qu'il apparaisse comme une suite de digressions. C'est tout le contraire.'[1] Surely we can take for granted by now the long meandering sentences that comprise Proust's style, and which have been so fully analysed by Milly, or Spitzer?[2] Whether we make grand overarching comments about how Proust's style contributes to the structure of the work, or descend into the minutiae of semantic analysis, making a move to the general from the exemplarity of a particular *phrase type*, evidence of digressiveness will be a constant conclusion of either approach, which might make it seem a superfluous tool with which to come at this novel, what amounts to a sledge-hammer. In ignoring digressions and digressiveness, however, we are blinding ourselves to one of Proust's most impressively stocked laboratories for experimental play with self-justification.

Digressiveness beyond this text has its own stylistic, even philosophical history, and we should supply ourselves with

---

[1] To René Blum, 20 Feb. 1913, *Corr.* xii. 26.

[2] See Jean Milly, *La Phrase de Proust* (1975); see, on the Proustian parenthesis as a delaying tactic, Leo Spitzer, *Études de style* (1988). Most recently, Pierre Bayard has used Randa Sabry's fusion of rhetoric to semiotics to produce an interesting contribution to Proustian digression studies: *Le Hors-sujet* (1996), which surprisingly, given its title, has nothing to say about the deconstruction of digression, choosing instead to capitalize, somewhat unfortunately, on the idea that 'Proust est trop long' (p. 11). He has made extensive use of Randa Sabry's *Stratégies discursives* (1992). Bayard's title seems to make reference to Jacques Derrida's metatextual 'Hors livre: préfaces', the exordium to *La Dissémination* (1972), 9–76, and to the Derridean dictum, 'il n'y a pas de hors-texte', a few years earlier, in *De la grammatologie* (1967), 227. Bayard, to my mind, errs on the side of sanitizing Proust's text, depriving digression of the very elasticity and incongruity which give it shape.

some information about several of its rule-makers and law-breakers. We can summarize its history as a shift over time in its conception from a rhetorical trope to a performative act, from Quintilian's warnings against unnecessary verbal excursions from the main thrust of argument, to Diderot's championing of a freely associative verbal drift as a direct correlation of the workings of the mind.[3]

Quintilian knows well the seductive uses of digression, both for speaker and audience: rhetoricians and lawyers, he notes, 'are in the habit, as soon as they have completed the *statement of facts*, of digressing to some pleasant and attractive topic with a view to securing the utmost amount of favour from their audience'.[4] He insists that 'such a practice confers great distinction and adornment on a speech, but only if the digression fits in well with the rest of the speech and follows naturally on what has preceded, not if it is thrust in like a wedge parting what should naturally come together'.[5] Digressions may make an appearance not only at the end of statements, he concedes, but may supply 'a second *exordium* with a view to exciting or mollifying the judge or disposing him to lend a favouring ear to our proofs'.[6]

The strict controls and divisions Quintilian demands for the appropriate manipulation of digression exact, however, their own toll, and this is where the subject of digressiveness starts to take on the fascinatingly tensile and malleable power with which Proust has charged his own narrative experiment: 'There are so many different ways in which a speech may leave the direct route. For whatever we say that falls outside the five divisions of the speech already laid down is a digression, whether it express indignation, pity, hatred, rebuke, excuse, conciliation

---

[3] Quintilian, *Institutio Oratoria*, ii. 120–31. See, on Diderot, David Berry, 'The Technique of Literary Digression in the Fiction of Diderot', *Studies on Voltaire and the Eighteenth Century*, 118 (1974), 115–272.

[4] 'Plerisque moris est prolato rerum ordine protinus utique in aliquem laetum ac plausibilem locum quam maxime possint favorabiliter excurrere.' *Institutio Oratoria*, ii. 122.

[5] '. . . sed si cohaeret et sequitur, non si per vim cuneatur et quae natura iuncta erant distrahit' (ii. 124).

[6] 'Est hic locus velut sequentis exordii ad conciliandum probationibus nostris iudicem, mitigandum, concitandum' (ii. 126).

or be designed to rebut invective.[7] Quintilian, as hearer of
digression's multiple identity shifts, its capacity to embody
many affective representations, and still remain the same
rhetorical device, has suddenly succumbed to a moment of
exhausted capitulation to his own discourse. There is a strenuous exertion to the supplementation of signifiers with passions,
or the forcible exclusion of passion from signifying processes:
digressiveness constantly threatens to deform the semantic
strictures within which Quintilian so resourcefully contains it.

Digressiveness is an informing rhetorical trope for the stylistically motley and knavish picaresque genre, coming out of
Spain in the sixteenth century. It finds a renewed habitat in the
French cultural imagination, after Rabelais and Montaigne,[8] in
the first European translation of the *Arabian Nights*, *Les Mille et
Une Nuits*, whose twelve-volume publication spanned the period
from 1704 to 1717, and was undertaken by the orientalist Antoine
Galland.[9] It was subsequently revised by another orientalist, and
medical doctor, Joseph Charles Victor Mardrus, as *Les Mille
Nuits et Une Nuit*.[10] Mardrus complained that the first translation had been 'systématiquement émasculée de toute hardiesse
et filtrée de tout le sel premier'.[11] His self-promotional argument gives away something beyond its own marketing strategy.
While Mardrus is referring to the restoration of the more scat-
ological or salacious elements of the Arabic original, a mode of
revision is being endorsed here which sees improvement as fill-
ing out, as restoring a lost truth through saturating what was
originally known with as much further material as possible. Yet
trammelled up in the concept of restorative vision comes the
unsightly. This new vision, the wide-eyed and the wide-angled,
implies a new pact made with faithfulness to the object. Not

---

[7] '. . . tot modis a recto itinere declinet oratio. Nam quidquid dicitur praeter
illas quinque quas fecimus partes, egressio est, indignatio, miseratio, invidia, convi-
cium, excusatio, conciliatio, maledictorum refutatio' (ii. 128).

[8] The complex publishing history of the works of both Rabelais and
Montaigne reflects their open-ended, loose narrative construction and high degree
of digressiveness: *Pantagruel* (1532); *Gargantua* (1534); *Tiers Livre de Pantagruel*
(1546); *Quart Livre* (1548) and the whole in 1552. Editions of Montaigne's *Essais* were
revised from initial publication in 1580, in 1588, and until his death in 1592.

[9] 4th edn. 8 vols. (The Hague: Husson, 1714–28).

[10] Its full title was *Le Livre des Mille Nuits et Une Nuit, traduction littérale et complète
du texte arabe* (Éditions de la Revue Blanche, 1899–1904; repr. 18 vols: Charpentier,
1920–4).   [11] Ibid. i, p. xviii (see *A la recherche*, iii. 230 and n. 2).

only must the late-nineteenth-century thinker, artist, writer be open to experience, Mardrus insists, he or she must note it all down, and not a detail may be *left out*. An always-threatened faithfulness to objects and subjects of discourse is a key component of Proust's digressiveness and the play it makes with self-justificatory desires.

We can take but a moment to remind ourselves of some of the other stars in our brief history of digression. In England, Laurence Sterne was bringing out *The Life and Opinions of Tristram Shandy* between 1759 and 1767. Diderot's *Jacques le Fataliste*, its final version published posthumously in 1786, was suggested to him by Sterne's work. Diderot's dialogic *Le Neveu de Rameau* is arguably even more significant for the history of digressiveness: first published posthumously like *Jacques*, it appeared in German in 1805, translated by Goethe and based on a copy of the manuscript that had been sent to Catherine II in St Petersburg on the death of Diderot in 1784.[12] This passage of the text into and out of different European languages enacts uncannily what Hegel will say about the *Neveu*. For in 1807, Hegel quotes from this text to illustrate what he is trying to say about the content of Spirit, its negativity, and perversion:

The content of what Spirit says about itself is thus the perversion of every Notion and reality, the universal deception of itself and others; and the shamelessness which gives utterance to this deception is just for that reason the greatest truth. This kind of talk is the madness of the musician 'who heaped up and mixed together thirty arias, Italian, French, tragic, comic, of every sort; now with a deep bass he descended into hell, then, contracting his throat, he rent the vaults of heaven with a falsetto tone, frantic and soothed, imperious and mocking, by turns'. To the tranquil consciousnes [*sic*] which, in its honest way, takes the melody of the Good and the True to consist in the evenness of the notes, i.e. in unison, this talk appears as a 'rigmarole of wisdom and folly, as a medley of as much skill as baseness, of as many correct as false ideas, a mixture compounded of a complete perversion of sentiment, of absolute shamefulness, and of perfect frankness and truth. It will be unable to refrain from entering into all these tones and running up and down the entire scale of feelings from the profoundest contempt and dejection to the highest pitch of admiration and emotion; but blended with the latter will be a tinge of

---

[12]   Goethe, *Rameaus Neffe: Ein Dialog von Diderot* (1805).

ridicule which spoils them.' The former, however, will find in their
very frankness a strain of reconciliation, will find in their subversive
depths the all-powerful note which restores Spirit to itself.[13]

For Hegel, the spiritedness of the Neveu's pastiche performs a
shameless and indiscriminate appropriation of disparate
elements and styles, which at once enacts and despoils a unified
totality.

When Michel Foucault also takes up this text, he is equally
admiring of the Neveu's unbridled rampaging, marking the
Neveu as a character of transition in the grand Comedy of
madness, a figural midway point between a lunatic *Nef des fous*
and a paranoid schizophrenic Artaud.[14] There is, however, a
hard edge to this fascinated reception of the Neveu's shamelessness, which we should keep in mind as we listen to Proustian
digression. The Neveu undergoes the external censure of those
who identify him with his *déraison*, but knows himself instead to
be *fou*. *Déraison* is a surface to his *folie*. This interdependence of
exuberance with censure tells us something vital about digression's relation to self-justification. Shameless self-exposure may
be enfolded in the generous arms of a narrative strong enough
to carry it; yet the demands of that narrative's own unfolding
will also enforce endings to digressions, moments of hair's
breadth reattachment to narrative concerns, a keeping up of
orderly appearances. However much the Proustian narrator
may desire to lose control of the plot, by exposing his deepest
concerns in rumpled corners of easily forgotten anecdote, he
may not, ultimately, exit from his own story into the darker
hinterlands of absolute insanity. Digression bears within it the
hallmarks of its own textual demise. The very demands by
digressions that their scandalous, scabrous, irrelevant interventions be heard are inscribed with the knowledge that this atten-
tion-seeking will bring about their ending.

2. ' "LUI, DU MOINS VA DROIT AU BUT!" '

This sounds like a world of madness (or at least unattainable
splendour) very far from the comfort of Combray's *Mille et Une*

---

[13] G. W. F. Hegel, *Phenomenology of Spirit* (1977), §522.
[14] Michel Foucault, *Histoire de la folie à l'âge classique* (1972), 363–72.

Nuits-patterned plates (i. 70; tr. i. 83), and maternal preferences for the sanitized Galland translation of that text (iii. 230; tr. iv. 271). We are, however, not as far from a certain kind of madness as we might think. Marcel's mother sends him both versions of Scheherazade's death-defying variations on a theme, to remind him of Combray and encourage his writing, but with some reservations:

> tout en craignant de m'influencer à cause du respect qu'elle avait de la liberté intellectuelle, de la peur d'intervenir maladroitement dans la vie de ma pensée, et du sentiment qu'étant une femme, d'une part elle manquait, croyait-elle, de la compétence littéraire qu'il fallait, d'autre part elle ne devait pas juger d'après ce qui la choquait les lectures d'un jeune homme. (iii. 230; tr. iv. 271)

If she has a binary logic to her explicitly gender-segregated reasoning about why she has no say in her son's reading, he is also, it should not be forgotten, in the throes of an analysis of love itself, figured in the same binary mutual exclusivity:

> 'Ne détournez pas la conversation,' me dit-elle [Albertine], 'soyez franc comme moi.' Je mentis. . . . je ne faisais—à cause d'une circonstance et en vue d'un but particuliers—que rendre plus sensible, marquer avec plus de force, ce rythme binaire qu'adopte l'amour chez tous ceux qui doutent trop d'eux-mêmes pour croire qu'une femme puisse jamais les aimer, et aussi qu'eux-mêmes puissent l'aimer véritablement. Ils se connaissent assez pour savoir qu'auprès des plus différentes, ils éprouvaient les mêmes espoirs, les mêmes angoisses, inventaient les mêmes romans, prononçaient les mêmes paroles, pour s'être rendu ainsi compte que leurs sentiments, leurs actions, ne sont pas en rapport étroit et nécessaire avec la femme aimée, mais passent à côté d'elle, l'éclaboussent, la circonviennent comme le flux qui se jette le long des rochers, et le sentiment de leur propre instabilité augmente encore chez eux la défiance que cette femme, dont ils voudraient tant être aimés, ne les aime pas. (iii. 222–3; tr. iv. 262–3)

The metronomic oscillations of the self-doubting lover are here characterized in a particular way, one which undoes, even in the saying of it, the steady-sounding heartbeat of turning now to this explanation of the beloved's infidelity, now that. This *rythme binaire* is not a regular ticking, but an exaggeratedly syncopated recognition that underlying difference there is sameness, and that relations are made up of avoided rather than consummated collisions. 'Lui, du moins va droit au but!',

Albertine reproaches Marcel, indicating a seabird flying 'sans dévier de son chemin, comme un émissaire qui va porter bien loin un message urgent et capital' (iii. 225; tr. iv. 265).

Getting straight to the point, however, is not possible for Marcel. What he is trying to understand is the spectacle of an unearthly chiasmus: the *danse contre seins* between Andrée and Albertine that Cottard has indicated marks the site of a sexual pleasure incomprehensibly different from the heterosexual male's conception of such things, entirely given over to the female libido, excluding him as it reflects his impotent gaze back at him, emptied of any claims upon pleasure he can see but not feel (iii. 191; tr. iv. 225).[15] Double deflection for Marcel, then, forced to move between two possibilities. He is either to *see* or to remain unsure of *what* he has seen.

This context lends Marcel's mother's double-edged doubt about her own capacity to judge either literature or her son, both, to her mind, inhabiting a male preserve, a new importance. The question turns now not on an analysis of hermeneutic questing, or the identification of epistemological modes and means of that quest, but on what one does when one has the material in hand. The really important question raised by the *danse contre seins*, and by Marcel's mother's hesitation, is, how can one judge what is *outside one's own province*? How, Marcel asks, and repeatedly finds ways to rehearse, can we judge what is beyond our understanding, when understanding is bounded, demarcated, and territorialized? Are we to suspend judgement, ephectically, in a spirit of Pyrrhonism?[16]

This very question of how to judge what lies beyond our understanding turns into a two-way shuffle in the central volumes of *A la recherche*, *Sodome et Gomorrhe* and *La Prisonnière*, as the narrator struggles incessantly with incommensurable needs. How is he to move mentally, morally, and logically,

---

[15] See Emma Wilson, *Sexuality and the Reading Encounter* (1996), who argues that it is 'through our enactment of the text and our involvement in its mirroring projections of our acts of decoding, rather than through the search for a single "truth" or an occluded subtext, that we may come to a rereading of Albertine's sexuality' (p. 92). Wilson's account of reader response theory argues for a reassessment of the role of the *reader's desire* in the reading process.

[16] See the writings of the sceptic Sextus Empiricus, in *Outlines of Pyrrhonism*. Samuel Beckett muses 'Can one be ephectic otherwise than unawares?', *The Unnamable* (1979), p. 267.

between conclusions that appear unavoidable (about Albertine, about homosexuality), and the burden (or the opportunity) of slowly accumulating and patiently elucidating proof? It is in these volumes that digressiveness presents its special significance for Proust's narrator, and its difference from a tradition which celebrates digression wholeheartedly.[17]

In order to demonstrate the interconnections that run between the rhetorical figure of digression, and the complexities that arise when self-justification is conceptualized in terms of inclusiveness, I want to look closely at one particular passage from *La Prisonnière* (iii. 708–22; tr. v. 227–40). It presents us with a paradigm of the self-justificatory functioning of digressiveness that forces us to assess its syntagmatic elements, as these grapple with the conflicting demands of textual inclusiveness and clemency, critical intolerance and indifference. Now gathering all the text's forces, maxims, themes, intuitions into a moment of clear insight, now letting that collected moment unravel, sag, become open to hostility, suspicion, doubt, whether of a self-inflicted or outwardly imposed kind, then aiming to rein narrative unfolding back in: this is where we can relate self- justification to digression.

3. A LIMINAL ENCOUNTER

The narrator meets Charlus on the doorstep of the Verdurins (iii. 708; tr. v. 227), where they are about to hear the Vinteuil Septet, a hearing which will reorient the direction of the narrative. This is a liminal moment that, instead of being characterized by an anxiety about narratorial assimilation into salon society, triggers quite different concerns. Homosexuality has been discovered, Albertines' untrustworthiness has been identified as a source of anxiety, though not definitively proven. The narrator's decision to go to the Verdurins' concert is predicated on an afternoon's independent thought about music, Wagner, and whether or not an artwork may ever be said to be

---

[17] See Appendix II for a necessarily terse tabular demonstration of the sheer variety of digressions and digression-types in *A la recherche*. Its purpose is to supply evidence which connects digressiveness, that is to say, evasive but inclusive linguistic manœuvring, to our overall understanding of the justification of self.

'complete' (iii. 664–7; tr. v. 173–8); and on the desire to undertake just one more piece of detective work before abandoning
Albertine:

Mais je me ravisais pour ce soir, car je voulais tâcher d'apprendre
quelles personnes Albertine avait pu espérer rencontrer l'après-midi
chez eux. A vrai dire, j'en étais arrivé avec Albertine à ce moment où
(si tout continue de même, si les choses se passent normalement) une
femme ne sert plus pour nous que de transition avec une autre
femme. (iii. 674; tr. v. 186)

The focus that his project gives him is almost immediately
held up by the spectacle of Charlus, lumbering towards Brichot
and himself, 'naviguant vers nous de tout son corps énorme'
(iii. 709; tr. v. 227). This particular digression opens on the
figure of a figure; and this obstacle, moment of anagnorisis,
nodal point in the progression of plot and narrative, this
textual *blocus*, is also an opportunity for deviation. It offers,
ready-made, as proairetic sequence, a departure from the
narrative teleology. Just as at parties, the narrator had let
himself be held up by Elstir's paintings, making him late for the
Guermantes's dinner (ii. 712–15; tr. iii. 483–7), and within its
narrative account had stalled again with a justificatory analysis
of the Guermantes's genealogical superiority (ii. 730–73; tr. iii.
505–58), so here, at the moment of rediscovering art's potential
value, in Vinteuil's music, he is pushed off course by intervening matter. The liminal meeting here is the moment not of
transgression, the breaching of some fixed social boundary, but
the entrance into a sphere of otherness, into a bubble of
chaotic phenomenal apperception, an experimental space in
which anything might be said, the closure for which comes only
with a determined wrenching of the narrative back to its previously appointed course, fourteen pages later: 'Mais il est temps
de rattraper le baron qui s'avance, avec Brichot et moi, vers la
porte des Verdurin' (iii. 722; tr. v. 240).
    Digressions in *A la recherche* trawl around in and catch a haul
of very properly *digressive* matter, comments on fat, on sexuality,
on the human detritus of the streets, the *voyous* that hang about
Charlus, 'traînant sans le vouloir à sa suite un de ces apaches ou
mendigots, que son passage faisait maintenant infailliblement
surgir' (iii. 709; tr. v. 227). What characterizes the Proustian

digression is not simply dreamy meandering or free associative-ness. It is instead an intense encounter with the difficulties of judgement, in which the desire to be detained and fascinated struggles with the desire to reject and exclude. Will, its control and its loss, the hubris of human planning and its high-minded protestations of charitable generosity suddenly ghost the inter-play here between diegesis and mimesis.

In the face of the transformation that has overcome Charlus, the narrator has recourse to a metaphor which strives to trans-late corporeality into astronomy, the movement of the spheres: 'il me sembla découvrir, accompagné de son satellite, un astre à une tout autre période de sa révolution et qu'on commence à voir dans son plein' (iii. 709; tr. v. 227). The sublimating gesture succumbs to a magnificent pratfall: this *astre* is a walk-ing *désastre*, the absolute inverse of the figure used to describe him. The language of the stars, however, signals to another metaphorical performance internal to the *narration*, that of the dinners at Rivebelle (ii. 165–76; tr. ii. 448–60).[18] The peculiar Proustian economy, where one figure fits all, star systems can represent both happy dining occasions and flabby ageing homosexuals, has a sinister side-effect: the jolly plenitude of metaphorical inclusiveness sometimes cannot bear the weight of what it attempts to transfigure. The metaphor that crashes to earth again does so into a lexical field very familiar to the Proustian reader: that of the cancerous illness, 'un malade envahi maintenant par le mal qui n'était il y a quelques années qu'un léger bouton qu'il dissimulait aisément et dont on ne soupçonnait pas la gravité' (iii. 709; tr. v. 227). Here again, the gravity of Charlus's earthbound degeneracy recalls another occasion, the serious attention paid to Swann's 'petits points bleu de Prusse' (iii. 98; tr. iv. 115). Marcel's fascination orbits about his indifference, his sidelong glances cannot help but see clearly, but what he sees has been made the matter of an aside.

---

[18] See Genette, 'Discours du récit', *Figures III* (1972), 72. *Narration*, for Genette, refers to 'l'acte narratif producteur et, par extension, l'ensemble de la situation réelle ou fictive dans laquelle il prend place'. If *récit* refers to 'le signifiant, énoncé, discours ou texte narratif lui-même' (and *histoire* to 'le signifié ou contenu narratif'), I take metaphorical *performances*, such as the one we are analysing, to align themselves with *narration*, even if they are substantively available as *récit*.

Accompanied by the nearly blind Brichot, the observant narrator *as protagonist* finds himself caught for many pages straining to do justice to the baron's subjective sexual experience, but comes continually into fraught contact with the security, or otherwise, of detached judgement *in writing*. He runs the risk either of failing to justify Charlus, or of being accused himself of a sexual tolerance which masks complicity. Brichot responds instinctively to Charlus: his uneasiness 'se rassurait en récitant des pages de Platon, des vers de Virgile' (iii. 710; tr. v. 229). Mme de Surgis le Duc, we are told, as part of an anecdote about Charlus's behaviour towards her sons, 'éprouva ce sentiment inquiet du mystère physique qui fait se demander si le voisin avec qui on avait de bons rapports n'est pas atteint d'anthropophagie' (iii. 709–10; tr. v. 228). Their gut-level apprehension of everyday, neighbourhood evil, socialized humanity's constant fear that eruptions of natural blight threaten to overpower its careful upkeep of a *bonne réputation* (iii. 709; tr. v. 228), calls for discrimination between such nebulous concepts as 'evil', and justifications on behalf of sexual choice. But when the narrator tries to supply this clear-sighted detachment from such instinctive fears, his terms of reference are themselves continually under threat by the very same primitive seepage which conditions instinct: 'L'irresponsabilité aggrave les fautes et même les crimes, quoi qu'on en dise. Landru (à supposer qu'il ait réellement tué des femmes), s'il l'a fait par intérêt, à quoi l'on peut résister, peut être gracié, mais non si ce fut par un sadisme irrésistible' (iii. 71; tr. v. 228–9).[19]

Sadism and irresponsibility mark an absolute indifference to the needs of others, a breach in social self-control which the sadist refuses to explain or regret. Reasoned explanation about human evil fails in the face of the inexplicability of human indifference. The narrator makes his own explanatory task impossible, by permitting homosexuality to come into close contact with the question of evil. What the digressive interlude constantly circles around and comes back to is whether or not

---

[19] See Gilles Deleuze, 'Présence et fonction de la folie: L'Araignée', *Proust et les signes* (1993), 205–19, for an analysis of Charlus as the conduit of madness in *A la recherche*. The example of the murderer Landru was appended to the *La Prisonnière* manuscript in 1921.

Charlus's moral irresponsibility, inscribed in the way his bodily proportions are escaping his conscious control, reflects an essential immorality in homosexuality:

Ce n'était pas d'ailleurs seulement dans les joues, ou mieux les bajoues de ce visage fardé, dans la poitrine tétonnière, la croupe rebondie de ce corps livré au laisser-aller et envahi par l'embonpoint, que surnageait maintenant, étalé comme de l'huile, le vice jadis si intimement renfoncé par M. de Charlus au plus secret de lui-même. Il débordait maintenant dans ses propos. (iii. 712; tr. v. 231)

Narratorial efforts at redeeming the spectacle of Charlus through metaphoric transfiguration here have not only given up all pretence at controlling language harnessed in the service of persuasion; they have instead themselves given way to a purely sadistic pleasure in linguistic play. Nouns may have their boundaries tampered with ('les joues, ou mieux les bajoues'); gender may be shifted with an unexpected supplementary adjective ('la poitrine tétonnière'); verb structures may enact rather than define a moral mobility that oozes instead of dancing: *envahi, surnageait, étalé, débordait.* 'The observer infects the observed with his own mobility', wrote Beckett.[20] Yet what we now find ourselves trying to understand is the reversal of that infection, Marcel's attempts to maintain at arm's length, but his simultaneous written desire to become embroiled in, another character's identity.

Narratorial implication in what he describes can only just manage to draw the line at insinuation. Digression as licentious trope permits incommensurability and dangerous implications to inhabit it. It allows into the Proustian narrative safety valves for engaging, indulging, and fending off, moral quirks which refuse to stop pestering Marcel. The blurring of cause and effect that this brings about, so that trope informs and forms its own content, harnesses in troublesome ways the undecidability of the narrator's *caractère.* Digressiveness, like Barthes's *biographèmes,* opens the *étroite brèche* (iii. 711; tr. v. 230) from the illusory spectacle of straightforward identity (that which never questions itself as identity) onto identity as ongoing confusion, disguise, stage-management, such as Charlus's (but also the

---

[20] *Proust* (1965), 17.

narrator's).[21] Proust cannot simply be characterized as a 'post-modern writer' as Margaret Gray would like, because there is a constant struggle *between* essentialism and existentialism that runs through the Proustian arguments about the nature of self-hood, identity, and *caractère*. Self, for Proust, is *both* stable and unstable, *both* the rootedness of the *nénuphar* and its surface wavering (i. 166–7; tr. i. 202).[22]

The 'petit déplacement de goût purement physique, à la tare légère d'un sens' (iii. 710–11; tr. v. 230) peeks through an *étroite brèche* onto more than just questions about the narratorial identity. Marcel adds to his array of arguments justifying homosexuality its commonplace close linkage to artistic experience.[23] Yet almost immediately, the connection is perverted, by injecting creativity with another of its topoi, insanity. The mad poet, even if he composes a *sublime poème* (iii. 711; tr. v. 230), says the narrator, is none the less mad, and drives sane people away if he insists that: 'Tenez, celui qui va venir me parler dans le préau, dont je suis obligé de subir le contact, croit qu'il est Jésus-Christ. Or cela seul suffit à me prouver avec quels aliénés on m'enferme, il ne peut pas être Jésus-Christ, puisque Jésus-Christ c'est moi!' (iii. 711; tr. v. 230). The very same joke is repeated, almost word for word, in *Albertine disparue*, but this time as Marcel dreams that his dead lover is alive: 'ce souvenir qu'Albertine était morte se combinait sans la détruire avec la sensation qu'elle était vivante. Je causais avec elle, pendant que je parlais, ma grand-mère allait et venait dans le fond de la chambre. Une partie de son menton était tombée en miettes

[21] See Roland Barthes, *Sade, Fourier, Loyola* (1971), 14, and *La Chambre claire*, 54, for *biographèmes* ('traits biographiques qui, dans la vie d'un écrivain, m'enchantent à l'égal de certaines photographies'). Compare *Roland Barthes par Roland Barthes* (1975), where Barthes contrasts *biographèmes* to *anamnèse*, a notion which sounds suspiciously like Proustian *mémoire involontaire*: 'l'action—mélange de jouissance et d'effort—que mène le sujet pour retrouver, *sans l'agrandir ni le faire vibrer*, une ténuité du souvenir: c'est le haïku lui-même' (p. 113). One of the wonders of Barthes is his fascination with the dangers of over-identification and complicity with his subjects. Compare the recordings of Barthes's voice, caressingly narrating a Proustian itinerary in Paris (Roland Barthes and Jean Montalbetti, 'Proust' (à Combray et à Paris), *Un homme, une ville* (France-Culture, Paris, 20 and 27 Oct. 1978 and 3 Nov. 1978), released as *Un homme, une ville: Marcel Proust à Paris par Roland Barthes*, audiocassette, Cassettes Radio France, 1978).
[22] Margaret E. Gray, *Postmodern Proust* (1992).
[23] See J. E. Rivers, *Proust and the Art of Love* (1980), 180–6, on this topos.

comme un marbre rongé' (iv. 120; tr. v. 616).[24] Metaphors are recycled in order to try to redeem the spectacle of Charlus's degeneracy; and jokes are recycled inside the Proustian text, signifying contradictory things. On the one hand, madness will cause revulsion in those who witness it. On the other, a joke about madness is appropriated in order to explain the hallucinatory disjunctions and disproportions that mourning requires in order to accomplish its work.

Digression allows play and speculation to go on within its confines. At moments, however, the narrator is not above gathering together such speculation and redirecting it into a subdigressive aside. These asides carry the inbuilt proviso *that their textual status as digression will allow them to pass unnoticed*. They are evasive self-justificatory claims. A sudden burst of serious thought threads together the set of references preceding it:

Le poète est à plaindre, et qui n'est guidé par aucun Virgile, d'avoir à traverser les cercles d'un enfer de soufre et de poix, de se jeter dans le feu qui tombe du ciel pour en ramener quelques habitants de Sodome. Aucun charme dans son œuvre; la même sévérité dans sa vie qu'aux défroqués qui suivent la règle du célibat le plus chaste pour qu'on ne puisse pas attribuer à autre chose qu'à la perte d'une croyance d'avoir quitté la soutane. Encore n'en est-il pas toujours de même pour ces écrivains. Quel est le médecin de fous qui n'aura pas à force de les fréquenter eu sa crise de folie? Heureux encore s'il peut affirmer que ce n'est pas une folie antérieure et latente qui l'avait voué à s'occuper d'eux. L'objet de ses études, pour un psychiatre, réagit souvent sur lui. Mais avant cela, cet objet, quelle obscure inclination, quel fascinateur effroi le lui avait fait choisir? (iii. 711; tr. v. 230–1)

The implicatedness in his or her subject-matter which makes of poets explorers without guides, makes defrocked priests paragons of celibate virtue; makes psychologists and psychia-

---

[24] Compare Proust's use of a case-study by Thomas Henry Huxley (1825–95), a biologist, palaeontologist, and doctor, in which a female patient would see 'un vieux monsieur' sitting in the armchair indicated to her to sit in, and had to struggle with 'un instant de pénible hésitation en se demandant si le signe aimable qu'on lui faisait était la chose réelle, ou si, pour obéir à une vision inexistante, elle allait en public s'asseoir sur les genoux d'un monsieur en chair et en os' (iii. 38; tr. iv. 44). The case is used as an analogy for the difficulties of locating a secure site for judgement, or the certain apprehension of phenomena, as either internal to the mind, or external.

trists suffer from all the mental aberrations they study, entails a correlative risk: that their occupations are merely the outward manifestations of much more primitive preoccupations. But if this is so, then nothing justifies the prolongation of the specta-tor sport of observation.

Yet far from confronting this sudden narratorial doubt, introduced into the heart of the digression, comes a three-page evasion from it.[25] In it, not the narrator's, but *Charlus's* gift for observation of the minute is taken up. The narrator breaks into his own reporting of Charlus's direct speech to assert the baron's absolute difference from him: 'Ici je dois dire que M. de Charlus "possédait", ce qui faisait de lui l'exact contraire, l'antipode de moi, le don d'observer minutieusement, de distinguer les détails aussi bien d'une toilette que d'une "toile" ' (iii. 712). Whether or not we extend readerly competence to knowledge that this statement opens a late addition to the text of *A la recherche*, what is so striking about it is the clamping of observation upon observation that grows outwards from this digression. In carefully watching Charlus watching carefully, a process that the reader is also tied into, the digression takes on greater volume as well as density: recessive and incestuous prox-imity to the subject of digression at the level of syntagmatic elements finds a paradigmatic corollary in the loosening of formal controls over its length.

The commentary on Charlus that follows has equally striking analogies with the obituary genre:

j'ai toujours regretté, dis-je, et je regrette encore, que M. de Charlus n'ait jamais rien écrit. Sans doute je ne peux pas tirer de l'éloquence de sa conversation et même de sa correspondance la conclusion qu'il eût été un écrivain de talent. Ces mérites-là ne sont pas dans le même plan. Nous avons vu d'ennuyeux diseurs de banalités écrire des chefs-d'œuvre, et des rois de la causerie être inférieurs au plus médiocre dès qu'ils s'essayaient à écrire. (iii. 713)

The use of the pluperfect subjunctive, which is identical with an archaic form of the past conditional, 'qu'il *eût été* un écrivain de talent' (iii. 713), marks a mode of regret for a past that never

---

[25] From 'Ici je dois dire . . .' (iii. 712, the passage has not been translated in the version I am using here) to '. . . sur mon épaule' (iii. 715) is a *paperole* addition to the manuscript, N. a. fr. 16716: 103.

was, always to be read as *Schadenfreude* when referring to the activities of another. To construct what another's past has never been is a quite extraordinarily virtuoso piece of self-justificatory reshuffling on the part of the narrator, bringing into eerie focus the crossover points between future-directed narratorial activity, on the way to claiming a writerly vocation, and its retrospective, writing counterpart. The narrator who claims still to be undecided about the *uses* of writing is here judging another's life as a failure for *not having used it to write.* If nothing matters in digressions then, by the same token, anything goes, and that includes Charlus's narrative destiny.

If the narrator is struggling to contain his digression, he is also struggling, and sometimes fails, to contain himself:

En effet, disons (pour anticiper de quelques semaines sur le récit que nous reprendrons aussitôt après cette parenthèse que nous ouvrons pendant que M. de Charlus, Brichot et moi nous dirigeons vers la demeure de Mme Verdurin), disons que, peu de temps après cette soirée, le baron fut plongé dans la douleur . . . par une lettre qu'il ouvrit par mégarde et qui était adressée à Morel. (iii. 720; tr. v. 237)

This proleptic moment cannot resist taking us into the intimate details of the relationship between Morel and Charlus, and another linguistic examination in the form of a letter. Yet the letter itself is coyly censored: 'Sa grossièreté empêche qu'elle soit reproduite ici, mais on peut mentionner que Léa ne lui parlait qu'au féminin en lui disant: "Grande sale! va!", "Ma belle chérie, toi tu en es au moins, etc." ' (iii. 720; tr. v. 237–8). Just as the narrator's proleptic revelation of painful intimacy has crossed conventional narrative limits, so this letter marks the explosive proliferation of Charlus's jealousy beyond all its previously known boundaries: 'la jalousie de M. de Charlus n'avait plus de raison de se borner aux hommes que Morel connaissait, mais allait s'étendre aux femmes elles-mêmes' (iii. 720; tr. v. 238). *En être* spells a 'signification nouvelle d'un mot', which creates a 'double mystère où il y avait à la fois de l'agrandissement de sa jalousie et de l'insuffisance soudaine d'une définition' (iii. 721; tr. v. 238). And at this moment of quivering vulnerability, we see the narrator make a stiletto-sharp lunge at another character:

M. de Charlus n'avait jamais été dans la vie qu'un amateur. C'est dire que des incidents de ce genre ne pouvaient lui être d'aucune utilité.

Il faisait dériver l'impression pénible qu'il en pouvait ressentir, en scènes violentes où il savait être éloquent . . . Mais pour un être de la valeur de Bergotte, par exemple, ils eussent pu être précieux. (iii. 721; tr. v. 238–9)

On the back of his own sly disclosure, the narrator closes judgement. Charlus can *only deviate* from his pain, jealousy, suffering, and incomprehension. For Charlus, the impossible suspicion that Morel might be a lesbian, contravening all known sexual laws, goes a step further beyond the pale even than the sight of Morel in bed with women (at the *palace de Maineville*, iii. 466; tr. iv. 550). But unlike a Bergotte, he cannot synthesize, accommodate, rewrite, transform this raw insight into art. Without standing firm against deviation, there is no compensation through artistic redemption, resounds the implication. You must be Jacob, haughtily cries Marcel, and wrestle with your incomprehension, not abandon it for fury, *Sturm und Drang*.

Like the pinprick which lets the air from the tyres of a hitherto smoothly rolling vehicle, however, Marcel's judgemental triumph lasts only a handful of lines. Just as the metaphor which opened the digression could not take the strain of what it should have transfigured, the syntax which closes it falls apart at the seams, and lets its grammatical contents spill out:

Il faut dire pour ce qui concerne M. de Charlus, que s'il fut stupéfait d'apprendre relativement à Morel un certain nombre de choses qu'il lui avait soigneusement cachées, il eut tort d'en conclure que c'est une erreur de se lier avec des gens du peuple et *que des révélations aussi pénibles (celle* qui le lui avait été le plus avait été celle d'un voyage que Morel avait fait avec Léa alors qu'il avait assuré à M. de Charlus qu'il était à ce moment-là à étudier la musique en Allemagne. . . .). (iii. 721–2; tr. v. 239; my emphasis)

Marcel condemns Charlus for thinking that it is a mistake to have relationships with *gens du peuple*. We have seen before the narrator's own ironic ambivalence about *divulging* secrets,[26]

---

[26] 'L'amitié, l'admiration que Saint-Loup avait pour moi, me semblaient imméritées et m'étaient restées indifférentes. Tout d'un coup j'y attachai du prix, j'aurais voulu qu'il les révélât à Mme de Guermantes, j'aurais été capable de lui demander de le faire. Car dès qu'on est amoureux, tous les petits privilèges inconnus qu'on possède, on voudrait pouvoir les divulguer à la femme qu'on aime, comme font dans la vie les déshérités et les fâcheux' (ii. 369; tr. iii. 72). *Divulguer*: to make known to the *vulgus* or common people.

given that it bears within it the risk of the vulgar, the display to
the common herd, a giving in to one's libidinal impulses that
makes one just the same as everyone else, just a body without a
mind. Here the vulgarity of intimate disclosures seems successfully to have been displaced onto Charlus's snobbery. Yet the
text itself pulls the plug. No amount of editing can retrieve a
textual omission here, that of semantic coherence: 'il eut tort
d'en conclure que c'est une erreur de se lier avec des gens du
peuple et que des révélations aussi pénibles . . .' leaves us hung
over the abyss of possibilities. For at the very moment when the
narrator seemed to be about to tell us what such painful revelations might signify, he opens a parenthesis to give us an example of one such revelation, and fails to finish the sentence, or
rather finishes it, but *within* a parenthesis. Rushed composition,
perhaps; but the opening onto some miasma of incompletion,
the unsayable, the forever irretrievable, is here passed on to the
struggling reader, thwarted of her competence, thrown onto
the nervous throat-clearing of an editorial apology for the
author's failure to be grammatical. And caught up in this head-
long rush, scrambling to cover his tracks, straining to gather in
more information before the deadline of the digression's end,
the narrator announces, proleptic moment within prolepsis,
one final forthcoming attraction, in which the baron will play
the leading role: 'The Baron is being Beaten' (iv. 394; tr. vi. 154),
brought to us by the good offices of the spying narrator, doing
his research diligently as ever: 'On verra, en effet, dans le
dernier volume de cet ouvrage, M. de Charlus en train de faire
des choses qui eussent encore plus stupéfié les personnes de sa
famille et ses amis, que n'avait pu faire pour lui la vie révélée
par Léa' (iii. 722; tr. v. 239).

4. CONCLUSION

Rhetoric, music, madness, perversion, shamelessness, motley:
all these terms emerge in the dance of digressiveness across
European literature and thought. At times demonized, at
others celebrated precisely for its demonic, invasive qualities,
digression as a verbal strategy may be manhandled and
constructed, but always threatens to deconstruct itself, to

unravel into literary flotsam and debris, the isotopes of former, seemingly stable and ungainsayable textual atoms. It draws attention to itself as a vehicle in which to carry ideas in language, but might at any moment turn into Jacques Lantier's runaway train.[27]

Digression is evidence, in the outside world, of flux into which pitiful linguistic interventions are made by men and women and, from an internal perspective, of instinctual processes which, like Charlus's upheavals of perception, 'de véritables soulèvements géologiques de la pensée' (iii. 464; tr. iv. 553), suddenly thrust themselves upon consciousness, overwhelming it with unwanted matter and chatter.

We can make here a terrific claim about first-person narrative fiction. In its Clytemnestrean nets, it builds up residues, internal to itself, of what has gone into the narrative before. The unfolding of plot, which in *A la recherche* is always a revision of unfolding, is planned but also propelled by the weight of matter that it accumulates.[28] Plot devices such as chance meetings, which are of course staged, reactivate chanciness, because even as they are stage-managed, the narrator (at the moment of writing, as at the moment of encounter) *does not know how the performance will come off.* While digressions in Sterne may make up the whole of the narrative playing field, Proust's narrator fights a strenuous battle for control over digressiveness. If digressions are rightly seen by Quintilian to be dangerous, because excessive, it is the nature of that excess, in its coprophilia, scatology, bawdiness, titillation, desperate grasping after high-mindedness, constant falling back into the degenerate and the obscene, which characterizes them in Proust's writing. And we must, I think, make a distinction between the digressions of the middle, the post-1914 sections of the novel, and the early sections, because this is also a question of reception, the deadening of metaphor, the habituation that Proust writes so intensely against. Combray has been naturalized. It is not a space into which renewal and resuscitation may infuse

---

[27] Émile Zola, *La Bête humaine* (1890). See Gilles Deleuze, 'Zola et la fêlure', *Logique du sens* (1969), 373–86.

[28] See the inspirational book by Peter Brooks, *Reading for the Plot* (1984), which picks up narratological concerns, and reads desire and dynamic back into the functioning and organization of some of the Western novel tradition's greatest plots.

new life. The *madeleine* is rockhard and no amount of dunking will soften it.

Digressions in *A la recherche* entail performance art, the setting up of momentary soapboxes, fleeting seductions, those of the thrill-seeking wartime 'Pompéiens sur qui pleuvait déjà le feu du ciel . . . dans les couloirs du métro' (iv. 413; tr. vi. 177). They will always be reined in, but with sexual unravellings and moral renegotiations to show for their time in the wild. What I hope I have taken us to are Proust's enactment strategies. The elastic boundaries of digressiveness put it, as a rhetorical device, within reach of the formal conventions of narratological demarcations, but allow self-contradiction to persist within it. It is the enabling trope of heterogeneous and disputatious voices; it allows delicate shades of difference between similar voices; and it maintains the dangerous proximity of immoral within moral voices in the text, so that different projects of self-justification may be stealthily packed away rather than bravely declared. If cathedral-like structures come into Proust's writing as explanatory narratological metaphors at all (iv. 610; tr. vi. 432), we should perhaps start to conceptualize them as we do Gaudí's *Sagrada Familia* in Barcelona, rather than as Ruskin's crumbling Gothic French objects of affection.[29] Building there certainly is, in the blocks of digressions that may be picked apart by careful, coralling attention to the respective statuses of textual additions, prolepsis, paralepsis, and analepsis, of basic narrative departures from a pregiven teleology. We may divide *A la recherche* up into its manifold digressions, rigorously and painstakingly on the grand scale either of the new Pléiade edition, or Alison Winton's immensely valuable research tool, *Proust's Additions*. But we should sound a warning note to ourselves as we do it. Because digressions are *attempts to fit in*, quite as much as entertaining departures, joke-telling, the capturing of attention either of an audience or of a beloved. They seek disguise, wish to perform like other kinds of text, bulge like the 'croupe rebondie de ce corps livré au laisser-aller' of Charlus's sagging body (iii. 712; tr. v. 231). Proustian

[29] This vast cathedral was begun by Francisco del Villar in 1882 to a Neo-Gothic design, taken over by Gaudí's undulating and membranous conception in 1883, and remained unfinished at his death in 1926.

digressions are inclusive textual spaces like overstuffed armchairs, and *belle époque* drawing-rooms, like Odette's crammed salon (i. 529; tr. ii. 130), and the rooms Marcel cannot get used to (ii. 27; tr. ii. 282). They are chaotic spaces of perceptual bombardment, where the horror of decay, of the spectacle of giving way to desire, gets closest to engulfing even the boundaries of grammatical steadiness.

To arrive at a fuller understanding of how they work, and what they contain shows self-justification in *A la recherche* in a new mode, and in a new light, pulling what we might previously have seen as disconnected regions of the text into a renewed coherence. Self-justificatory hold-ups are precisely what hold the novel up.

Having seen self-justification in large-scale operation as a set of attempts to integrate into a hostile social environment, and as an organizing principle holding vast areas of the novel in play, another question comes into view. Does self-justification take place on a much smaller, more intimate scale, and if it does, under what kind of conditions?

3

Moments of Attachment: The *Cloison*

Soudain les cloisons ébranlées de ma mémoire cédèrent.

(*CSB* 212)

I. INTRODUCTION

'Judging', Freud tells us, 'is the intellectual action which decides the choice of motor action, which puts an end to the postponement due to thought and which leads over from thinking to acting.'[1] Lacan begins his final class on *L'Éthique de la psychanalyse* by announcing that: 'L'éthique consiste essentiellement—il faut toujours repartir des définitions—en un jugement sur notre action, à ceci près qu'elle n'a de portée que pour autant que l'action impliquée en elle comporte aussi ou est censée comporter un jugement, même implicite. La présence du jugement des deux côtés est essentielle à la structure.'[2] Lacan (inadvertently) refines Freud's statement by introducing an idea of ethical action, a process of making a judgement which also looks at itself as the process of making a judgement, and so is simultaneously inward-looking and

---

[1] 'Negation' *SE* (1925), xix, 235–9 (p. 238). Freud discusses the 'postponement due to thought' repeatedly as one of the main functions of the ego, a kind of scaled-down, pre-emptive version of acting. See, among other papers, the 'stock-taking' of 'Formulations on the Two Principles of Mental Functioning', *SE* (1911), xii, 215–26 (p. 221), the paper that draws on previous thinking about the distinction between a pleasure and a reality principle. This distinction was written about both in 'A Project for a Scientific Psychology', *The Origins of Psycho-Analysis, SE* (1950 [1895]), i. 283–359, and in Ch. 7 of *The Interpretation of Dreams, SE* (1900), v. 509–621. See on 'postponement', part i. section 17 of the 'Project' (and on judgement, part i. sections 16, 17, and 18). See also *The Ego and the Id, SE* (1923), xix. 3–66 (p. 55). Lecture 32 of *New Introductory Lectures*, 'Anxiety and Instinctual Life', *SE* (1933 [1932]), xxii, 81–111 (p. 89) gives a list of references to 'postponement due to thought'.

[2] Jacques Lacan, 'Les Paradoxes de l'éthique', *L'Éthique de la psychanalyse* (1986), 359.

outward-looking. Freud's definition makes the world revolve around just one person, the Hamlet figure who is deciding what action to take. Lacan, as he ponders how to define ethical activity, reminds us that making judgements is not as simple as Freud's account seems to summarize here, since outcomes in the form of action come up against both internal and external resistances. We do not pass judgements in isolation, but in dynamic, interpersonal, and often fraught situations, in which there is not enough time to reflect. It is this aspect of judging under fraught conditions in *A la recherche*—the ways it produces self-justification, what form that self-justification takes, and where it is to be located—that forms the next stage of my argument.

Bersani's psychoanalytic interest in the constitution and validation of redemptive attempts by literature and other art forms for the human subject that undertakes them, relaunches another, more neglected, strain of Proustian criticism, that of moral epistemologies: 'In the work of art, a certain type of representation of experience will operate both as an *escape* from the objects of representation and as a *justification* (retroactive, even posthumous) for having had any experiences at all. In Proust, art simultaneously erases, repeats, and redeems life. Literary repetition is an annihilating salvation.'[3] Proust's attention to the interconnectedness of mental and material phenomena through the retrieving powers of metaphor[4] is

3 Leo Bersani, *The Culture of Redemption* (1990), 11; my emphasis.

4 Gérard Genette, in 'Métonymie chez Proust', sparked off a grand debate on Proust's metaphorical systems, showing that metaphor, despite Proust's rule that the two objects used to construct it should be 'deux objets différents' (iv. 468; tr. vi. 246), were almost invariably in contagious, metonymic contact, citing, among other examples, (i) the duchesse de Guermantes's gaze at Combray, 'bleu comme un rayon de soleil qui aurait traversé le vitrail de Gilbert le Mauvais' (i. 175; tr. i. 213); (ii) the description of Giotto's Vices and Virtues in the Arena Chapel at Padua: 'si bleus qu'il semble que la radieuse journée ait passé le seuil elle aussi avec le visiteur et soit venue un instant mettre à l'ombre et au frais son ciel pur' (iv. 226–7; tr. v. 744). Compare 'les mouches qui exécutaient devant moi, . . . comme la musique de chambre de l'été . . . unie à l'été par un lien plus nécessaire; née des beaux jours, ne renaissant qu'avec eux, contenant un peu de leur essence' (i. 82; tr. i. 97) that accompany Marcel's early reading afternoons, given a brilliant deconstructive reading by de Man, 'Reading (Proust)', *Allegories of Reading* (1972). See also Jean-Pierre Richard, *Proust et le monde sensible*; Barthes's 1978 paper, ' "Longtemps, je me suis couché de bonne heure . . ." ', *Le Bruissement de la langue* (1984), 313–25; Philippe Lejeune, who discusses *allitération* in 'Les Carafes de le Vivonne', in G. Genette and

much celebrated and pored over as a linguistic phenomenon in its own right. Work on Proust's stylistics has brought the dynamics of the Proustian text into close focus, so that it is, as it were, 'better', but more partially, read than was previously fashionable, and this has led to a degree of prurience about the ethical questions that Proust's absorbing textual experiments in representation consistently strive to master.

What Bersani terms the operation of an *escape from* and a *justification for* experience reminds us of what we have seen of Proustian digression, its evasions, and attempts at impossible inclusiveness. But it also makes us turn our attention to the multiple experiments that Proust conducts into an acutely painful ethical dilemma throughout *A la recherche*, asking how it is possible to take account of otherness in a (narrative) world structured and apprehended by a singular perceiving self.

Such a question moves my argument into a new realm, one in which we must look at how reassurance is sought, not through public tokens of esteem, respect, or acceptability, or through convenient or helpless evasion by digression, but through moments of difficult, sometimes dangerous intimacy, encounters not with those whom Marcel is most like, but those whom he most likes.

What I am about to present is Proust's flexible graphic representation of a thought process, a vital two-way switch to be found distributed at irregular intervals, and in various clusterings and constellations throughout *A la recherche du temps perdu*, functioning here as a prop, there as a prompt, now goading and now inhibiting moral judgement. It is Proust's spectacularly economical mnemonic for self-justification under intimate conditions.

2. THE *CLOISON*

The organization of modern urban space was of paramount importance to Proust. In 1919, on having to leave his apartment on the boulevard Haussmann, he wrote: 'Je ne crains pas du

T. Todorov (eds.), *Recherche de Proust* (1980), 163–96; and Jonathan Culler, 'The Turns of Metaphor', *The Pursuit of Signs* (1981).

tout le bruit de la rue . . ., je recherche les bruits extérieurs et continus parce qu'*ils m'assourdissent les bruits des voisins, les bruits intermittents et auxquels on cherche une explication.*'[5] The *bruits des voisins* were audible through the interior walls of Proust's apartment. His irritated desire to know what the sounds signify directs us to the composition of those walls themselves.

The noun *cloison* first came into the French language in around 1160, according to *Le Grand Robert,* and signified at that time an *enceinte fortifiée.* Its root was the Latin *clausio, -ionis,* derived from *clausus,* a *clos,* or enclosure. Towards 1538, a *cloison* had come to mean a 'paroi qui limite une pièce et l'isole du reste de la maison', or the 'séparation (sur un navire)'. By around 1732, an additional meaning had crept into the language: 'ce qui divise naturellement l'intérieur d'une cavité, détermine des cases, des compartiments, des loges' (where *loges* presumably means a stall in a stable, rather than its other meaning of box at the theatre, or dressing room, behind the scenes). In botany, *cloison* denoted the membranous 'lames séparant les loges à l'intérieur de certains fruits'. It could refer to 'ce qui divise un objet fabriqué'. In the language of firearms, it meant the 'partie pleine qui sépare deux rayures, à l'intérieur du canon d'une arme à feu'. The term also carried a readily available figurative significance of *barrière* or *séparation.*

Its word history shows that, despite originally designating what *surrounded* and protected the whole, the uses of the *cloison* were shifted *inside* spaces, now enclosed by quite different materials, to accommodate new architectural (and shipbuilding) naming needs: *cloisons* came to refer to internal division. The division of internal space produces a multiplication of spaces: 'room' becomes 'rooms', but at the same time, the permanence and stability of the *cloison* becomes fraught and fragile. Unlike their sibling *clôture,* which has remained solidly cloistering monasteries, *cloisons* turn into expediently erected partitions. But if *cloisons* come to be needed to divide space internally, in a cheap, makeshift way, a new mode of social interaction finds itself dogging their installation; for *cloisons* are permeable, and

[5] *Corr.* xviii. 85; my emphasis. See *Esquisse* II [Le Réveil et les rêves], ii. 1: 'Une sorte de participation à l'obscurité de la chambre, à la vie inconsciente de ses cloisons et de ses meubles, tel était mon sommeil' (i. 640).

they provide room for manœuvre. Makeshift internal division introduces a newly won privacy and secrecy, but it is secrecy that is enticingly available for decipherment.

Luc Fraisse tries to find evidence from a letter of 1910, written to Gabriel Mourey to congratulate him on his translation of Edgar Poe, for his own idea that Proust thinks of *cloisons* as *translucide*: 'depuis tant d'années que j'espère (et je n'ai toujours pas renoncé!) vous connaître, c'est du moins une compensation à mon isolement, de causer avec vous de Poe à travers la translucide cloison du texte irisé.'[6] This seems a convincing interpretation until Fraisse goes on to attach *translucide* to *vitrail*, *vitrages*, and *vitraux*, as he finds these terms in both letters and the text of *A la recherche*. There is a confusion of terms here, though: it is not the *cloison* that is translucent, but the material *cloisons* contain when they act as boundaries, when they signify the lead piping around stained glass.[7] *Cloisons* admit of noise, but do not transmit light.

When we come to think about internal division in other spheres of activity, we are quickly reminded that it is both vital and deadly. If cell division did not occur, the human body would be unable to repair itself or reproduce. But retold in parable form, Christ's encounter with the Pharisees explains internal division very differently:

And knowing their thoughts he said unto them, Every kingdom divided against itself is brought to desolation; and every city or house divided against itself shall not stand: and if Satan casteth out Satan, he is divided against himself; how then shall his kingdom stand? And if I by Beelzebub cast out devils, by whom do your sons cast them out? therefore shall they be your judges. But if I by the Spirit of God cast out devils, then is the kingdom of God come upon you.[8]

In stark terms, splitting, when seen through the focus of modern cell biology, is one of the principal self-preservative forces. Through the perspective of an allegory intended both as explanatory psychomachia and as Christian political provocation, on the

---

[6] *Corr.* x. 38. See Fraisse's recent selection and thematic distribution of Proust's letters, *Proust au miroir de sa correspondance* (1996), 154–8.

[7] In another form, they give their name to the separations between pools of enamel, shaping them into the patterns we call *cloisonnement*.

[8] Matthew 12: 25–8.

other hand, splits are threats and prophecies of doom. United we stand, divided we fall.

In 'Splitting of the Ego in the Process of Defence', Freud speculates that it is a conflict *within the ego*, and not one between the id and the ego, which produces splitting in the face of intolerable danger, preserving on the face of it a pleasurable activity that has been proscribed, but simultaneously generating a fetish, a displaced symptom of the fear (of castration).⁹ Lacan, in redramatizing Freud, stages internal division as radically inescapable: 'cette forme situe l'instance du *moi*, dès avant sa détermination sociale, dans une ligne de fiction, à jamais irréductible pour le seul individu,—ou plutôt, qui ne rejoindra qu'asymptotiquement le devenir du sujet, quel que soit le succès des synthèses dialectiques par quoi il doit résoudre en tant que *je* sa discordance d'avec sa propre réalité.'¹⁰

Both outside and inside the human mind, then, division of an internal variety offers high-risk solutions to the imposition of different pressures; and we are very nonchalant, when reading *A la recherche*, about the ways in which Proust so effortlessly seems to permit merging, permeation, and the crumbling of barriers and boundaries, in response to affective pressures, without asking ourselves about the dangers of such infringement of limits.

Social, amicable, familial, and sexual love are, in *A la recherche*, amorous areas that constantly shift and merge into one another, even as the differences in their contexts are adumbrated. The mother's goodnight kiss (i. 23; tr. i. 25) is replicated in Albertine's kiss (ii. 281–5; tr. ii. 592–4; ii. 660; tr. iii. 420; iii. 585; tr. v. 79; iii. 900–2; tr. v. 458). The young Marcel is brought to orgasm merely by touching both Gilberte and Albertine's bodies (i. 484–5; tr. ii. 76–7; and iii. 581; tr. v. 74). Telegrams arrive that fuse Gilberte and Albertine's names together (iv. 234; tr. v. 753). Charlus's offer to the young narrator to be his

⁹ *SE* (1940 [1938]), xxiii. 273–8. Freud's thinking on internal division in his models of mind can, of course, be traced throughout his work, not only in this late paper; perhaps most dramatically in *The Ego and the Id, SE* (1923), xix. 3–66, where he revises and reorganizes what had been largely a bipartite mental model into not only a tripartite but also a dynamic and systemic description of mental functioning.
¹⁰ Jacques Lacan, 'Le stade du miroir comme formateur de la fonction du Je' (1949), *Écrits I* (Éditions du Seuil, 1966), 89–97 (p. 91).

guide is exactly the same as a moment of sexual opportunism, but can be translated either way, one neutrally, the other appetitively (ii. 581; tr. iii. 326). Saint-Loup's difficulties with Rachel Quand du Seigneur are the same as those experienced by Marcel with Albertine. Only male homosexuality is radically and unspeakably different from female homosexuality (iii. 533; tr. v. 17). Otherwise, friendship can substitute for love: witness the narrator's evening out with Saint-Loup, instead of Mme de Stermaria (ii. 688–708; tr. iii. 455–79), taking the spurned narrator spinning from weeping on rolled-up carpets, through revolving doors. Conquests without consequence (the 'petite fille pauvre qui me regardait avec de grands yeux et qui avait l'air si bon que je lui demandai si elle ne voulait pas venir chez moi' (iv. 15; tr. v. 495), as well as life-diverting tragic love affairs, can and do both end in *oubli*.[11]

These endless permeations and permutations also make up the forward-directed, vocation-discovering drive of the novel, however: 'jamais rien ne se répète exactement' (iv. 80; tr. v. 570). Each recurring event is painstakingly remapped, and processed, as though it were absolutely new. It is not *recurrence* which gives us our ethical mainspring here, but the *renewability* of the encounter with others, either in groups, or in the multiple guises of singular individuals, and this renewability has as much to do with the unexpected sharpness and pain of suddenly imposed barriers as it does with the permissiveness of fluid interconnectivity. The self-justificatory activity signalled in such moments of attachment is still bound up with the desire to hear and the desire to please, but in the mode of deprivation.

Proust's early thinking about the release of affective states to writing was highly compacted and dense. All the instances of *mémoire involontaire* occur together in the early 'Projets de préface', as the 1971 editors of *Contre Sainte-Beuve* have christened its opening pages, and it is a breached mental *cloison* that precipitates them: 'les cloisons ébranlées de ma mémoire cédèrent, et ce furent les étés que je passais dans la maison de campagne que j'ai dite qui firent irruption dans ma

---

[11] Although there is a hilarious consequence to the narrator's absent-minded propositioning of the young girl, when he is brought to book by the girl's parents and the chef de la Sûreté, a police chief who doubles as knowing lecher himself (iv. 27–8; tr. v. 506–7).

conscience' (*CSB* 212). The dissolution of barriers to the retrieval of affective knowledge is presented as a fantastic piece of mental good fortune, as it will also be in *A la recherche*.

Yet what is so striking about the textual moments where *cloisons* appear in the novel is that they take us to moments where far less salubrious and meritorious narratorial activity than epiphanic remembrance is going on. In the argument that follows, I will take us to some of these moments, encounters, and activities.[12] We can divide them up, loosely, for the time being, into public and private moments, and literal and figurative uses of our key term, although the way in which each of these spheres and uses is constructed will be very much a part of how these moments of particular moral scrutiny function.

3. PUBLIC *CLOISONNEMENT*

Grouping together one kind of occurrence of permeable partitions, we find that in contexts of public display, they are used figuratively to signify transparency and untouchability. They focus our attention specifically on the ways in which those with social pretentions see boundaries as ends in themselves, rather than as media of communication. The visibility and transparency apparently afforded by *cloisons* when they are figuratively erected between a lowly viewing public, and figures whose existence is played out in public, enacts a one-way communication whose purpose is to show without telling. When there is nothing there to be said, silently appreciated spectacle carries out a protective function, which arranges exposure to an audience without giving away anything but what is perfectly plain for all to see, that is, exclusivity. Mme Swann, for example, carefully arranges her flowers, imported from the countryside so that the passer-by will be intrigued at the hothouse acceleration of the passing of the seasons: 'Car la châtelaine de Tansonville savait qu'avril, même glacé, n'est pas dépourvu de fleurs, que l'hiver, le printemps, l'été, ne sont pas séparés par des cloisons aussi hermétiques que tend à le croire le boulevardier' (i. 623; tr. ii. 244).

---

[12] The table to be found in Appendix III at the end of the study adumbrates the context of each *cloison* moment.

When Mme de Villeparisis travels, she, as much as the envi-
ously spectating fellow occupants of the Grand Hôtel at Balbec,
does so clad about with all her own trappings: 'sa chambre où
des rideaux personnels, remplaçant ceux qui pendaient aux
fenêtres, des paravents, des photographies, mettaient si bien,
entre elle et le monde extérieur auquel il eût fallu s'adapter, la
cloison de ses habitudes, que c'était son chez elle, au sein
duquel elle était restée, qui voyageait plutôt qu'elle-même' (ii.
39; tr. ii. 296–7). But if the omniscient narrator as *passe-muraille*
can here see through the walls of Mme de Villeparisis's hotel
bedroom, at other moments Marcel's desire to preserve the
mystery located in names ensures that none of the liquid of the
duchesse de Guermantes's life is either poured out or evaporated in the glare of its own footlights. Just before the narrator's
second visit to watch la Berma play Phèdre, enthralled by the
spectacle of the Guermantes *baignoire* 'où Mme de Guermantes
transvasait sa vie' (ii. 335; tr. iii. 32), he tries to establish the location of the particular gap she represents between the continuous and the contiguous:

Les noms de Guise, de Parme, de Guermantes-Bavière, différenciaient
de toutes les autres les villégiatures où se rendait la duchesse . . . S'ils
me disaient qu'en ces villégiatures, en ces fêtes consistait successive-
ment la vie de Mme de Guermantes, ils ne m'apportaient sur elle
aucun éclaircissement. Elles donnaient chacune à la vie de la duchesse
une détermination différente, mais ne faisaient que la changer de
mystère sans qu'elle laissât rien évaporer du sien, qui se déplaçait
seulement, protégé par une cloison, enfermé dans un vase, au milieu
des flots de la vie de tous. (ii. 335; tr. iii. 32)

What is visible through the *cloison*, which here extends its
protective enclosure about the duchesse as its medieval sense
intended it to, is a transportable reproduction, a public life
represented intact and in miniature, impressed upon the body
of the aristocrat.

At the theatre itself, the transportable *cloison* is again in
evidence, but this time the enclosure is a *loge*, an ambiguous
word that covers both high and low status, a box both for
horses and at theatres. Its boundaries are properly established by the modern definition of the *cloison*, rather than the
medieval all-enclosing surround that the duchesse likes to
take with her, but once inside the theatre, the *loge* doubles

once again, as being at once off-stage and the only thing
worth looking at:

c'était parce que les gens du monde étaient dans leurs loges (derrière
le balcon en terrasse) comme dans des petits salons suspendus dont
une cloison eût été enlevée . . .; c'est parce qu'ils posaient une main
indifférente sur des fûts dorés des colonnes qui soutenaient ce temple
de l'art lyrique, c'est parce qu'ils n'étaient pas émus des honneurs
excessifs que semblaient leur rendre deux figures sculptées qui
tendaient vers les loges des palmes et des lauriers, que seuls ils
auraient eu l'esprit libre pour écouter la pièce si seulement ils avaient
eu de l'esprit. (ii. 339; tr. iii. 36–7)

While students of theatre think only of not spoiling their gloves,
or of not stepping on people's toes, apprehensively aware of not
quite fitting in, the *gens du monde* take their justification from
the contours of the space that demarcates them, are indifferent
to the sweatmarks of their own hands on the auditorium's
panelling, take their cue from the carved figures that hand up
carved honours to them—and may be toppled only by writing
that describes their self-enclosure as stupidity.[13] Against social
indifference, what recourse is there but to a poisoned pen?
What real or political difference is possible against apparently
fixed class boundaries? These are questions that we have seen
emerge before, during Marcel's navigation of the salon territories, and they are brought into intimate focus here through the
variable permeability of panelling that, when it functions trans-
parently, in fact shows only fixation, the human organism as
prearranged and recyclable symbol of class difference. When
the *cloisons* of *A la recherche* seem to let light through, or are
partially withdrawn, and when we are invited to look through
them, or the opening their removal leaves behind, at what is
going on visibly but silently on their other side, they are doing
no work. Public *cloisons* are a focus for social jealousy and snobbery, but there are other faces to Proustian jealousy, and other
emotions organized by the intimacy of partitions.

---

[13] Compare the writing of exposure through which the marquis de Palancy is
inflected: 'le cou tendu, la figure oblique, son gros œil rond collé contre le verre
du monocle, se déplaçait lentement dans l'ombre transparente et paraissait ne pas
plus voir le public de l'orchestre qu'un poisson qui passe, ignorant de la foule des
visiteurs curieux, derrière la cloison vitrée d'un aquarium' (ii. 343; tr. iii. 41).

4. UNCONDITIONAL LOVE

Cloisons which let light through them are also, it should be recalled, figurative separations. When Marcel encounters *material* partitions, their effect on communication is substantially altered. The pattern we are about to see plots an uncanny course for itself through the novel, bringing into line seemingly quite disparate parts of the text, and establishing what amounts to a confident causality that sends us forwards and backwards in the narrative's unfolding and re-enfolding chronology.

When Marcel first visits the Grand Hôtel at Balbec, in the company of his grandmother, he is famously unable to sleep in the strange new room. He feels invaded by the very smells of his surroundings: 'c'était presque à l'intérieur de mon moi que celle du vétiver venait pousser dans mes derniers retranchements son offensive, à laquelle j'opposais non sans fatigue la riposte inutile et incessante d'un reniflement alarmé' (ii. 28; tr. iii. 283). What is often missed by critics writing on intense moments of Proustian sensorial apprehension is that the writing of them is simultaneously absolutely comic and absolutely straight-faced. The writing narrator implicitly justifies his hyperbolic style as being the result of conveying the intensity of childhood experience, but an opportunistic self-pity is also resident in this reactivating of a personal past. In order to show the way forward for the narratorial *moi*, to bring into view an account of formative markers, the writing narrator never misses a chance to inflect the detail of past experiences through a deftly mature adult writing style, which at once shows its distance from those past events, but pleasurably and tirelessly replays them under the heading of necessary recall. That Marcel's grandmother should be alerted to her beloved charge's suffering by repeated sniffing does not sit easily with the monumentality of her status in the novel, and yet what else should unconditional love respond to but sniffing? The portrait of the grandmother which follows her entrance into Marcel's room continues this hyperbolic style:

je savais, quand j'étais avec ma grand-mère, si grand chagrin qu'il y eût en moi, qu'il serait reçu dans une pitié plus vaste encore; que tout ce qui était mien, mes soucis, mon vouloir, serait, en ma grand-mère, étayé sur un désir de conservation et d'accroissement de ma propre vie autrement fort que celui que j'avais moi-même; et mes pensées se prolongeaient en elle sans subir de déviation parce qu'elles passaient de mon esprit dans le sien sans changer de milieu, de personne. (ii. 28; tr. ii. 283–4)

The unmediated, unconditional love that is written about here inaugurates a kind of writing that we have not yet examined closely. As readers we are faced with a difficult question: in the context of a novel which is capable of retaining a glaring focus on each and every one of its objects, what are we to make of sincerity? Criticism has come this way before, the first-person confessional *récit* or novel demands that it do so, but the question never goes away. This, presumably, is because it is impossible to answer. We can neither take at face value the authenticity of the narrator's portrait of his grandmother, nor decry it in utter cynicism. What is so shocking about this passage is not that it is about love, but that it is about love *in writing*.

The discomfort of 'reading love' on the page deflects readerly attention in an oblique direction, onto two objects to be found in the hotel room: Marcel's *bottines* (ii. 29; tr. ii. 284) and the *cloison* which separates his room from his grandmother's.[14] As he tries to undress for bed, his grandmother stops 'd'un regard suppliant mes mains qui touchaient aux premiers boutons de ma veste et de mes bottines' (ii. 29; tr. ii. 284). *Touchaient, boutons, bottines* diffuse the soft sound of a kiss across this sentence, through a *bouche* whose syllables ghost it. Built into the phonemes of the touching of buttons and *bottines*, overriding the loving kiss, however, is the verb phrase *toucher au bout*. Even as we are shown a moment of familial privacy, the movements of language are urgently signalling what is to come.

Practical arrangements for neediness are made. This is the first time in the text that the *cloison* is named in direct speech:

---

[14] Lacan has given us a brilliant analogy for how this deflection of focus from subjects to objects functions, in 'La demande du bonheur et la promesse analytique', where he tells the story of Professor D*, *L'Éthique de la psychanalyse*, 337–48. The recognition of the professor's old boots is, for Lacan, 'la manifestation visible du beau' (p. 344), but this beauty 'n'a rien à faire avec ce qu'on appelle le beau idéal. C'est seulement à partir de l'appréhension du beau dans la ponctualité de la transition de la vie à la mort, que nous pouvons essayer de restituer le beau idéal' (p. 344). We apprehend beauty, Lacan is saying, only as a *ponctualité*, an exactitude, an on-timeness, in a plotting of endless such points headed deathwards.

' "Oh, je t'en prie," me dit-elle. "C'est une telle joie pour ta grand-mère. Et surtout ne manque pas de frapper au mur si tu as besoin de quelque chose cette nuit, mon lit est adossé au tien, la cloison est très mince." ' (ii. 29; tr. ii. 284). The injunction to *frapper au mur*, to transmit a signal of need, is rehearsed that night. It becomes a habitual and wordless act of communication between the narrator and his grandmother: 'à peine j'avais frappé mes coups que j'en entendais trois autres, d'une intonation différente ceux-là, empreints d'une calme autorité' (ii. 29; tr. ii. 285).[15] And within a page, we find the *cloison* transubstantiated into an immaterial and angelic singer, itself now the agent of the *trois autres coups*:

doux instant matinal qui s'ouvrait comme une symphonie par le dialogue rythmé de mes trois coups auquel la cloison pénétrée de tendresse et de joie, devenue harmonieuse, immatérielle, chantant comme les anges, répondait par trois autres coups, ardemment attendus, deux fois répétés, et où elle savait transporter l'âme de ma grand-mère tout entière et la promesse de sa venue, avec une allégresse d'annonciation et une fidélité musicale. (ii. 30; tr. ii. 286)

More disturbing yet than the depiction of unconditional love is this quasi-religious discourse. Disturbing not necessarily because of the register of the over-wrought language chosen to express this once habitual daily exchange, but because its wildness throws into relief the relative paucity of unconditional encounters with a familial other in this text. Incidents such as the 'baiser de paix' (i. 13; tr. i. 13), or the 'conduite . . . arbitraire'

---

[15] Compare David R. Ellison, 'The Self in/as Writing', *The Reading of Proust* (1984), 133–85. Ellison writes about the *cloison* as womb ('The womb is a "cloison" that protects without separating'), being inverted to become the symbol of a barrier against incest with the mother (p. 160). For Doubrovsky, the *cloison* is a screen between Marcel Proust and his desire to *be* his mother (*La Place de la madeleine* (1974), 73, 119–45). The *cloison* signifies a screen between a subject and his mother for Jacques Derrida, too, writing on Rousseau and the *supplément* in *De la grammatologie*: 'La disposition topographique de l'expérience n'est pas indifférente. Jean-Jacques est dans la maison de Mme de Warens: assez près de *Maman* pour la voir et pour en nourrir son imagination mais avec la possibilité de la cloison. C'est au moment où la mère disparaît que la suppléance devient possible et nécessaire. Le jeu de la présence ou de l'absence maternelle, cette alternance de la perception et de l'imagination doit correspondre à une organisation de l'espace' (p. 220). These are interesting readings. But my focus is upon the *cloison* as an epistemological modelling tool for Proust, a sign indicating areas of the novel where finding out how knowledge is discovered, acquired, or maintained is privileged.

of the narrator's father (i. 37; tr. i. 42) have strings attached,
social constraints which prevent the 'hostie pour une communion de paix où mes lèvres puiseraient sa présence réelle' (i. 13;
tr. i. 13) from being more than a textual instant long.
A moment later, and all the desperation of this idealized
transmission is exposed, in the collapse of style to simplicity.
There follows a long sentence, structured by the triple repetition of *refus*. I reproduce the sentence in its entirety:

Peut-être cet effroi que j'avais—qu'ont tant d'autres—de coucher
dans une chambre inconnue, peut-être cet effroi n'est-il que la forme
la plus humble, obscure, organique, presque inconsciente, de ce
grand *refus* désespéré qu'opposent les choses qui constituent le
meilleur de notre vie présente à ce que nous revêtions mentalement
de notre acceptation la formule d'un avenir où elles ne figurent pas;
refus qui était au fond de l'horreur que m'avait fait si souvent éprouver la pensée que mes parents mourraient un jour, que les nécessités
de la vie pourraient m'obliger à vivre loin de Gilberte, ou simplement
à me fixer définitivement dans un pays où je ne verrais plus jamais mes
amis; *refus* qui était encore au fond de la difficulté que j'avais à penser
à ma propre mort ou à une survie comme celle que Bergotte promet-
tait aux hommes dans ses livres, dans laquelle je ne pourrais emporter
mes souvenirs, mes défauts, mon caractère qui ne se résignaient pas à
l'idée de ne plus être et ne voulaient pour moi ni du néant, ni d'une
éternité où ils ne seraient plus. (ii. 30–1; tr. ii. 286–7; my emphasis)

This extraordinary sentence moves from a consideration of the
future, to the death of others, specifically his parents, and finally
to the idea of an afterlife, advertised by Bergotte, but unsatisfac-
tory to Marcel. All moments of unconditional love, even those
joyfully handled by intervening walls, have suddenly been seen
but as presages and instigators of a time when such moments
will have failed the self, and been fully withdrawn. The shifting
responsibility for the *refus*, first a resistance thrown up by objects
to their own disappearance, then a refusal that underlies the
thought of parental death, finally a refusal by Marcel to accept
survie in Bergotte's terms, opens the refusal of the *cloison* to be
the grandmother in any other but gaudily inappropriate terms
onto a much larger question of self-justification in language. If a
doux instant matinal is to have any meaning, it must be recorded
for posterity, but the writing narrator demonstrates, in the
excess and bathos of his attempt to configure the *cloison* here,

that moments of attachment cannot easily be imported wholesale into writing. The last part of the long sentence above expresses Marcel's continued doubt about what could be carried over into an afterlife, but rides the echo of an ambiguity. Bergotte promises men an afterlife in his books, but it is not clear whether this means that it is the promise or the afterlife itself which is to be found in his works. The *cloison* carries sound through a barrier in the narratively resurrected present, but, the narrator asks, what can carry and then preserve 'mes souvenirs, mes défauts, mon caractère' across a barrier that in no way guarantees the fanfares his writing can give *partitions* here?

Self-justification at a moment of attachment focused through a *cloison*, then, can broaden and develop to take on far larger spheres of human activity and preoccupation than merely knocking for attention might at first glance predict. From everyday neediness and the desire for reassurance frustrated by knocking up against intervening room partitions, terrifying amplifications of mental activity may uncontrollably occur, predicting and speculating upon an utter *loss* of limits.

What happens, however, when the very object of the narrator's affections herself, unexpectedly, turns into a self-justifying subject? Later on during this first visit to Balbec, Saint-Loup elects to take a photograph of the narrator's grandmother:

quand je vis qu'elle avait mis pour cela sa plus belle toilette et hésitait entre diverses coiffures, je me sentis un peu irrité de cet enfantillage qui m'étonnait tellement de sa part. J'en arrivais même à me demander si je ne m'étais pas trompé sur ma grand-mère, si je ne la plaçais pas trop haut, si elle était aussi détachée que j'avais toujours cru de ce qui concernait sa personne, si elle n'avait pas ce que je croyais lui être le plus étranger, de la coquetterie. (ii. 144; tr. ii. 423)

Photography embarrasses Marcel, because it implies modelling, posing, a wilful staging of the self that immobilizes one's availability as sexual entity, a distorted self-promotional activity which, while it inscribes 'words of light', tells only half a story as it does so. He feels it incumbent upon him to transmit this impression to his grandmother, exposing the truth of her *coquetterie* to her, to

faire preuve de pénétration et de force en lui disant quelques paroles ironiques et blessantes destinées à neutraliser le plaisir qu'elle

semblait trouver à être photographiée, de sorte que si je fus contraint
de voir le magnifique chapeau de ma grand-mère, je réussis du moins
à faire disparaître de son visage cette expression joyeuse qui aurait dû
me rendre heureux. (ii. 144–5; tr. ii. 424)

This language of surgical correction, *pénétration, force*,
'paroles ironiques et blessantes destinées à neutraliser',
contraint, faire disparaître, in which a renewed balance of human
behaviour is sought through verbally punishing its excesses, has
a direct correlation with the ensuing *absence* of the sign system
which has come to represent the grandmother since the arrival
of the pair in Balbec. For Barthes, the photograph has the
potential power to make demands upon us, to hail us: 'piqûre,
petit trou, petite tache, petite coupure—et aussi coup de dés.
Le *punctum* d'une photo, c'est ce hasard qui, en elle, *me point*
(mais aussi me meurtrit, me poigne).'[16] And we might expect
the appearance of a photograph of the grandmother to cause a
measure of repentance in Marcel for his incisive cruelty. It is,
however, not photography which touches the narrator now, but
the interruption of the *cloison*'s good offices. Later that night,
on returning from an evening out with Saint-Loup, and more
and more aware that his grandmother 'avait paru me fuir' (ii.
145; tr. ii. 424), we are told that:

j'avais beau attendre qu'elle frappât contre la cloison ces petits coups
qui me diraient d'entrer lui dire bonsoir, je n'entendais rien; je finis-
sais par me coucher, lui en voulant un peu de ce qu'elle me privât,
avec une indifférence si nouvelle de sa part, d'une joie sur laquelle
j'avais tant compté, je restais encore, le cœur palpitant comme dans
mon enfance, à écouter le mur qui restait muet et je m'endormais
dans les larmes. (ii. 145; tr. ii. 424)

The *cloison* carries responsibility for the grandmother's access
to communication, a communication which, if it came, would
be the sign for unconditional love. Its silence effects the transmission of her *indifférence si nouvelle*: the surgical interventions
of the narrator's words neutralize not only the pleasure she

---

[16] *La Chambre claire*, 49. For Coventry Patmore, writing in 1898, the *punctum* in
works of art meant something rather different: he takes from Coleridge the idea
that all 'busy' works of art have a 'point of rest', a *punctum indifferens*, matter 'to
which all that is interesting is more or less unconsciously referred', 'The Point of
Rest in Art', *Principle in Art* (1898), 14.

takes in being photographed, but her capacity for boundless love. And the excessive *force* used by the narrator to rein back in behaviour by his grandmother which he interprets as her attempt to *be something she is not*, her attempt to justify herself in the guise of an inappropriate reinvention of herself as coquette (rather than continue to find her habitual justification in being his 'unconditional lover'), and the resulting failure of the sign system of unconditional love, kickstarts the dynamic for a vital bipartite sequence in *A la recherche*.

5. 'DES COUPS TROP BRUYANTS': SEXUAL RESEARCH

Before we turn to this pendant to the first Balbec visit, however, we should take a moment or two to look over our set of *cloison* moments, and gather together what we have discovered about their impact on our understanding of self-justification in *A la recherche*.

The twinkling mosaic effect rendered during walks by the Vivonne ('un bleu clair et cru, tirant sur le violet, d'apparence cloisonnée et de goût japonais': i. 167; tr. i. 203), or tea with Gilberte ('elle extrayait pour moi du monument écroulé tout un pan verni et cloisonné de fruits écarlates, dans le goût oriental': i. 497; tr. ii. 91), for all their *belle époque* good taste, are, very precisely, *sujets cloisonnés*: like duchesses at theatres, and unseasonal hothouse flowers, they do not work hard, but simply sit there on the surface of the text, looking gorgeous. The narrator can snatch up any number of these glittering set-pieces, large and small, and sprinkle them across the text for our delectation. But *cloison* moments which stage a moment of attachment, whether a seemingly low-level narrative incident, like Saint-Loup's quarrelling with Rachel Quand du Seigneur (ii. 578; tr. iii. 323–4), or the narrator's doubts about the uses of friendship ('serments d'amitié qui, nés dans les cloisons de cette heure, restant enfermés en elle, ne seraient peut-être pas tenus le lendemain': ii. 691; tr. iii. 458) contain their own microdrama of self-justification, compacted into the moment of encounter with the *cloison* itself—but which also resonates across the narrative.

In *A la recherche*, its myriad stories are compounds, built up of blocks or units, perhaps of other stories, but they invariably come with attachments: they nest one inside another, compacted into cups of tea, bifurcating into two pathways, carried by coastal trains, reduced down into the 'temps incorporé' (iv. 623; tr. vi. 449) of a former beloved's daughter, or the corner of a Carpaccio or a Vermeer. Self-justificatory shards, the *sujets cloisonnés* that are prettily and complacently self-regarding have no textual power. What makes *cloison* moments of attachment textually active and effective is their clamorous provocativeness, the way in which they appear in the text with moral dubiousness attached, the way each of their appearances reminds us of all the others, and positively demands interpretation. Let me give an example of this particularly Proustian chain of reaction.

When Marcel meets Morel for the first time it is recorded as a digression from the main narrative (of Mme de Villeparisis's salon), and it concentrates into the space of three pages an extraordinary density of information with a slow-release timer to it. Morel has brought the narrator Oncle Adolphe's collection of naughty photographs, 'de nature à intéresser un jeune homme de mon âge': 'C'étaient les photographies des actrices célèbres, des grandes cocottes que mon oncle avait connues, les dernières images de cette vie de vieux viveur qu'il séparait, par une cloison étanche, de sa vie de famille' (ii. 561; tr. iii. 303). Morel is immediately identified as a transmitter of information. He penetrates accounts of parties, brings photographs which expose another man's uncle to have been of dubious sexual morality, wants to 'couper le câble avec la domesticité d'où il sortait' (ii. 561; tr. iii. 303), talks to Marcel 'comme à un égal' (ii. 561; tr. iii. 303), asks for information about any poets 'ayant une situation importante dans le monde "aristo"' (ii. 562; tr. iii. 304), does not baulk at asking for an introduction to Jupien's niece, commissions a waistcoat from her, and seems singularly well-informed as to the identity of Miss Sacripant. Like Saint-Loup, he moves at speed (compare Saint-Loup's flailing fists in response to an improper advance (ii. 480; tr. iii. 205), or his exit from Jupien's *hôtel* (iv. 389; tr. vi. 148). If Oncle Adolphe had kept his private life to himself, Morel is the vehicle of its exposure.

One of the ways Morel talks to the narrator *comme à un égal* is by forcing him to justify himself over why he does not keep a photograph of his uncle in his room. The narrator does not record his response to Morel. But instead we are told something else: 'comme je n'avais même pas une photographie de mon père ou de ma mère dans ma chambre, il n'y avait rien de si choquant à ce qu'il ne s'en trouvât pas de mon oncle Adolphe' (ii. 562; tr. iii. 303). While the *cloison* panelling at Balbec had exposed Marcel's vulnerability by refusing to transmit the unconditional love demanded of it, the breaching of Oncle Adolphe's figural *cloison*, so carefully separating public from private, by an unexpected legacy, forces unwanted transmissions which leave the narrator vulnerable in a new way. The association of photography with exposure (of sexually liberated women, of louche behaviour and its fetishization as a collection of images), with the consequent exposure *of* this behaviour to a nephew, when in this novel 'On n'est pas toujours impunément le neveu de quelqu'un' (iii. 94; tr. iv. 110),[17] also catches in its associative net the spectacle of parental desecration viewed by the narrator at Montjouvain (i. 159–63; tr. i. 190–8). We are returned to the photographing of the narrator's grandmother, and the narrator's prim disapproval, otherwise interpretable as his fear, of the potential photography might have to tell more than it properly should.

Marcel's remembering of a *cloison étanche* which exposes the private life of a member of his family looks not only backwards into his own past, but can be seen to effect a mnemonic link, through repetition, with other private lives, the contents of which are exposed through *cloisons*. What at first sight look like innocent partitions in his own front yard, the screens separating workshops belonging respectively to an *ébéniste* and to Jupien, acquire an erotic force because of the intensity of the intratextual resonances that transmit a libidinal energy between them: 'l'ébéniste de notre cour, dont les ateliers

---

[17] 'On pourrait faire ainsi toute une galerie de portraits, ayant le titre de la comédie allemande *Oncle et neveu*, où l'on verrait l'oncle veillant jalousement, bien qu'involontairement, à ce que son neveu finisse par lui ressembler' (iii. 94; tr. iv. 110). The play is Schiller's *Der Neffe als Onkels* (1803), an adaptation of *Encore des Ménechmes* (1791) by Louis-Benoît Picard, itself referring to *Ménechmes* (1705), by Jean-François Regnard. Nepotism in *A la recherche* circulates exclusively about sexual inheritance, the clearest example, of course, being Charlus and Saint-Loup.

n'étaient séparés de la boutique de Jupien que par une cloison fort mince, allait recevoir congé du gérant parce qu'il frappait des coups trop bruyants. ... Jupien y mettrait son charbon, ferait abattre la cloison et aurait une seule et vaste boutique' (ii. 667; tr. iii. 429). Again, a repetition occurs, this time of the *cloison* that will be knocked down to accommodate Jupien's coal. The current occupier has been dismissed for knocking *too loudly*, and Jupien's goal will be achieved by knocking *down* the thin separation that at present frustrates him. This prefigures the kind of architectural liberties that Jupien will take with buildings later, when he turns a hotel into a brothel (iv. 388–411; tr. vi. 147–75). Just as Morel demonstrates a principle of accelerated movement and concentration of activity into a reduced space, so Jupien is an exponent of expansion, accommodation, and refitting. As if this were not overdetermined enough, the deal is struck with the otherwise reluctant owner of the property through the diligent spying of Françoise, who 'ayant remarqué que, même après l'heure où on ne visitait pas, le concierge laissait "contre" la porte de la boutique à louer, flaira un piège dressé par le concierge pour attirer la fiancée du valet de pied des Guermantes (ils y trouveraient une retraite d'amour) et ensuite les surprendre' (ii. 667–8; tr. iii. 430). The workshop is thus thoroughly saturated with an erotic charge from the moment of its discovery. Some two hundred pages further on, this apparently redundant little textual detail affords a handily ready-made protective space for the chance sexual encounter between Charlus and Jupien, in the opening chapter of *Sodome et Gomorrhe.*

Here, the *histoire* attempts to chart, step by step, the protagonist's exploration of a sexual arena purportedly hitherto completely unknown to him, while the *narration* mercilessly gives the game away ahead of time. What I want to draw attention to is the means by which the narrator effects his revelatory encounter. The celebrated alternation of focus, either on a bee which may or may not pollinate an orchid left in the courtyard, or on the activities of Jupien and Charlus, starts to look blurred well before the narrator has a chance to get to the *boutique* and discover what the couple are doing. In the middle of a sentence which purports to be the culmination of the alternation, but which itself precedes the narrator's heroic trip across the

courtyard to Jupien's workshop, we find the following parenthesis: '(simple comparaison pour les providentiels hasards,
quels qu'ils soient, et sans la moindre prétension scientifique
de rapprocher certaines lois de la botanique et ce qu'on
appelle parfois fort mal l'homosexualité)' (iii. 9; tr. iv. 8).[18]

In 'Negation', Freud famously says of the condemnatory
judgement that it is 'the intellectual substitute for repression;
its "no" is the hall-mark of repression, a certificate of origin—
like, let us say, "Made in Germany" '.[19] He goes on:

The other sort of decision made by the function of judgement—as
to the real existence of something of which there is a presentation
(reality-testing)—is a concern of the definitive reality-ego, which
develops out of the initial pleasure-ego. It is now no longer a question
of whether what has been perceived (a thing) shall be taken into the
ego or not, but of whether something which is in the ego as a presentation can be rediscovered in perception (reality) as well. It is, we see,
once more a question of *external* and *internal*. What is unreal, merely a
presentation and subjective, is only internal; what is real is also there
outside. (p. 237)

The important point about reality-testing, he asserts, is not that
we should find objects 'out there', but that we should relocate
objects external to ourselves that have already been present to
perception.[20] We will see later in this chapter how this idea fits
with the pendant of the early Balbec *cloison* encounters, but it is
no less important here: Marcel's physical behaviour enacts the
claim I will be making for the functioning of the tympanic *cloison*. For Freud says later in 'Negation': 'The ego periodically
sends out small amounts of cathexes into the perceptual system,
by means of which it samples the external stimuli, and then
after every such tentative advance it draws back again.'[21] The

---

[18] The term *homosexualité* was introduced in 1869 by the Hungarian doctor
Karoly Maria Benkert (see iii. 1278).   [19] *SE* xix. 236.
[20] Freud's thinking on reality-testing goes back at least as far as the 1895 'A
Project for a Scientific Psychology', part i, section 16. In Essay III, section 5, of the
Three Essays, he says 'The finding of an object is in fact a refinding of it', *Three Essays
on the Theory of Sexuality, SE* (1905), vii. 125–243 (p. 222).
[21] *SE* xix. 238. Compare Freud's extraordinary 1920 experimental essay *Beyond
the Pleasure Principle, SE*, xviii. 1–64 (p. 28) and 'A Note upon the "Mystic Writing
Pad" ' *SE* (1925 [1924]), xix. 225–32 (p. 231), where he connects intermittent
cathexis with a foundation for our conscious perception of time. Jacques Derrida's
essay 'Freud et la scène de l'écriture', *L'Écriture et la différence* (1967), 293–340, reads
the 'Project' with the 'Mystic Writing-Pad' essay and *The Interpretation of Dreams*, and

way in which Marcel makes his discovery is entirely dependent, not on his will, or his fantasies of heroic enterprise, which intervene to hold up the drama of the staging here, but on the practical steps he takes, then retakes, to collect his evidence once inside the *boutique*. Having revealed knowledge of the term *homosexualité* so casually in an aside, the narratorial voice swiftly reverts to sexual innocence: 'Ce que je viens de dire d'ailleurs ici est ce que je ne devais comprendre que quelques minutes plus tard, tant adhèrent à la réalité ces propriétés d'être invisible, jusqu'à ce qu'une circonstance l'ait dépouillée d'elles' (iii. 9; tr. iv. 8). Determined to listen to the conversation between Jupien and the baron, he is reminded of 'la boutique à louer séparée seulement de celle de Jupien par une cloison extrêmement mince' (iii. 9; tr. iv. 8). To get to it, he tells us, 'Je n'avais pour m'y rendre qu'à remonter à notre appartement . . . toute ma route se ferait à couvert, je ne serais vu de personne' (iii. 9; tr. iv. 8–9). Instead of this comparative safety, however, he chooses the high-risk, open-air route: 'longeant les murs, je contournai à l'air libre la cour en tâchant de ne pas être vu' (iii. 9; tr. iv. 9). Once in the *atelier*, the dramatic tension increases: 'Je n'osais bouger. Le palefrenier des Guermantes, profitant sans doute de leur absence, avait bien transféré dans la boutique où je me trouvais une échelle serrée jusque-là dans la remise. Et si j'y étais monté j'aurais pu ouvrir le vasistas et entendre comme si j'avais été chez Jupien même. Mais je craignais de faire du bruit' (iii. 10–11; tr. iv. 10). The unidentified sounds transmitted through the *cloison* which *was to have been demolished* do not become clear to the narrator until later: 'J'en conclus plus tard qu'il y a une chose aussi bruyante que la souffrance, c'est le plaisir' (iii. 11; tr. iv. 10). Again, the writing gives away the secret which has yet to be disclosed, while, in narrative terms, Marcel is still engaged in a short-circuited repetition of his own complex strategies for revelation: 'Enfin au bout d'une

homes in on just this temporal dimension of the intermittent functioning of consciousness. Derrida, in a paper of some brilliance, is keen to promote the non-recuperable, non-foundational perpetual shifts and slippages of signification which he terms *différance*, and tends to subsume all Freud's concepts, memory as trace, intermittent functioning of neurones of perception (consciousness arising instead of a memory-trace), *Nachträglichkeit*, that is, late-coming reinterpretations of traumatic events, the non-sitability or 'betweenness' of any location of psychical representation, and so forth, to it.

demi-heure environ (pendant laquelle je m'étais hissé à pas de loup sur mon échelle afin de voir par le vasistas que je n'ouvris pas), une conversation s'engagea' (iii. 11; tr. iv. 10–11).

What is it? What is Marcel telling us? The *vasistas* is a German import from around 1784, a word that performs the function of the object it designates, *Was ist das?* Like Freud's 'Made in Germany', the opening that Marcel does not look through is a certificate of negation. He does not see what he has elected to hear. Later, he will proclaim proudly: 'Jusque-là, parce que je n'avais pas compris, je n'avais pas vu. Le vice (on parle ainsi pour la commodité du langage), le vice de chacun l'accompagne à la façon de ce génie qui était invisible pour les hommes tant qu'ils ignoraient sa présence' (iii. 15; tr. iv. 15). The discovery of homosexuality does not *take place*. In terms of locating the event itself, both the pre-emptive writing that relentlessly gives the revelation away, but also the narrator's inability to co-ordinate his desire to see, with the *external* screens that intervene, operate a deft game of jack straws, narrative act and signifying moment sliding past one another, avoiding any kind of confrontation, even as we are being told that this is the most important confrontation of the narrator's developing insight.

The *vasistas* through which Marcel hears but does not see sets off a chain reaction of bewildering intensity in the writing, sustained in a brilliant range of references which move effortlessly from the literary to the political to the religious, mapping and remapping homosexuality against the Dreyfus Affair, Christ's persecution, revisitings of literary classics, Greek mythology, and botanical analogies, over spans of single sentences that cover up to two pages (iii. 17–19; tr. iv. 17–18).[22] He will, for example, reconfigure his discovery in terms of another story:

Rien, sur le visage privé de caractères de tel ou tel homme, ne pouvait leur faire supposer qu'il était précisément le frère, ou le fiancé, ou l'amant d'une femme dont elles allaient dire: 'Quel chameau!' Mais

---

[22] The exordium to *Sodome et Gomorrhe* is a highly complex piece of writing, much commented on in recent years. See, for commentary on sexuality in *A la recherche*, J. E. Rivers, *Proust and the Art of Love* (1980); Eve Kosofsky Sedgwick, *Epistemology of the Closet* (1991); Kaja Silverman, *Male Subjectivity at the Margins* (1992); Emma Wilson, *Sexuality and the Reading Encounter*, and Nicola Luckhurst, *Science and Structure in Proust's A la recherche du temps perdu* (1999), to name only a very few.

alors, par bonheur, un mot que leur chuchote un voisin arrête sur
leurs lèvres le terme fatal. Aussitôt apparaissent, comme un *Mané,
Thécel, Pharès*, ces mots: il est le fiancé, ou il est le frère, ou il est
l'amant de la femme qu'il ne convient pas d'appeler devant lui:
'chameau'. (iii. 15–16; tr. iv. 16)[23]

His exemplary essay technique carries with it, however, the
freight of anxiety attendant upon listening at *cloisons extrêmement minces.* The reference to the Book of Daniel, *Mene mene
tekel upharsin*, which signifies the writing on the wall for King
Belshazzar, his imminent downfall, contains written within it a
near anagram of 'Marcel Proust'.[24] Like a miniature version of
Proust's enormous digressions, hoping to conceal themselves
among all those other words as just normal old bits of text, this
camouflaged authorial signature fits in, and signals itself, at one
and the same time.

Travelling at speed into explanatory abstraction away from
the narrative incident which provokes this dense matting of
justificatory declamation, however, the narrator encounters the
cloison once again, transposed into the register of scientific
observation:

Comme tant de créatures du règne animal et du règne végétal,
comme la plante qui produirait la vanille, mais qui, parce que, chez
elle, l'organe mâle est séparé par une cloison de l'organe femelle,

[23] But see Ch. 1 for other desecratory connotations that *chameau* bears in *A la
recherche.*

[24] 'Numbered, numbered, weighed, and divisions': in Daniel's interpretation,
'*mene*, God hath numbered thy kingdom, and brought it to an end. *Tekel*; thou art
weighed in the balances, and art found wanting. *Peres*; thy kingdom is divided' (5.
25). Serge Gaubert has written about the distribution of Marcel Proust's authorial
signature across various characters in the text, although he does not spot this
outstandingly proximate anagram. See 'Le Jeu de l'Alphabet', Genette and
Todorov (eds.), *Recherche de Proust*, 68–87. His work may be seen to be part of a
French structuralist debate on Proustian onomastic cryptography that is to be
traced back through work undertaken by Milly, Genette, and Barthes. See *La Phrase
de Proust*, (1975), 67–97 for Milly's analysis of the *hypogramme*, Starobinski's borrow-
ing from Saussure that designates the *mot-thème*, or fragmentation, dispersal, and
dissemination of the letters of a proper name or noun across a text (see Jean
Starobinski, *Les Mots sous les mots*, 1971). Genette, in 'Proust et le langage indirect',
is distracted by the extent to which names may be said to be motivated by phonetic
influences on the imaginary. Roland Barthes's essay 'Proust et les noms' (1972),
discusses the genetic primacy of Proust's 'name system', or cratylistic desire and
subsequent disappointment, impressed across the plan and execution of *A la
recherche.*

demeure stérile si les oiseaux-mouches ou certaines petites abeilles ne transportent le pollen des unes aux autres ou si l'homme ne les féconde artificiellement, M. de Charlus (et ici le mot fécondation doit être pris au sens moral, puisqu'au sens physique l'union du mâle avec le mâle est stérile, mais il n'est pas indifférent qu'un individu puisse rencontrer le seul plaisir qu'il soit susceptible de goûter, et 'qu'ici-bas toute âme' puisse donner à quelqu'un 'sa musique, sa flamme ou son parfum'), M. de Charlus était de ces hommes qui peuvent être appelés exceptionnels, parce que, si nombreux soient-ils, la satisfaction, si facile chez d'autres, de leurs besoins sexuels, dépend de la coïncidence de trop de conditions, et trop difficiles à rencontrer. (iii. 28; tr. iv. 31–2)

This time, the encounter with a *cloison* is of a newly material, but also a newly figurative, kind: its technicalization inside the language of botany. The *cloison* is real, but intercepted within a justificatory language which enables a moral outcome to be predicated on the great risk of sterility run by the vanilla plant, with its compartmentalized reproductive system, so elegantly constructed and yet so vulnerable to performance failure. Intimate proximity is no guarantee of any kind of sexual success, the narrator is arguing, whether in the plant kingdom, or the human world, whether in terms of fertilization, morality, or pleasure. The great difficulty of fertilization in vanilla plants maps out onto and justifies the risks that men of Charlus's kind run to obtain their pleasure. But that pleasure, conversely, obtains its certificate of moral probity because the fertility model does not ultimately apply to the homosexual's situation. In homosexual practice, as the narrator seeks to explain it through the *cloison*, the agent of moral exoneration is *difficulty*, and sterility is the enabler of the quest for personal pleasure, yet the analogy that brings the two universes of botany and homosexuality together is itself no perfect fusion, but a delicate and partitioned construction, hoping to prove fertile, and aware of its vulnerability and potential sterility.[25]

Cloison partitioning, in workshops that are the scene of

[25] See *Proust et les signes*, (1993), 163–7, 207–13, on the *cloisonnement* of the sexes in some plants, which Deleuze sees as *pathos*, suffering: 'un végétal fait de parties cloisonnées' (p. 210). Julia Kristeva has used the same idea in *Le Temps sensible*, (1994), 110–29: *l'autofécondation* (which Lejeune celebrates in 'Écriture et sexualité') carries within it, for Deleuze and Kristeva, the madness of its potential *stérilité* (iii. 31; tr. iv. 35).

homosexual encounters, and in arguments designed to protect, enable, or justify such encounters, in writing, or in social situations where their exposure would be intolerable, shows us the intense risks being run by a mind trying to accommodate information which threatens its self-preservative instinct. It dramatizes in graphic form Proust's willingness to face the terrible fear that accompanies justificatory arguments of any kind, especially those that seek to justify the self's desires and actions: that they will crumble from the inside, and not only be *found* wanting, but ultimately, *be* wanting. Partitions are the obstacle to insight, but simultaneously the means by which insights are encapsulated as language, and the tireless repetition of this paradox, together with the strenuous efforts Proust makes to move forward out of its relentless grasp, is at the base of his brilliance and his despair.

This sense of being gripped in the clamp of contexts, with all forward motion, revolutionary activity, attempts at explanation suddenly somehow thwarted by a *cloison*, seems a very desperate place to have reached. It needs to be set against the pendant I promised earlier, when the *cloisons* of unconditional love at Balbec are met with what it will turn out they have been preparing for all the time.

6. 'POUR VOUS FATIGUER LE TRÉPAN': MISSED CONNECTIONS

Marcel returns to Balbec a second time, and is met by the *directeur*, who announces that the narrator has been put 'tout en haut de l'hôtel': ' "J'espère," dit-il, "que vous ne verrez pas là un manque d'impolitesse, j'étais ennuyé de vous donner une chambre dont vous êtes indigne, mais je l'ai fait rapport au bruit, parce que comme cela vous n'aurez personne au-dessus de vous pour vous fatiguer le trépan" (pour tympan)' (iii. 148; tr. iv. 174). The narrator informs us that 'Les chambres étaient d'ailleurs celles du premier séjour. Elles n'étaient pas plus bas mais j'avais monté dans l'estime du directeur' (iii. 148; tr. iv. 174). The *directeur*'s celebrated *cuirs*, or false connections, which here invert, by putting in the negative, his attempts at sincerity and *politesse*, end with a slip whose connotations could not be more significant, for the *trépan* is a medieval surgical instrument in the form of a drill, used to pierce holes in the skull and thus relieve pressure, and the narrator's supercilious correction of the *directeur*'s error, his assertion that he knows better than the manager what the latter has in mind, will prove disastrously wrong.

In the act of bending over to take off his shoes, Marcel experiences the famous 'Bouleversement de toute ma personne' (iii. 152; tr. iv. 179). Former self, thought, memory, and grandmother become fused, and return to his present self, taking it over. The narrator introduces the theory of 'les intermittences du cœur' (iii. 153; tr. iv. 181):

C'est sans doute l'existence de notre corps, semblable pour nous à un vase où notre spiritualité serait enclose, qui nous induit à supposer que tous nos biens intérieurs, nos joies passées, toutes nos douleurs sont perpétuellement en notre possession. Peut-être est-il aussi inexact de croire qu'elles s'échappent ou reviennent. En tous cas si elles restent en nous, c'est la plupart du temps dans un domaine inconnu où elles ne sont de nul service pour nous, et où même les plus usuelles sont refoulées par des souvenirs d'ordre différent et qui excluent toute simultanéité avec elles dans la conscience. Mais si le cadre de sensations où elles sont conservées est ressaisi, elles ont à leur tour ce même pouvoir d'expulser tout ce qui leur est incompatible, d'installer seul en nous, le moi qui les vécut. (iii. 153–4; tr. iv. 181)[26]

---

[26] The genesis of the 'Bouleversement de toute ma personne' section was intense and protracted (see *Notice*, iii. 1225–33 and *Esquisses* XIII (iii. 1032–48); XII (iii. 1030–2) based on *Carnet* I (publ. as *Le Carnet de 1908* (Gallimard, 1976) and *Cahiers* 48 and 50). The concept of the intermittent functioning of the self (self standing for 'consciousness', here) in fact predates *mémoire involontaire* as aesthetic and metaphysical 'key' to *A la recherche*. See K. Yoshikawa, 'Marcel Proust en 1908: Comment a-t-il commencé à écrire *A la recherche du temps perdu*', *Études de langue et littérature françaises*, 22 (1973), 135–52, for an analysis of *Carnet* I, in which a novelistic project was sketched out, but then abandoned in favour of the *Contre Sainte-Beuve* literary critical essay. Unlike *mémoire involontaire*, however, *intermittence* is not turned into a Proustian law, and remains an ephemeral and unstructured concept. In the *Esquisses*, its genesis is fundamentally intertwined with the dream-state, in which an unwanted but apparently unavoidable horror is revisited upon the narrator. The dreams were originally intended to demonstrate the principle of *intermittence* functioning in the service of self-preservation: overwhelming affect being transmittable in a vulnerable sleep state, but shut off again by the waking state. These dreams are populated with resurrected members of Marcel Proust's real-life family in the first instance, and their location in a future novel is constantly displaced throughout the writing of *A la recherche*, at one point intended for the Venice section. See Antoine Compagnon's *Proust entre deux siècles* (1989), p. 155—effectively a fuller version of his

The theory of *intermittence* has attracted critical attention, because it lends itself to what have become known as 'cryptanalytic' readings, or deconstructive readings of episodes of mourning in literary texts.[27] But these readings do not do justice to Proust's model of consciousness and the way he links consciousness with writing. *Intermittence*, astonishingly, emphasizes mental *disconnection*, sporadic blanks in a morse code, rather than being a representation of Time as agent of its own smoothly joined-up looping and spiralling effects on human activity. *Intermittence* is as much a theory of blank spaces on a page, as it is of mental systems. It is about mistimed interventions into the narration of suffering, and the deficient gobbets and gaps of speech by which suffering signifies in language.

At first, the way in which Marcel's *bouleversement* is written up bears the marks which cryptanalysis hunts down: 'Mais si le cadre de sensations où elles sont conservées *est ressaisi*' (iii. 154; tr. iv. 181; my emphasis), is an important half-sentence that is supposed to do the work of getting us from one side of the framework within which painful memories are stored to the other. Its agency here is expressed in the passive, rendering the source of the return of a past unknown, though its movement is one of recapture and domination. Time, moreover, is altered by the state the narrator tells us he has entered, or by the past self that has re-entered him, 'comme s'il y avait dans le temps des séries différentes et parallèles—sans solution de continuité' (iii. 154; tr. iv. 181): 'Le moi que j'étais alors et qui avait disparu si longtemps, était de nouveau si près de moi qu'il me semblait encore entendre les paroles qui avaient immédiatement précédé et qui n'étaient pourtant plus qu'un songe, comme un

own editorial notes to vol. iii. of the Pléiade edn. of *A la recherche*. See also Appendix II (variant *a* of iii. 369–74) for notes on an excised dream about the grandmother: a moment, suppressed from the text, of intense self-justificatory activity, a narratorial appeal to a dead grandmother and his almost simultaneous recognition of the futility of such self-justificatory vulnerability.

[27] Informed by Freud's 1915 paper 'Mourning and Melancholia', *SE* xiv. 239–58, and his 'Wolf Man' case-study, 'From the History of an Infantile Neurosis', *SE* xvii. 3–122. It is Nicolas Abraham and Maria Torok's work on the 'Wolf Man' case and mourning which has paved the way for cryptanalytic readings; see their *Cryptonomie* (1976) and *L'Écorce et le noyau* (1978). Angela Moorjani has written extremely perceptively on this: 'A Cryptanalysis of Proust's "Les Intermittences du cœur" ', *MLN* 105 (1990), 875–88. Leo Bersani's essay in *The Culture of Redemption*, cited above, is another case in point.

homme mal éveillé croit percevoir tout près de lui les bruits de son rêve qui s'enfuit' (iii. 154; tr. iv. 181). From now on, however, a very different set of terms is introduced and lodges itself into the narration. What is compelling about the narrator's recognition of the loss of his grandmother is not the loss itself, but the attempt to sustain the pain transmitted by *souffrance*, to prolong an instant both because it is privileged, and in order to privilege it: 'je venais, en la sentant pour la première fois, vivante, véritable, gonflant mon cœur à le briser, en la retrouvant enfin, d'apprendre que je l'avais perdue pour toujours. Perdue pour toujours; je ne pouvais comprendre *et je m'exerçais à subir la souffrance de cette contradiction*' (iii. 155; tr. iv. 182; my emphasis). There are no less than *four* repetitions of this same thought within the space of a page (iii. 155–6; tr. iv. 182–4). The involuntary resurrection of the grandmother must apparently cause real rather than imaginary *souffrance* in Marcel, in order that his attempt to respect its originality by continuing to endure it may be justified. Time spent suffering must seemingly be accounted for. Yet stigmata, the best proof of the suffering caused by the death of the grandmother—not her suffering, but Marcel's—are representable only in the form of similes ('*comme* un double et mystérieux sillon': iii. 156; tr. iv. 184), or as metaphorically flesh-impaling *clous* (iii. 156; tr. iv. 183). Marcel's fear that he would not be able to sustain the pain caused by involuntary *bouleversement* over time is directly analogous to the failure of the metaphors and similes that represent suffering in writing to *be* suffering. The unjustifiability of time spent suffering in the past is governed by the unjustifiability of figurative language coined at a later date, which fails to transmit the temporality of suffering, since suffering is always endured in the present tense.

Just as the writing of unconditional love had become embarrassed, and as significance had sheered off into local objects, the *bottines* and the *cloison*, so here again, the scene attaches itself to, and death is signified by, a displacement:

Pour ne plus rien voir, je me tournai du côté du mur, mais hélas! ce qui était contre moi c'était cette cloison qui servait jadis entre nous deux de messager matinal, cette cloison qui, aussi docile qu'un violon à rendre toutes les nuances d'un sentiment, disait si exactement à ma grand-mère ma crainte à la fois de la réveiller, et si elle était éveillée déjà, de n'être pas entendu d'elle, et qu'elle n'osât bouger, puis aussitôt comme la réplique d'un second instrument, m'annonçant sa venue et m'invitant au calme. Je n'osais pas approcher de cette cloison plus que d'un piano où ma grand-mère aurait joué et qui vibrerait encore de son toucher. Je savais que je pourrais frapper maintenant, même plus fort, que rien ne pourrait plus la réveiller, que je n'entendrais aucune réponse, que ma grand-mère ne viendrait plus. Et je ne demandais rien de plus à Dieu, s'il existe un paradis, que d'y pouvoir frapper contre cette cloison les trois petits coups que ma grand-mère reconnaîtrait entre mille, et auxquels elle répondrait par ces autres coups qui voulaient dire: 'Ne t'agite pas, petite souris, je comprends que tu es impatient, mais je vais venir,' et qu'il me laissât rester avec elle toute l'éternité, qui ne serait pas trop longue pour nous deux. (iii. 159–60; tr. iv. 187–8)

The *cloison* is referred to no less than four times, and an ascending scale of theatricality makes itself apparent in this passage, between the two players, narrator and grandmother, the three knocks which signify unconditional love (but also the commencement of Classical French drama), and the fourth wall, which opens the scene to the scrutiny of an audience. Where the *madeleine* retrieval of the past is a fulsome and joyous regaining of plenitude, here, the *souvenir involontaire* is set up to perform as a one-way *via negativa* enabling death to enter the living.[28] This mortuary aesthetic works, the narrator is at pains

---

[28] Compare Lacan's brilliant revisiting of one of the dreams that most puzzled Freud, that of the 'burning child' (see Freud's *The Interpretation of Dreams*, *SE* v. 509–11, 533–4; 542, 550, 571, and Lacan's reading in 'Tuché et automaton', *Les quatre concepts fondamentaux de la psychanalyse* (1964), 53–62). Freud found it strange that the dream did not seem to contain much dream-work, but was instead apparently an absolutely straightforward account of reality, warning a sleeping father that his dead child in the next room was being burnt by a candle that had fallen over, unnoticed by the man set to watch over the body who had himself fallen asleep. Freud's analysis runs: 'The dream was preferred to a waking reflection because it was able to show the child as once more alive' (*SE* v. 510). But for Lacan, another, more dreadful, interpretation is available: 'Car ce n'est pas que, dans le rêve, il se soutienne que le fils vit encore. Mais l'enfant mort prenant son père par le bras, vision atroce, désigne un au-delà qui se fait entendre dans le rêve. Le désir s'y présentifie de la perte imagée au point le plus cruel de l'objet. C'est dans le rêve seulement que peut se faire cette rencontre vraiment unique. Seul un rite, un acte toujours répété, peut commémorer cette rencontre immémorable—puisque personne ne peut dire ce que c'est que la mort d'un enfant—sinon le père en tant que père— c'est-à-dire nul être conscient' (*Les quatre concepts*, 58). The burning child dream is, for Lacan, an opportunity for the child's father to imagine him *dead*, not dead as he will surely see the boy once he reawakens, but dead in terms of an unknowable

to assert, because he has not embellished it, but the writing undoes itself. Despite his insistent methodological provisos and repetitions, nothing emerges so clearly from the presentation of the *bouleversement* as its staginess, and a residue of this stock-in-trade portrayal of authenticity will hang about the narrator's emergence from it. When the narrator's mother arrives, the narrator feels that he has won the right to special consideration because of his trial by personal *souffrance*: 'Il me semblait que j'étais moins indigne de vivre auprès d'elle, que je la comprendrais mieux, maintenant que toute une vie étrangère et dégradante avait fait place à la remontée des souvenirs déchirants qui ceignaient et ennoblissaient mon âme' (iii. 165; tr. iv. 193–4). He goes on:

comme un récitant qui devrait connaître son rôle et être à sa place depuis bien longtemps mais qui est arrivé seulement à la dernière seconde et n'ayant lu qu'une fois ce qu'il a à dire, sait dissimuler assez habilement quand vient le moment où il doit donner la réplique, pour que personne ne puisse s'apercevoir de son retard, mon chagrin tout nouveau me permit quand ma mère arriva, de lui parler comme s'il avait toujours été le même. (iii. 165; tr. iv. 194)

What price authenticity of expression when any fool can ad lib, the narrator shamefacedly concedes, in a passage which shows us that even in the hoisting aloft of memorable moments as privileged vehicles of meaning in the writing of *A la recherche*, doubt as to both their authenticity and their success continues to haunt Proust. Better to undermine his own text than let anyone more critical see through it, mutters the narratorial voice; and we are to see in the final part of this study the importance of such a self-debunking gesture in the presentation of the self persuading and justifying the self.

The fortuitous, and the arbitrary, the permeable and the opportunistic, all these wholly unexpected conditions and qualities afford purchase for the self-justificatory urges of the narrator, in his moral and epistemological sallies. Marcel's

---

significance, a meaning that simply cannot be formulated in language, which is absolutely lost to consciousness—an absolutely *other* kind of awakening to reality. The dream functions for Lacan himself as well, of course, for it gives him in quite literally the most fortuitous possible way, an opportunity to demonstrate the opportunism of his own concept, the *réel*, the 'order' that designs itself as unmodellability.

bouleversement, like the revelation of homosexuality, does not *take place* where the writing narrator wants it to, but does shore up against the transferable representation of self-justificatory mental processes that Proust has constructed in the form of the *cloison*. For in its untransformability, in its material resistance, and repeated refusal to act as transmitter between the narrator and a reality in which his grandmother would still be unconditionally available, or in which homosexuality would still be a discovery, by being the agency of conditional and therefore intermittent *Besetzung*,[29] the *cloison* is like a blinking eye, an on–off switch, the tap-tapping of a morse-code machine, a camera's shutter action, or the second hand on a watch: movements that in not knowing what they do, effect another action. The *cloison* repetitions make available in manageable doses a recognition that absolute entitlement, totally successful self-justification, pure forgiveness, is a mirage or a fiction that has been shredded by death.

7. CODA

Freud speculates at the end of 'Negation' that: 'The performance of the function of judgement is not made possible until the creation of the symbol of negation has endowed thinking with a first measure of freedom from the consequences of repression and, with it, from the compulsion of the pleasure principle.'[30] Self-justification when undertaken in close proximity to other human subjects, available only in their partiality, is a very different mode from its manifestation as the various means by which to gain admittance to a group perceived as hostile; different too from the kind of self-justification that strains to hold together wholly incommensurable moral and psychological pressures. The *cloison* moments that precipitate

---

[29] See the entry under 'Investissement' in Jean Laplanche and J.-B. Pontalis, *Vocabulaire de la psychanalyse* (1994), 211–15, for a thoroughgoing explanation of *Besetzung*, whose meanings vary from the military act of occupying (a town etc.), to the casting of a play, but which Freud often used with the sense of 'investment', both economically and energetically. The French *investissement* preserves the economic sense, while the usual English translation, 'cathexis', rather unfortunately loses the metaphorical play of the original German.

[30] *SE* xix. 239.

their cumulative and resonant domino effect across the text of *A la recherche* function, painfully and pitiably, to protect Marcel from unwanted knowledge, and they both serve and are manipulated for this protective quality. Self-justification in relation to intervening and permeable screens can thus be heard as temporary, and often necessary self-protection, but can be seen as wilful blindness. For Proust's *cloisons*, with their tympanic rather than their translucent properties, signal sites of sensory overload, tell the dreadful and unwanted story that selves are indifferent, that they do not live in dependence upon one another, or necessarily offer one another unconditional love, justifications, answers, or absolutions. Mourning is botched and mistimed, sexuality is squeezed into abandoned workshops. The self can be restaged, but importantly, it is the permeable partition, that shaky prop, which shows Marcel that loss is the underlying cause of restaging, not volition. Selves are slung by contingent disaster against their own volition into contexts which no longer include the props they once thought reflected reality, they are abandoned helplessly to the censure of indifferent judgement, forced into justifying themselves as a way of keeping disaster at bay, *even as* they thought themselves entitled to displays of helplessness.

The status of the *cloison* as an impermanent and porous barrier gives a temporary anchorage to flailing self-justification, seen here in a third manifestation, that of wilful self-protection against unwanted, painful knowledge, but like the social indifference which infects subjective moral choices, or digressions which cannot stave off their own demise, the figure of the *cloison* only averts the full consequences of self-justification's other possible mutations in the short term. And in the next chapter, the last of this section, we will see that as we examine a particular aspect of Proust's experimentation in characterization, the three kinds of self-justification we have so far been shown, necessary for the purposes of assimilation, to accommodate contradictions, and to ward off danger, are all contributing factors to a fourth kind.

4

Dangerous Proximity: The Reverses of Character

La nature recommençait à régner sur le Bois d'où s'était
envolée l'idée qu'il était le Jardin élyséen de la Femme; au-
dessus du moulin factice le vrai ciel était gris; le vent ridait
le Grand Lac de petites vaguelettes, comme un lac; de gros
oiseaux parcouraient rapidement le Bois, comme un bois.[1]

(i. 419; tr. i. 512–13)

I. INTRODUCTION

Methods of integration into a society of hostile others, the
attempt to accommodate incommensurable or uncomfortable
facts, or the attempt to sidestep them: each separates out into a
distinct aspect of self-justificatory activity, but cumulatively, they
beg the question of how to state one's *own* case, take a stand
against another, or justify oneself *by differentiation* from others.
This chapter considers the narrator's negotiation of the
dangers of being too close for comfort to the representation of
personal beliefs, needs, or desires in others, from whom a
distinguishing mechanism is demanded if self is to be constituted and preserved.

What I want to show now is self-justification when it is working as the imposition of a necessary separation from like-
minded others; a wilful, or deliberate outsidedness to the act of

[1] In a letter of 6 Feb. 1914, to Jacques Rivière, Proust states that this conclusion
to the first volume of the *Recherche*, in which the narrator seems resigned to the
disappointment of the world, was imposed by an editorial constraint on the length
of *Du côté de chez Swann*, and 'est le contraire de ma conclusion. Elle est une étape,
d'apparence subjective et dilettante, vers la plus objective et croyante des conclusions' (*Corr.* xiii. 43).

observing them; and a viscous, sado-masochistic contagion of characteristics that, while they pass between the series of men, are never fully reversible, or fully detachable from the narrator. The chapter will culminate with a study of how Marcel encounters Saint-Loup and Bloch: it will look closely at the work of differentiation from them undertaken by the narrator in his own justification.

2. THE PROBLEM OF PROUST'S CHARACTERIZATION

There is something peculiar about the logistics of characterization in *A la recherche*: about the way Proust moves from the technical use of free indirect speech, for example, or from ironic discrepancies between what a character thinks of him or herself and the signals they actually present which hint at their mental activities, to, on the other hand, caricature, an altogether sharper edged writerly tool, which deforms and manipulates alterity sadistically, and is the outcome of a one-way, observer-to-observed perceptual relationship.

Edmund Wilson's magisterial meditation on *A la recherche* reminds us that:

Proust, like Dickens, was a remarkable mimic: as Dickens enchanted his audiences by dramatic readings from his novels, so, we are told, Proust was celebrated for impersonations of his friends; and both, in their books, carried the practice of caricaturing habits of speech and of inventing things for their personages to say which are outrageous without ever ceasing to be lifelike.[2]

But this appreciation of a clever comic talent does not resolve my question about characterization. Beckett notes that: 'It will be necessary, for example, to interrupt (disfigure) the luminous projection of subject desire with the comic relief of features.'[3] Yet question, for a moment, that necessary truncation, that interruption of flow with feature, insist that its necessity is nothing more than a novelist's self-dispensation, an abdication of responsibility for others, a merriment with figures of speech which act as a convenient stopgap before the overwhelming

---

[2] *Axel's Castle* (1984), 137.   [3] *Proust* (1965), 11–12.

enormity of other people. Beckett nonchalantly reduces to a sentence what Proust struggles with for many thousand.

We should be on our guard against taking as read that the series of laws of literary creation drafted in the Guermantes library before the *Bal de têtes* sequence are Proust's final legislation on the writing of character. He talks there of fictional characters as amalgamations of fragments ('il n'est pas un nom de personnage inventé sous lequel il ne puisse mettre soixante noms de personnages vus': iv. 478; tr. vi, 259), and of listening to others only when 'si bêtes ou si fous qu'ils fussent, répétant comme des perroquets ce que disent les gens de caractère semblable, ils s'étaient faits par là même les oiseaux prophètes, les porte-parole d'une loi psychologique' (iv. 479; tr. vi. 260). It is hard not to plump for the comfort of conclusions such as 'characters in novels are distillations and compounds of people the author met'. This kind of conclusion, however, begs all the questions about expressing an accurate relation between what we can only name in figurative ways when we use language to do so, the flesh of psychology, and the way in which it meets the flat porcelain shell of outer appearance, which Proust is at such pains to understand. It is as much a difficulty of criticism on Proust as it is part of the Proustian phenomenology of self-justification that concerns us here: the vices and virtues of differentiation.

We need, at this juncture, to give ourselves a brief overview of some of the transitions through which a notion of 'character' has passed, in both French and English. The term in both languages is derived from the Greek χαρακτηρ, an instrument for marking or engraving. In English, it literally means a distinctive stamp, a graphic symbol standing for a sound, a syllable, or a notion, used in writing or printing.

If 'character' stands for whatever is the formal contour, the hollowed-out husk by which representation of a graphic or written kind may be attempted, a symbol that may pass into circulation as an enabler of communication between users of a sign system, its passage into the desires and flesh of human beings is very far from being so convenient.

Kristeva points out that the Greeks did not have a conception of 'character' but of actant, *prattontes*, or *èthos*, a habitual way of being, that which belongs to, is appropriate to an individual, or a group of individuals.[4] Let us home in on this a little more closely. In the fourth century BC Aristotle tells us that in Greek tragedy, 'Speech or action will possess character if it discloses the nature of a deliberate choice; the character is good if the choice is good.'[5] Aristotle's logic relies on binary oppositions, either a choice is made or it is not, either it is the right choice or it is not. In any case, tragedy being what it is, the inexorability of the plot will see to the outcome. Character arises as an attempt to do something about plot, so that personality in some sense arises in the face of impersonality. What is good about choice, essentially, is that its starkness is what will produce pity in spectators. One very good reason for the persistence of binary oppositional logic, or stark choices, certainly in occidental cultural production, is that the reduction of the world's plenitude to either/or possibilities of action is, as Aristotle makes clear, inherently dramatic. The seductive fascination of a stark choice, both for protagonist and for spectator, which pitilessly strips out the confusion of ambiguity from the notion of *character* in Greek tragedy, thereby also *prompts* identificatory pity in the spectator (a blend of commiseration and lust for sacrifice). Greek tragedy's minimalist plot structures, high degree of acceleration, and its intense focus on only a very few, high-status participants, hardly seems comparable to the development of modern notions of 'character' in the heterogeneous patchwork of the novel genre.[6] But let us store it up for a moment, as one kind of understanding of 'character', that which arises to cross the space between the awed but indifferent spectator and the far-off figure on stage who moves in helpless response to colossal and indifferent pressures imposed upon him or her.

---

4 In seeking to situate 'lost' Proustian characters, she locates Proust's work in a classical rhetorical tradition which has taken its cue on character definition from Greek tragedy, via the 17th-cent. rhetorician, Scaliger. She likens this to the psychoanalytic conception of character as a space waiting to be filled by the analysis: 'la parole analytique mime une figure', *Le Temps sensible*, 152–6 (p. 154).

5 Aristotle, 'Other Aspects of Tragedy: *Character*', *Poetics*, tr. M. Heath (1996), 24–5 (p. 24).

6 Bakhtin finds Aristotle's pared-down model 'monologic', and wants us to see the novel genre overall as wildly subversive, transgressive, and contestatory of limitations on 'plot', 'theme', and 'character'. See M. M. Bakhtin, *The Dialogic Imagination* (1981).

The occidental conception of 'character' has not only developed from Greek tragedy. Theophrastus's *Characters* (*c.*300 BC) has been taken as the progenitor of that solitary spectator-sport, moralizing commentary. If Aristotle is the rationalizer of Greek tragedy's attempt to put man and his gods into the same kind of space, Theophrastus begets an altogether more secular history of people-watching. A Latin translation of *Characters* by Isaac Casaubon in 1592, closely followed by an English translation of Casaubon's Latin version by John Healey (1616), did much to spread the popularity of the character genre in England.[7] In France, La Bruyère translated Theophrastus from the Greek in 1688, and published it together with his own *Mœurs de ce siècle*.[8] There were eight subsequent editions of this work, involving substantial revisions and expansions, until his death in 1696. From the seventeenth and eighteenth centuries, in France as in England, the areas the term character or *caractère* could cover slipped dizzyingly inside and outside the human, speaking subject. *Caractère* could refer to the 'ensemble des manières habituelles de sentir et de réagir qui distinguent un individu d'un autre'.[9] It could also refer to an individual's moral disposition: *avoir du* or *manquer de caractère* implies an external perspective, arrogating the right to pass judgement about another individual. It is not far from this self-appointedly objective critical stance to a formulation of types, a set of individuals captured under a governing series of *mœurs*. The interest in defining the characteristics of groups extended in the eighteenth century to attempts to define the behavioural, mental, and moral contours of the nation-state and its nationals.

In highly schematic terms, a decisive intervention is made in the history of 'character' twenty-two centuries after Aristotle, which brings back into play that lost dialectic between man and his gods. Nietzsche's horrified, fascinated 'Attempt at a Self-Criticism', turning on his own *The Birth of Tragedy* fourteen years after the latter's publication (but turning on it in some ways only to *repeat* its tenets), knows something devastatingly new and different about both tragedy and character:

[7] Isaac Casaubon, *Theophrasti Notationes* (repr. De Harsy, 1617).

[8] Jean de La Bruyère, *Les Caractères de Théophraste traduits du Grec avec Les Mœurs de ce siècle* (1688), *Œuvres de La Bruyère*, ed. M. G. Servois (1865), i.

[9] *Le Grand Robert* takes this definition from Lalande.

In fact, the entire book knows only one overt and implied artistic meaning behind all events—a 'god', if you will, but certainly only an entirely thoughtless and amoral artist-god, who in both creating and destroying, in doing both good and ill, wishes to experience that same joy and glory; who, creating worlds, rids himself of the *affliction* of abundance and *super-abundance*, of the *suffering* of his internal contradictions. The world: at every moment the *successful* redemption of God, the ever-changing, ever-new vision of the most afflicted, contrary, contradictory being, who can find redemption and deliverance only in *illusion*.[10]

The clean-limbed vertical hierarchies with their neat distinctions, drawn between the gods and mankind of Aristotle's vision, have mutated in Nietzsche's conception into a glutinous impossibility of safe separations and detachments between what is internal and what is external in the tragic, magic mode. Nietzsche's coagulated, imbricated collapse or confusion of the psychological with the elemental acts with the devastatingly unexpected impact of a landmine upon our sketch of 'character', blowing the safe assimilation of typeface to type of face into oblivion.[11] If there is no way of saying that choice is imposed upon us from without, then there is, by extension, no safe way of assessing where the stamp of character leaves off and subjective self begins, where good judgement has overbalanced into judgemental intolerance. But again, let us put this difficult thought by for the time being, keeping it in mind when we return to Proust's worries about characterization.

In France, by the twentieth century (after a hundred years of post-revolutionary French nationalism, and the various attempts and failures at territorial expansionism), the adjectival offshoot *caractériel* starts to take precedence over previous more general definitions. Rooted in observation of the ways in which an individual exceeds or falls short of the norms imposed by a well-policed society, *caractériel* indicates a fascination with internal,

---

[10]   Friedrich Nietzsche, *The Birth of Tragedy* (1872), 8.

[11]   René Girard's argument in *Mensonge romantique et vérité romanesque* (1961) is essentially a post-Nietzschean understanding of the transition inwards of 'gods' originally conceived of as external mediators, roving satellite transmitters reflecting back internal human desires—desires justified by taking the form of a return journey from the will of the gods, but ultimately laid bare as what they were all along: petty spite and envy.

psychological processes. This fascination tends itself to be marked by an ideological motivation: to gauge what reasons the *individuel instable, dépressif* or *mythomane* might legitimately have for failing to adapt to (and thus maintain) the social conditions in place—the early handling of hysteria by Charcot, and then his disciple, Freud, is a prime example of this.[12]

'Character', in other words, has slipped its moorings as an externally verifiable marker of individuality, usually with a one-way moral purpose in the observer's mind (a demonstration of the vile self-interestedness of man and the frivolousness of woman, in the main), to become the contested site of conflict-ual *inner* forces, most of which we must take on trust, their visi-bility available only to the psychologically wise, the linguistically attuned, or to practitioners of physiognomy.[13] This adds infor-mation to the problem we are trying to solve about self-justifi-cation, detachment, and characterization in *A la recherche*, but sends us back to the text to start excavation in earnest for exam-ples of it.

A familiar sequence in the novel shows the narrator seeking reassurance that the world has *mystère* to reveal, first in natural miracles, then in the *cogito's* capacity to capture the world, then in the superior intermediary who will transmit the world. From hawthorn blossom, to la Berma's Phèdre, who will not stand still enough for the narrator to 'immobiliser longtemps devant moi chaque intonation de l'artiste' (i. 441; tr. ii. 22), we come to Norpois in the act of correcting Marcel's defective vision ('il justifierait ainsi ce désir que j'avais eu de voir l'ac-trice': i. 448; tr. ii. 31). And this is where the peculiarity makes itself apparent:

[12] See John Forrester, *The Seductions of Psychoanalysis* (1990), for an excellent account of psychoanalysis and fascination. If hysteria is a limit case, hovering phan-tasmatically and provocatively between a genuine internal neurosis and hostile, external prejudice, neither a reality nor easily dismissed, it is also, and as a result of this, the condition which most persuaded Freud to think against his own early perceptual and ideological assumptions, however much the charge of misogyny is levelled at him.

[13] See A. J. Krailsheimer, *Studies in Self-Interest* (1962), and the collection of essays G. Craig and M. McGowan (eds.), *Moy Qui Me Voy* (1989), which study other French practitioners of the moralizing and self-reflexive art of the essay, and offer extremely interesting perspectives on the development of the modern conception of self.

Peut-être par habitude professionnelle, peut-être en vertu du calme qu'acquiert tout homme important dont on sollicite le conseil et qui, sachant qu'il gardera en mains la maîtrise de la conversation, laisse l'interlocuteur s'agiter, s'efforcer, peiner à son aise, peut-être aussi pour faire valoir le caractère de sa tête (selon lui grecque, malgré les grands favoris), M. de Norpois, pendant qu'on lui exposait quelque chose, gardait une immobilité de visage aussi absolue que si vous aviez parlé devant quelque buste antique—et sourd—dans une glyptothèque. (i. 444; tr. ii. 27)

Even as Marcel tries hard to grasp what Norpois has to say, his passive listening is caught up in an active narratorial characterization of Norpois's listening, and produces three alternative readings. The use of *peut-être* to introduce and separate out versions of a deferred narratorial judgement is a favourite Proustian device (as we have seen, at parties, again with Norpois). By innocently putting forward three hypotheses to explain one observable fact, all three are layered into what is often a satirical portrait.[14] Norpois's *immobilité de visage* is a mark of *caractère*, but, pecked at by *peut-être*, is whittled into a mark of caricature.

Let us listen to Proust's treatment of another minor character, one we will also recall from party-going. Legrandin's 'croupe . . . que je ne supposais pas si charnue' (i. 123; tr. i. 148), and his invitation to dinner: 'faites-moi respirer du lointain de votre adolescence ces fleurs des printemps que j'ai traversés moi aussi il y a bien des années' (i. 124; tr. i. 150), read, on the face of it, so to speak, perfectly simply. Legrandin is a snob. How is it that we *know* about Legrandin's insincere snobbery without its being meticulously spelt out? Why do we not concentrate on his articulate invitation, especially since it sounds not unlike a Proustian wistfulness: 'leur parfum s'étendait aussi onctueux, aussi délimité en sa forme que si j'eusse été devant l'autel de la Vierge' (i. 136; tr. i. 165), for example? This is a question about a generalized hermeneutic activity which might demand a thesis of its own: how does irony work?

---

[14] The *rythme binaire* (iii. 223; tr. iv. 263) of jealous love reduces to an either/or dichotomy the possible alternatives of character in the Albertine volumes. *Peut-être* is a signature of speculation in a generous or relaxed mode. The binary rhythm 'soit . . . soit', however, is a Proustian presentation of comic alternatives in deciding how to read another's actions: 'moyens violents que ces psychiatres transportent souvent dans les rapports courants avec des gens bien portants, soit par habitude professionnelle, soit qu'ils croient tout le monde un peu fou' (i. 22; tr. i. 23).

There are several objections to trying to solve our peculiarity by going down this road, however. One is that the *eirōn* or dissembler has been a feature of occidental thought since at least the Platonic dialogues; the second is that every intellectual from Theophrastus to Kierkegaard to Rorty has formulated an understanding of what it means and how it works, registering it more or less favourably as a locus of dissent, a place with no footholds, not even for the ironist.[15]

The third is that irony just works. Before embarking on ambitious claims on behalf of Proust, we must remind ourselves that the expert handling of irony and proximity to one's characters cannot but be an attribute of those novelists we choose to call great. Dickens, Dostoevsky, Austen, Flaubert, Eliot, Stendhal, and others, all share the facility of reaching up through the imagined skin of their creations to ventriloquize their voices and inflate the universe in which they are deemed to exist.[16]

The problem of characterization that is ceaselessly reinvoked in *A la recherche*, then, is not resolved by pointing out who Proust ironizes, pastiches, or caricatures, or by concluding that the caricaturist is the more impressive for having the skill to manipulate and contain what he parodies in a cartoon deformation and concentration of features. Neither Proust nor his narrator are content to allow irony to pre-select an appreciative audience, able to distinguish between comic and serious characters without having such an interpretation explained for them. There is an ethical dilemma raised by the workings of caricature in a first-person novel that is an intrinsic part of the phenomenology of self-justification as it is inscribed in the movements of this text. Secondary characters in *A la recherche* do not merely exhibit themselves as textual demonstrations of doubtful language use: pedantry, poor joke-cracking, endless etymologies, vapid literary opinions, or pompous self-aggrandizement through literary appropriations. The exhibitionist

---

[15] See Søren Kierkegaard, *The Concept of Irony* (1841); Richard Rorty, *Contingency, Irony, and Solidarity* (1989). The former's we might summarize as anxious irony, the latter's as lax irony. What I mean by this is that Kierkegaard finds himself in the grip of an ironic universe, while Rorty's ironist swaggers amiably over it. Wayne C. Booth's *A Rhetoric of Irony* (1974) gives much more insight into the functioning of irony than I can hope to here.

[16] See Eric Griffiths, *The Printed Voice of Victorian Poetry* (1989) for an excellent study of the ideas surrounding ventriloquism in the 19th cent. in English poetry.

self-promotion by which a Cottard, a Mme Verdurin, a Brichot, Legrandin, or Norpois hang on to an identity in the novel also has the capacity to overwhelm, agitate, or silence the narrator. Marcel mocks his characters, has the ear of his reader, as any self-respecting first-person narrator should. But he also takes to extraordinary, and immensely dangerous, lengths a serious study of the effects that surrounding others have upon him. When Mme Verdurin expels Swann from the *petit clan,* for instance, we find the narrator cannibalizing his own experience for analogies to her verbal reaction:

Et elle ajouta encore, un instant après, avec colère: 'Non, mais voyez-vous, cette sale bête!' employant sans s'en rendre compte, et peut-être en obéissant au même besoin obscur de se justifier—comme Françoise à Combray quand le poulet ne voulait pas mourir—les mots qu'arrachent les derniers sursauts d'un animal inoffensif qui agonise, au paysan qui est en train de l'écraser. (i. 281; tr. i. 343)

The 'mots qu'arrachent les derniers sursauts d'un animal inoffensif qui agonise' perform their own assassination by piling on the description of death throes. In imitating Mme Verdurin's squawk, the narrator is allowing himself a moment of self-directed flagellation, and his question resounds right through the novel: 'If I abuse my characters in justifying myself and my vocation, by reducing them to caricature, how can I be sure that my own justification of myself is ever legitimate? How can I be sure that the revelation of my vocation will compensate the maliciousness of the portraits I have painted, on the strength of which I have been able to discard proximate others along the way?' The provisional but rigorously explored answer, for Marcel, is to allow himself to be cut on the sharp edges of his own caricatures.

3. TOO CLOSE FOR COMFORT

Risky proximities that would well repay close attention crop up everywhere, once the search for thinning writing, scarcely disguised malevolence, or opportunities for exposure begins; we must select from these only a handful. First, some fictional intertexts: Swann's obituary is grafted from a newspaper into the narrative (iii. 704; tr. v. 222), but details such as 'ses relations

choisies mais fidèles', 'la finesse avisée de son goût le faisait se
plaire', 'physionomie spirituelle', ' "vernissages" dont il avait
été l'habitué fidèle', rendered as panegyric, knit the language
of Swann's social and artistic failures into euphemism.
Disingenuous wholesale reporting by the narrator paratactic-
ally passes the responsibility for the success or failure of
Swann's life, and the event of his death, on to a public paper,
rather than integrating Swann's death into the narrative of *A la
recherche*. As a detachable cutting, the obituary is a keepsake that
could more kindly have been lost.[17]

The Goncourt journal pastiche (iv. 287–95; tr. vi. 23–32)
provokes the kind of differential self-justification under examination here, in the shape of a celebratory recuperation of
subjective procedure: 'mon incapacité de regarder et d'écouter,
que le journal cité avait si péniblement illustrée pour moi,
n'était pourtant pas totale. Il y avait en moi un personnage qui
savait plus ou moins bien regarder, mais c'était un personnage
intermittent, ne reprenant vie que quand se manifestait
quelque essence générale' (iv. 296; tr. vi. 33). Here, another
ready-made—and home-grown—import is the necessary but
artificial condition for a retaliatory reaffirmation of the narrator's order of priorities.[18] As interior monologue, however, the
complicity of the reader is still being sought. Counter-claims
under the duress of attack only masquerade as decisions, or
certainties, and may fade away again into doubt.

Imported pastiche makes us think of the host of performers
and wordsmiths in *A la recherche*. Morel, musician and bisexual,

---

[17] The notorious ekphrasis of Tissot's *Le Cercle de la rue Royale* (1868), from
which Proust is apparently singling out Charles Haas as the real-life model for
Swann usually obscures the uncanny obituary, and the fact that Swann's death is
mentioned as an accidental aside, well after the event.

[18] Proust was well aware of the pitfalls of pastiche. In the *Nouvelle Revue française*
(Jan. 1920), Proust's essay on Flaubert carried a health warning on weaning oneself
off its addictions: 'Heureux ceux qui sentent ce rythme obsesseur; mais ceux qui ne
peuvent s'en débarrasser, qui, quelque sujet qu'ils traitent, soumis aux coupes du
maître, font invariablement "du Flaubert", ressemblent à ces malheureux des légen-
des allemandes qui sont condamnés à vivre pour toujours attachés au battant d'une
cloche' ('A propos du "style" de Flaubert', *CSB* 586–600, p. 594). Yet even in self-
castigation Proust is still tongue-tied, tolling a lament that echoes through
Flaubert's novels: 'la parole humaine est comme un chaudron fêlé où nous battons
des mélodies à faire danser les ours, quand on voudrait attendrir les étoiles'
(*Madame Bovary*, 219).

aims to please all of the people all of the time, undoing his own identity to perform another's: 'Morel imitait Bergotte à ravir. Il n'y eut même plus besoin au bout de quelque temps de lui demander d'en faire une imitation. Comme ces hystériques qu'on n'est plus obligé d'endormir pour qu'ils deviennent telle ou telle personne, de lui-même il entrait tout d'un coup dans le personnage'[19] (iv. 278; tr. vi. 12). Dangerously close to artistic success, as is Octave 'Dans les choux' (iv. 185, tr. v. 693; iv. 309, tr. vi. 49),[20] his imitative capability must be destroyed by the narrator, but in the action of destruction, he picks up the adjective used of himself by Norpois, and reported to him by Odette: 'un flatteur à moitié hystérique' (ii. 568; tr. iii. 311). Which way is our reading to go? Hysteria signifies both the sadistic opinion passed on another (our hero) by Norpois, and a label which silences and disparages within a clinically appraisable aetiology the condition facilitating Morel's performative ability.

Or consider this minor character with a capacity to trip the narrator up in the zeal of his characterization: Brichot, the academic who thinks he can disguise academia's worst habit, that of pedantry, by displaying a 'un certain scepticisme'. He hunts down analogies 'dans ce qu'il y avait de plus actuel quand il parlait de philosophie et d'histoire', and imagines that he is seeing 'en action dans le petit clan ce qu'il n'avait connu jusqu'ici que dans les livres', but: 's'étant vu inculquer autrefois, et ayant gardé à son insu, le respect de certains sujets, il croyait dépouiller l'universitaire en prenant avec eux des hardiesses qui, au contraire, ne lui paraissaient telles, que parce qu'il l'était resté' (i. 247; tr. i. 302). The narrator makes merciless inroads into Brichot's constructed nonchalance, bottling him inside the very test tube he thought he had left behind.[21]

---

[19] Michael R. Finn draws attention to this moment in *Proust, the Body and Literary Form* (1999), 38.

[20] The narrator damns Octave's genius with faint praise: 'Il pouvait être très vaniteux, ce qui peut s'allier au génie, et chercher à briller de la manière qu'il savait propre à éblouir dans le monde où il vivait et qui n'était nullement de prouver une connaissance approfondie des *Affinités électives*, mais bien plutôt de conduire à quatre' (iv. 185; tr. v. 694). Proust himself had written on Goethe's *Elective Affinities* ('Sur Goethe', *CSB* 647–50).

[21] Malcolm Bowie points out the self-reflexive cruelty that attends the sight of Brichot's new spectacles (iii. 703; tr. v. 220) in 'Proust, Jealousy, Knowledge': they are compared to 'laboratoires trop richement subventionnés'. See *Freud, Proust and Lacan*, (1987), 60–1.

We might want to label this 'satire of an institution', or 'caricature of one of its representatives', but a comment on Brichot's later career confounds such labelling in the very act of confounding our impression of Brichot. When his articles during the First World War make him famous, Mme Verdurin criticizes him for using *je* too often: 'A partir de ce moment Brichot remplaça *je* par *on*, mais *on* n'empêchait pas le lecteur de voir que l'auteur parlait de lui et permit à l'auteur de ne plus cesser de parler de lui, de commenter la moindre de ses phrases, de faire un article sur une seule négation, toujours à l'abri de *on*' (iv. 371; tr. vi. 127). In a novel whose first-person protagonist has the same Christian name as its author, whose signature appears threaded into his characters' names (Morel), and in anagrammatic form in biblical references to apocalyptic warnings (*Mané, Thécel, Pharès*: iii. 16; tr. iv. 16), this blatant redistribution of narrative responsibility for an uncomfortably proximate possibility of criticism straddles exhibitionism quite as much as it does diverted confession.

Pitiless stripping of Brichot's cover, which exposes the same authorial gambit that Proust uses to found his own novel, is akin to the dangerous flaunting of sexual proclivities practised with increasing obsessiveness by Charlus. When Charlus infantilizes Morel, 'Il faut qu'il rentre se coucher, comme un enfant bien obéissant' (iii. 355; tr. iv. 422), the narrator, in commenting, 'il trouvait *quelque sadique volupté* à employer cette chaste comparaison et *aussi à appuyer au passage sa voix sur ce qui concernait Morel*, à le toucher, à défaut de la main avec des paroles qui semblaient le palper' (iii. 355; tr. iv. 422; my emphasis), lays himself open to exactly the same charge. For nothing recurs so frequently in *Sodome et Gomorrhe* as fascinated narratorial reappraisals of Morel's character:

Il ressemblait à un vieux livre du Moyen Âge, plein d'erreurs, de traditions absurdes, d'obscénités, il était extraordinairement composite. J'avais cru d'abord que son art, où il était vraiment passé maître, lui avait donné des supériorités qui dépassaient la virtuosité de l'exécutant. Une fois que je disais mon désir de me mettre au travail: 'Travaillez, devenez illustre,' me dit-il. 'De qui est cela?' lui demandai-je. 'De Fontanes à Chateaubriand.' Il connaissait aussi une correspondance amoureuse de Napoléon. Bien, pensai-je, il est lettré. Mais cette phrase qu'il avait lue je ne sais pas où, était sans doute la seule qu'il connût de toute la littérature ancienne et moderne, car il me la répétait chaque soir.[22] (iii. 420–1; iv. 499)

And if Morel is forever being repackaged, at other points in the novel, the narrator's magnanimous mitigation of the spectacle of sadism (in the form of parental desecration), in which he urges the reader not to take 'evil' at face value, but see some of its manifestations as performances, harmless short circuits, in which staging evil offers sufficient titillation to preclude any attempts at the real thing, start to sound rather like special pleading. After eavesdropping and spying at Montjouvain, the narrator tells us of Vinteuil's daughter:

Une sadique comme elle est *l'artiste du mal*, ce qu'une créature entièrement mauvaise ne pourrait être car le mal ne lui serait pas extérieur, *il lui semblerait tout naturel*, ne se distinguerait même pas d'elle; et la vertu, la mémoire des morts, la tendresse filiale, comme elle n'en aurait pas le culte, elle ne trouverait pas *un plaisir sacrilège* à les profaner. (i. 162; tr. i. 196; my emphasis)

The way we can tell the difference between real sadism and adopted sadism, the narrator argues, is by the degree of self-consciousness that accompanies the act. Thus gay abandon would signify utter perversion, while coyness would supply a moral escape hatch. As general maxims go, this is peculiarly akin to wish fulfilment; for effectively, the profession of guilt is being forced to function as an entitlement to and a justification of sexual pleasure, when nothing guarantees the authenticity of that guilt.

In repeatedly remarking on Charlus's behavioural tendencies: 'Il est singulier qu'un certain ordre d'actes secrets ait pour conséquence extérieure une manière de parler ou de gesticuler qui les révèle' (iii. 356; tr. iv. 423), an automatic reflexivity is engineered between the revelations of Charlus's proclivities and the delayed revelation of vocation promised by the structure of a retrospective first-person account. Self-exposure is pantographically displayed and delayed in *A la recherche*, arranged as local spectacle within the narrative procedures, and dangled as the enticement of terminability: the moment

---

[22] The citation is from a 1798 letter from Louis de Fontanes to Chateaubriand, quoted by the latter in *Mémoires d'outre-tombe* (1849–50).

when self-exposure will reveal itself to *be* the naked truth about the value of writing. But local self-exposure riddles this always deferred grand revelation, with its repeated failure to add up to any apodictic truth about the positive benefits of baring one's secrets.

There are even minor one-act plays, staged as train rides and pre-party conversations, where Proust throws all the minor characters together, just to see what happens. Brichot outdoes himself during the long conversation on the *petit train* to La Raspelière (iii. 437–40; tr. iv. 519–23), by pastiching Rabelais: 'vous voulez dire que je suis moult sorbonagre, sorbonicole et sorboniforme' (iii. 438; tr. iv. 520–1), but is matched by Charlus, announcing, 'Quand je parlais de ce côté "hors nature" de Balzac à Swann, il me disait: "Vous êtes du même avis que Taine"' (iii. 440; tr. iv. 522). Left to their own devices, the secondary characters are not only subject to caricature, but can come out with subsidiary literary justifications, counter-caricatures, and pastiches all by themselves.

On the subject of Brichot's repeated recourse to learned etymology the narrator is at pains to spell out that he is the only listener 'à ne pas remarquer qu'en énumérant ces étymologies, Brichot avait fait rire de lui' (iii. 339; tr. iv. 402).[23] He goes on:

> Et comme les impressions qui donnaient pour moi leur valeur aux choses étaient de celles que les autres personnes *ou n'éprouvent pas, ou refoulent sans y penser comme insignifiantes*, et que par conséquent si j'avais pu les communiquer elles fussent restées incomprises ou auraient été dédaignées, elles étaient entièrement inutilisables pour moi et avaient de plus l'inconvénient de me faire passer pour stupide aux yeux de Mme Verdurin. (iii. 339–40; tr. iv. 402–3; my emphasis)

The long pages of etymology and toponymy find an a posteriori justification in the narrator's approval, but in inverting this appreciation to deprecate himself as their only admirer, a direct challenge to the reader is being formulated. Find strings of word histories dull, and we are in danger of aligning ourselves with a Mme Verdurin. We are not allowed to laugh at a distance. By reflexively performing the inclusiveness of all that is at first glance *insignifiante*, retrospectivity and attention in reading is in

---

[23] Brichot's etymologies may be found at: iii. 280–4, tr. iv. 330–4; iii. 316–17, tr. iv. 379; iii. 321–3, tr. iv. 381–3; iii. 327–9, tr. iv. 388–9; iii. 484–6, tr iv. 579.

turn demanded of us, as well as a legitimation and valorization of the narrator's diligence in communicating everything he notices. If 'dans tout clan, qu'il soit mondain, politique, littéraire, on contracte une facilité perverse à découvrir dans une conversation, dans un discours officiel, dans une nouvelle, dans un sonnet, tout ce que l'honnête lecteur n'aurait jamais songé à y voir' (iii. 340; tr. iv. 403), if habit orders interpretation, 'l'instinct d'imitation et l'absence de courage gouvernent les sociétés comme les foules' (iii. 325; tr. iv. 385), where does externally verifiable opinion begin? The narrator is here momentarily, and slyly, arrogating the position of the anthropologist and the *moraliste*, relying on an implicit reference to a tradition of self-styled observation from without to justify the inclusion of digressions and *longueurs*. He is pointing to a methodology of tolerant speculative inclusiveness, which might be useful to protect him from charges of solipsism at some future point in the narrative, a point when perhaps the anthropologist's stock of observation, eaten up from the inside, might have cut out the spectacle of middle men, and reduced itself to the self-apologist's internal monologue.[24]

Norpois the diplomat is famously opinionated, pompous, and dull. But there is one moment of dangerous proximity to the narrator's interests which stands out. As he gives his views on the value of Bergotte's writing, a complex self-justificatory paradigm makes its appearance: 'Il n'empêche que chez lui l'œuvre est infiniment supérieure à l'auteur. Ah! voilà quelqu'un qui donne raison à l'homme d'esprit qui prétendait qu'on ne doit connaître les écrivains que par leurs livres' (i. 465; tr. ii. 53). Here is Norpois pre-emptively harnessing for his own rhetorical purposes one of the most dearly held narratorial opinions of *À la recherche*—appropriating indeed Proust's own position—that books should be judged by their contents and not by their authors.[25]

[24] See Ch. 5.
[25] The most important intratext for this being the much-cited passage: 'cette méthode qui consiste à ne pas séparer l'homme et l'œuvre, à considérer qu'il n'est pas indifférent pour juger l'auteur d'un livre, si ce livre n'est pas "un traité de géométrie pure", d'avoir d'abord répondu aux questions qui paraissent le plus étrangères à son œuvre (comment se comportait-il . . .), à s'entourer de tous les renseignements possibles sur un écrivain, à collationner ses correspondances, à interroger les hommes qui l'ont connu, en causant avec eux s'ils vivent encore, en

What is astonishing about Marcel's response is that it does not occur. He crumples in the face of what in other instances are very clearly his own views: 'Je me sentais consterné, réduit; et mon esprit comme un fluide qui n'a de dimensions que celles du vase qu'on lui fournit, de même qu'il s'était dilaté jadis à remplir les capacités immenses du génie, contracté maintenant, tenait tout entier dans la médiocrité étroite où M. de Norpois l'avait soudain enfermé et restreint' (i. 466; tr. ii. 54). Rather than retaliate by mocking Norpois implicitly for giving away some trademark pomposity, the narrator here allows his own judgements to be overriden, or taken over, in the writing of the narrative. There is a gap where the self-justification of differentiation should be, where, in other words, a robust resistance to undermining from a dangerously proximate source should or could have taken place. It is as though, in this huge novel all about jealous scrutiny, on every subject, from Albertine's lesbianism to whether the narrator's grieving is as authentic as his mother's (iii. 165; tr. iv. 193–4), at moments when the narrator is put to the test of his own standards, he simply collapses.

What kind of self-justificatory moral imperative drives the abdication of self-preservation in the face of criticism directed at the narrator which is too like the criticisms the narrator has of others? This is vulnerability fuelled by jealousy, or dangerous proximity. Marcel's two suspicions, that 'mon existence était déjà commencée' and that 'je n'étais pas situé en dehors du Temps' (i. 473; tr. ii. 62 and 63) cause him the same pain as though: 'j'avais été non pas encore l'hospitalisé ramolli, mais ces héros dont l'auteur, sur un ton indifférent qui est particulièrement cruel, nous dit à la fin d'un livre: "Il quitte de moins en moins la campagne. Il a fini par s'y fixer définitivement, etc."' (i. 474; tr. ii. 63). To recognize himself as caught up in time would be to accept that others may pass definitive judgements upon him, but also to accept that a state of enforced self-justification, as an

lisant ce qu'ils ont pu écrire sur lui s'ils sont morts, cette méthode méconnaît ce qu'une fréquentation un peu profonde avec nous-même nous apprend: qu'un livre est le produit d'un autre moi que celui que nous manifestons dans nos habitudes, dans la société, dans nos vices. Ce moi-là, si nous voulons essayer de le comprendre, c'est au fond de nous-même, en essayant de le recréer en nous, que nous pouvons y parvenir. Rien ne peut nous dispenser de cet effort de notre cœur' (*CSB* 221–2).

ongoing, unavoidable differentiation from otherness too like himself, is the state in which representation takes place. An original authenticity of experience, life as one long goodnight kiss, would then be revealed as a wholly death-driven instinct, with which the narrator would have to do battle, and perpetually defeat, in order for life *as* painful differentiation to take place.[26] Collapse in the face of his own judgements coming back at him is not one side of a conveniently two-faced coin, the other side being successful differentiation from hostile alterity, but part of a complex, endlessly re-undertaken engagement with the dangers of identification, over-hasty rejection, and the surprise of finding that others constantly overstep the limits laid down for them by the first impressions they leave behind, continue to have opinions, change their minds:

Tout ce qui nous semble impérissable tend à la destruction; une situation mondaine, tout comme autre chose, n'est pas créée une fois pour toutes mais aussi bien que la puissance d'un empire, se reconstruit à chaque instant par une sorte de création perpétuellement continue. . . . La création du monde n'a pas eu lieu au début, elle a lieu tous les jours. (iv. 247–8; tr. v. 770–1)

The multifarious workings of the minor characters, sabotaging now themselves, now each other, and occasionally the narrator, are seen to be part of a much larger project only at the end of *Le Temps retrouvé*:

Et même si je n'avais pas le loisir de préparer, chose déjà bien plus importante, les cent masques qu'il convient d'attacher à un même visage, ne fût-ce que selon les yeux qui le voient et le sens où ils en lisent les traits, et pour les mêmes yeux selon l'espérance ou la crainte, ou au contraire l'amour et l'habitude qui cachent pendant trente années les changements de l'âge, même enfin si je n'entreprenais pas, ce dont ma liaison avec Albertine suffisait pourtant à me montrer que sans cela tout est factice et mensonger, de représenter certaines personnes non pas

---

[26] Marcel Muller, in 'Charlus dans le métro ou pastiche et cruauté chez Proust', *Cahiers Marcel Proust, 9, nouvelle série, Études Proustiennes III* (1979), 9–25, makes this point: 'c'est bien à la mémoire involontaire que le *je* est redevable d'avoir conservé, vivace, l'image du drame du coucher quotidien. Mais, lié au mal, ce souvenir l'est aussi à la finitude. L'authenticité en est toute provisoire, parce que fragmentaire. De plus, ce souvenir n'étant pas sujet à l'oubli, aucun hasard n'a été nécessaire pour le faire sortir de la nuit. L'image mémorielle est protégée contre les vicissitudes de l'existence: autant dire qu'elle est morte' (p. 23).

au-dehors mais au-dedans de nous où leurs moindres actes peuvent
amener des troubles mortels, et de faire varier aussi la lumière du ciel
moral, selon les différences de pression de notre sensibilité, ou quand,
troublant la sérénité de notre certitude sous laquelle un objet est si
petit, un simple nuage de risque en multiplie en un moment la
grandeur, si je ne pouvais apporter ces changements et bien d'autres
(dont la nécessité, si on veut peindre le réel, a pu apparaître au cours
de ce récit) dans la transcription d'un univers qui était à redessiner tout
entier, du moins ne manquerais-je pas d'y décrire l'homme comme
ayant la longueur non de son corps mais de ses années, comme devant,
tâche de plus en plus énorme et qui finit par le vaincre, les traîner avec
lui quand il se déplace. (iv. 622–3; tr. vi. 448)

This long, rhythmically pulsed sentence demonstrates performatively that the rigours of definition are in direct proportion
to the *longueurs* of explanation. Readings of character cannot
but be drawn out. The exaggeration of a Norpois caricature
turns out to be the same piece of rhetorical equipment needed
to jot down change over time, a writerly tool quick enough to
outline self's continually plotted difference from itself *as it takes
place*. Proust has his tussle between the synchronic and the
diachronic, and the latter wins, though not without repeated
punctuation at the local level of seemingly final words on the
morality and banality of this or that character, even Marcel's:

Car, peu à peu, je ressemblais à tous mes parents, à mon père qui—de
tout autre façon que moi sans doute, car si les choses se répètent, c'est
avec de grandes variations—s'intéressait si fort au temps qu'il faisait;
et pas seulement à mon père, mais de plus en plus à ma tante Léonie.
. . . ce qui me faisait si souvent rester couché, c'était un être, non pas
Albertine, non pas un être que j'aimais, mais un être plus puissant sur
moi qu'un être aimé, c'était, transmigrée en moi, despotique au point
de faire taire parfois mes soupçons jaloux, ou du moins d'aller vérifier
s'ils étaient fondés ou non, c'était ma tante Léonie. (iii. 586; tr. v. 81)

Inclusiveness is the Möbius Strip flypaper that Proust is striving
for.[27] This tireless unpicking of the contours around things runs

[27] Compare Walter Benjamin's felicitous parable in 'The Image of Proust': 'the
stocking which has the structure of this dream world when, rolled up in the laundry hamper, it is a "bag" and a "present" at the same time. And just as children do
not tire of quickly changing the bag and its contents into a third thing—namely a
stocking—Proust could not get his fill of emptying the dummy, his self, at a stroke
in order to keep garnering that third thing, the image which satisfied his curiosity',
Illuminations (1968), (207).

into a particular problem when otherness turns out to be rather like self, and we should turn now to the more sustained examination of the processes of discrimination promised at the beginning of this chapter.

4. DISCRIMINATION

Balbec is a coastal resort, half-marine, half-terrestrial, a *société mêlée*, according to Tadié.[28] Elstir's vision of the port at Carquethuit reshapes Marcel's vision of the interchangeability of maritime, earthly, and aerial landscapes (ii. 190–8; tr. ii. 478–87). More urgent, perhaps, for the narrator's emerging libidinal energies, is the sighting of the *petite bande* (ii. 146; tr. ii. 425). These fabulous revisionings and super-mobile set-pieces of writing have tended to obscure the fact that there is an equally carefully introduced series of men, within a continuous section of text, appearing even before the young girls are seen for the first time.[29] There is an important difference between the sketching of the *bande zoophytique* (ii. 210; tr. ii. 502), the 'liaison invisible, mais harmonieuse comme une même ombre chaude, une même atmosphère, faisant d'eux un tout aussi homogène en ses parties qu'il était différent de la foule' (ii. 151; tr. ii. 431), the 'théorie qu'elles déroulaient le long de la mer' (ii. 153; tr. ii. 434), and the series of young men. The girls are overt objects of sexual desire, and this desire is expressed as the need to assimilate the alterity of their *théorie* into the narratorial self:

Or, chaque fois que l'image de femmes si différentes pénètre en nous, à moins que l'oubli ou la concurrence d'autres images ne l'élimine, *nous n'avons de repos que nous n'ayons converti ces étrangères en quelque chose qui soit pareil à nous*, notre âme étant à cet égard douée du même genre de réaction et d'activité que notre organisme physique, lequel ne peut tolérer l'immixtion dans son sein d'un corps étranger sans qu'il s'exerce aussitôt à digérer et assimiler l'intrus. (ii. 159; ii. 441; my emphasis)

[28] Jean-Yves Tadié, *Proust*, (1983), 54.
[29] ii, 87–144; tr. ii. 355–423: the section comprises a first meeting with Saint-Loup; meeting Bloch after an implied period of separation; encountering Charlus for the first time; and a dinner party at Bloch's father's house. I will concentrate here on Saint-Loup and Bloch.

As we shall see, however, a very different order and logic of discovery is applicable to the cycle of meetings with men, and its intricate movements act out the principle we are exploring here, that of dangerous proximity, of action, intention, beliefs, desires, *caractère*, as an incitement to self-justificatory differentiation. The rest of this chapter, then, devotes itself to a close analysis of how this finely tuned calibration works, looking at Marcel's developing friendship with Robert, marquis de Saint-Loup-en-Bray, and then at their joint encounter with Bloch, Marcel's childhood comrade.

Even before Marcel has seen Saint-Loup, a complete set of expectations are articulated about the future of their relationship: 'déjà je me figurais qu'il allait se prendre de sympathie pour moi, que je serais son ami préféré' (ii. 87; tr. ii. 355). Within a page, the narrator has also pre-emptively sketched out his imaginary conception of the tragic parabola Saint-Loup's life will take as a result of that friendship, on the skimpiest of details supplied by Mme de Villeparisis:

comme j'étais persuadé que ce genre d'amour finissait fatalement par l'aliénation mentale, le crime et le suicide, pensant au temps si court qui était réservé à notre amitié, déjà si grande dans mon cœur sans que je l'eusse encore vu, je pleurai sur elle et sur les malheurs qui l'attendaient comme sur un être cher dont on vient de nous apprendre qu'il est gravement atteint et que ses jours sont comptés.[30] (ii. 88; tr. ii. 355)

When the first sighting takes place, it is securely framed and contained as a painterly portrait, 'dans la travée centrale qui allait de la plage à la route' (ii. 88; tr. ii. 356).[31] Saint-Loup is figured as a montage of external accoutrements, 'un jeune homme aux yeux pénétrants et dont la peau était aussi blonde et les cheveux aussi dorés que s'ils avaient absorbé tous les rayons du soleil' (ii. 88; tr. ii. 356). The narrator attempts a metaphoric transformation of the unknown man's clothing, in a familiar Proustian rhetorical gesture, the chiasmatic exchange

[30] This is not the only time we witness Marcel crying over Saint-Loup. At Doncières, when permission is granted for the pair to sleep in the same room, the narrator tells us, 'je me détournais pour cacher mes larmes' (ii. 378; tr. iii. 82).

[31] And again, 'la mer qui remplissait jusqu'à mi-hauteur le vitrage du hall lui faisait un fond sur lequel il se détachait en pied, comme dans certains portraits' (ii. 89; tr. ii. 357).

of external for internal: Saint-Loup is dressed in 'une étoffe souple et blanchâtre comme je n'aurais jamais cru qu'un homme eût osé en porter, et dont la minceur n'évoquait pas moins que le frais de la salle à manger, la chaleur et le beau temps du dehors' (ii. 88; tr. ii. 356). The metaphoric gearchange sticks, however, caught up in the scrap of disapproval lodged in the same sentence: 'comme je n'aurais jamais cru qu'un homme eût osé en porter'. The narrator immediately compensates for this troublesome effeminacy by introducing a ready-made idea that falls beyond the logic of the instantaneous impression: 'A cause de son "chic", de son impertinence de jeune "lion", à cause de son extraordinaire beauté surtout, certains lui trouvaient même une air efféminé, mais sans le lui reprocher, car *on savait combien il était viril* et qu'il aimait passionnément les femmes' (ii. 88–9; ii. 356; my emphasis). Saint-Loup's unmanly dress is given absolution through paraleptic reported gossip about his (hetero)sexual prowess, and the narrator's discriminatory *conscience* is displaced and redistributed to take its place among those uncertain *certains* who override their sexually inquisitive first impressions to give others the benefit of the doubt.

Saint-Loup seems at first to be utterly indifferent to the narrator, and it is his trademark monocle, the still centre around which Saint-Loup gravitates, 'équilibrant perpétuellement les mouvements de ses membres autour de son monocle fugitif et dansant qui semblait leur centre de gravité' (ii. 89; tr. ii. 357), and mentioned no less than three times, which functions as carrier for the narrator's initial disappointment. Marcel's first conclusion is that he is witnessing a spectacle of aristocratic indifference, an exercise in 'la morgue que devait ... pratiquer impitoyablement un jeune marquis' (ii. 89; tr. ii. 358): 'Mon intelligence aurait pu me dire le contraire. Mais la caractéristique de l'âge ridicule que je traversais—âge nullement ingrat, très fécond—est qu'on n'y consulte pas l'intelligence et que les moindres attributs des êtres semblent faire partie indivisible de leur personnalité. Tout entouré de monstres et de dieux, on ne connaît guère le calme' (ii. 89–90; tr. ii. 358). The interstitial comment, *âge nullement ingrat, très fécond*, mitigating the severity of *l'âge ridicule que je traversais*, prepares the way for: 'Plus tard on voit les choses d'une façon plus pratique, en pleine conformité avec le reste de la société, *mais* l'adolescence est le seul temps où l'on ait appris quelque chose' (ii. 90; tr. ii. 358; my emphasis). Saint-Loup's apparent indifference is balanced by the narrator's disappointment, in an apparently straightforward causal relationship. 'Mon intelligence aurait pu me dire le contraire', however, is doing battle here with 'mais l'adolescence est le seul temps où l'on ait appris quelque chose': we are suspended between two kinds of hindsight, that of *intelligence pratique* and that of *adolescence*. The adolescent rebellion that is being staged is resolved to shunt aside the reasonable intelligence of social practice's polite formalisms. First impressions, of Saint-Loup's effeminacy and his indifference, are not only to count, they are to form the foundation of Saint-Loup's entire future development.

To make a point about first impressions counting might seem a truism in a text famous for its promotion of a 'retour sincère à la racine même de l'impression', of choosing to 'représenter une chose par cette autre que dans l'éclair d'une illusion première nous avons prise pour elle' (ii. 712; tr. iii. 484). We are given repeated indications of what Marcel privileges in aesthetic accounts of the world: the 'côté Dostoïevski des *Lettres de Madame de Sévigné*' (twice referred to, on the train to Balbec (ii. 14; tr. ii. 267); and again during a literary discussion with Albertine, when she quotes Marcel referring to Mme de Sévigné in this way (iii. 880; tr. v. 432)), for example. His explanation is that 'Mme de Sévigné, comme Elstir, comme Dostoïevski, au lieu de présenter les choses dans l'ordre logique, c'est-à-dire en commençant par la cause, nous montre d'abord l'effet, l'illusion qui nous frappe' (iii. 880; tr. v. 432).[32] When the young narrator visits Elstir and studies his work, he notices that: 'l'effort d'Elstir de ne pas exposer les choses telles qu'il savait qu'elles étaient, mais selon ces illusions optiques dont notre vision première est faite, l'avait précisément amené

---

[32] See Descombes, *Proust: Philosophie du roman* (1987), 257–71, for a discussion of how this equation of Mme de Sévigné, Elstir, and Dostoevsky collapses. Descombes shows how both viewers of paintings and readers of novels bring what they know to what they see, even if the point of view they have been given is impressionistic, or unfolds in a subjective rather than a linear order. This fact renders the question of the nature of judgement unclear, if not impossible. Controlling the distribution of epistemological breakthroughs—where the reader beats the narrator to the novel's conclusion—is simply unfeasible.

à mettre en lumière certaines de ces lois de perspective, plus frappantes alors, car l'art était le premier à les dévoiler' (ii. 194; tr. ii. 483). But aesthetic impressions and rule-making for their viewing may not apply to the first impressions of others and the portfolio they supply of themselves, and this is what interests us here: narratorial reactions of a particular self-justificatory variety in response to like-mindedness.

The first conversation between Marcel and Saint-Loup passes uncommented: 'Je crus qu'il s'agissait au moins d'un duel, quand le lendemain il me fit passer sa carte. Mais il ne me parla que de littérature, déclara après une longue causerie qu'il avait une envie extrême de me voir plusieurs heures chaque jour' (ii. 91; tr. ii. 359). The disproportion between the text devoted to an anticipated *meeting* with Saint-Loup, during which he is observed, objectified (the use of the definite article depersonalizes him in the following example (ii. 90; tr. ii. 358): 'chaque fois qu'il passait à côté de nous, le corps aussi inflexiblement élancé, la tête toujours aussi haute, le regard impassible'), and judged ('la mauvaise impression que nous avaient causée ces dehors révélateurs d'une nature orgueilleuse et méchante' (ii. 90; tr. ii. 358–9) causes Mme de Villeparisis to justify her nephew), and the ellipsis that replaces an account of their first *conversation*, reveals obliquely a differential prioritizing that takes place repeatedly in *A la recherche*. 'Literature', reduced to an unspecific cipher, the subject of the conversation between Saint-Loup and Marcel, goes at first unnoticed by the narrator. More important for Marcel, in terms of text space devoted to it, is the classification of visual signals, the outward manifestations of moral or social codes, emitted by Saint-Loup, and demanding detailed specification and organization, as well as an account of how such signals relate to the narrator's capacity for interpretation. It is only Marcel's self-characterization as *victim* that prompts further investigations of Saint-Loup's identity, a further attempt to separate the proximities of Saint-Loup's class from his being: 'Bon, me dis-je, je me suis déjà trompé sur lui, j'avais été victime d'un mirage, mais je n'ai triomphé du premier que pour tomber dans un second, car c'est un grand seigneur féru de noblesse et cherchant à le dissimuler' (ii. 91–2; tr. ii. 360).

Saint-Loup's *air d'un aristocrate* is belied by his intellectual

interests, but their abstraction bores or irritates the narrator.
What fascinates Marcel instead are the *Mémoires* (of Saint-
Simon), 'tout nourris d'anecdotes sur ce fameux comte de
Marsantes en qui se résume l'élégance si spéciale d'une époque
déjà lointaine, l'esprit empli de rêveries' (ii. 92; tr. ii. 361). Saint-
Loup, by contrast, is: 'un de ces "intellectuels" prompts à l'admiration qui s'enferment dans un livre, soucieux seulement de
haute pensée. Même, chez Saint-Loup l'expression de cette
tendance très abstraite et qui l'éloignait tant de mes préoccu-
pations habituelles, tout en me paraissant touchante m'en-
nuyait un peu' (ii. 92; tr. ii. 360–1). Saint-Loup, 'au lieu de se
contenter d'être le fils de son père', has hoisted himself (*se fût
élevé*) to 'l'amour de Nietzsche et de Proudhon' (ii. 92; tr. ii.
361). What seems at first to be an acknowledgement of Saint-
Loup's intellectual superiority over a low-brow sentimentality
and nostalgia, written as vertical hierarchization of their respective intellectual projects, is immediately subverted: 'Saint-Loup
n'était pas assez intelligent pour comprendre que la valeur
intellectuelle n'a rien à voir avec l'adhésion à une certaine
formule esthétique' (ii. 93; tr. ii. 361). This direct attack on
Saint-Loup's judgement is, of course, embedded in the opposition that traces itself throughout *A la recherche*, and that can be
seen even in early projects, from the first words of the essay plan
for *Contre Sainte-Beuve*, for example: 'Chaque jour j'attache
moins de prix à l'intelligence' (*CSB* 211), the opposition
between objective and subjective intelligence. But the attack
reorients the alignment of vision, tolerance, and mutuality of
ideas that is the usual definition of friendship into a process of
differentiation between the narrator's interests and those of his
direct peers. The narrator insists upon the distinction:

si je trouvais Saint-Loup un peu sérieux, lui ne comprenait pas que je
ne le fusse pas davantage. Ne jugeant chaque chose qu'au poids d'intelligence qu'elle contient, ne percevant pas les enchantements
d'imagination que me donnaient certaines qu'il jugeait frivoles, il
s'étonnait que moi—moi à qui il s'imaginait être tellement inférieur—
je pusse m'y intéresser. (ii. 93; tr. ii. 362)

What Saint-Loup encounters, he judges, twice in the space of
this sentence. The plaintive 'moi–moi' repetition, drawing
attention to the narrator, also draws attention to a reversal

contained within the parenthetical comment it casually introduces. Everything that has led up to this point has insisted upon
the vertical binary opposition structuring the two men's intellectual orientation. Yet the inversion announced by Saint-
Loup's recourse to his own imaginary, that the *narrator* is
superior in some way to him ('moi à qui il s'imaginait être tellement inférieur'), tells of a third possibility. Leaked into the text
as a momentary lapse of narratorial self-effacement is the
notion that a received idea of what constitutes high-brow intel-
lectualism (here given in the form of *manifestations modernistes,
déclamations socialistes,* the reading of Nietzsche and Proudhon,
and a love of Wagner) might not be in a simple oppositional
relation to *enchantements d'imagination,* or a *roman démodé.* But
the existence of this third option goes missing, it is not ratified
by articulation in the text. Instead it marks a site of contestation, an agon played out through oscillations and inversions,
without producing a solution or a hero. What Saint-Loup thinks
of Marcel, and what Marcel thinks of Saint-Loup are not name-
able judgements, but are subject both to vertical inversions of
superiority and inferiority, and lateral exchanges, an incessant
reassessment, that is written into the text of *A la recherche* here,
of the flimsy boundaries between intellectual subject and
human subject.

The narrator's grandmother is a reference point for a particular kind of self-justificatory behaviour, particularly clearly
here, but everywhere she is mentioned in *A la recherche.* As a
reminder of Combray, a past point of stasis and immobility, site
of repetitions unspoilt by the fear that repetition is necessarily
neurotic, unproductive, or terminally driven, the grandmother
represents a particular scale of judgements and criteria for
judgement:

Dès les premiers jours Saint-Loup fit la conquête de ma grand-mère,
non seulement par la bonté incessante qu'il s'ingéniait à nous
témoigner à tous deux, mais par le naturel qu'il y mettait comme en
toutes choses. Or le naturel—sans doute parce que, sous l'art de
l'homme, il laisse sentir la nature—était la qualité que ma grand-
mère préférait à toutes, tant dans les jardins où elle n'aimait pas qu'il
y eût, comme dans celui de Combray, de plates-bandes trop
régulières, qu'en cuisine où elle détestait ces 'pièces montées'. (ii. 93;
tr. ii. 362)

The grandmother values what is unspoilt, what is natural. Her scale of value judgements depends on one stable criterion, and she is confident of being able to identify it in any material presented to her. Justification to the grandmother is not a process dependent on self-differentiation in the moment of decision-making about objects and people that come her way, but an a priori reliance on one known quantity to which experience must hold itself accountable. But here we have a parenthetical comment, which, like the interruption which displaced Saint-Loup's fixed judgements, turns her methodology against her: 'Or le naturel—sans doute parce que, sous l'art de l'homme, il laisse sentir la nature' calls into question through an ambiguity of signification the very possibility of attributing naturalness to nature, whether in humans, or flowerbeds. The deconstruction exposes the grandmother's blind reliance on the watertightness of her assumptions when she sets out to judge the world.

The parenthetical reflection that turns nature back on itself pre-emptively launches a series of confirmatory examples of Saint-Loup's 'naturalness'. His clothing, his negligent way of living in luxury 'sans "sentir l'argent"' (ii. 94; tr. ii. 363), and his inability to hide his emotions (a Keatsian physiological inscription of the flushes of spontaneity), all indicate, to the grandmother at least, a lack of pretention which guarantees his moral probity.[33] For the narrator, however, the spectacle of Saint-Loup's blush, his 'plaisir si brusque, si brûlant, si volatil, si expansif, qu'il lui était impossible de le contenir et de le cacher' (ii. 94; tr. ii. 363) at unexpected compliments, prompts a very different resonance. Just as it is impossible for Saint-Loup to conceal his pleasures, so the narrator-in-the-future finds it impossible not to give way to the pressure of knowledge still to come, already known and demanding exposure:

Mais j'ai connu un autre être et il y en a beaucoup, chez lequel la sincérité physiologique de cet incarnat passager n'excluait nullement la duplicité morale; bien souvent il prouve seulement la vivacité avec laquelle ressentent le plaisir, jusqu'à être désarmées devant lui et à être forcées de le confesser aux autres, des natures capables des plus viles fourberies. (ii. 94; tr. ii. 363)

[33] Christopher Ricks has analysed with great brilliance this embodied reflexivity in *Keats and Embarrassment* (1974).

In microcosmic form, Saint-Loup's entire future revelatory transformation is seeded here, his gradual unravelling from his own powers of discriminating and performing what is *naturel* for others. *Naturel*, the narrator cannot resist hinting, even in the moment of describing the cementing of one of the longest-running friendships in the novel, is only as strong as its performer's competence at imitating what is conventional.[34]

Saint-Loup's *vive rougeur*, which marks the site of an uncontrollable admission to his personal preferences (finding their disclosure in the future of the novel), sets off a further reflection in the narrator, that of controlling the admission of external stimulation, in the form of friendship. Saint-Loup characterizes the time they spend together as 'la meilleure joie de sa vie' (ii. 95; tr. ii. 364). It provokes in the narrator, on the other hand, 'une sorte de tristesse': 'car je n'éprouvais à me trouver, à causer avec lui—et sans doute c'eût été de même avec tout autre—rien de ce bonheur qu'il m'était au contraire possible de ressentir quand j'étais sans compagnon' (ii. 95; tr. ii. 364). There follows an extended and repetitive meditation on this problem: 'Seul, quelquefois, je sentais affluer du fond de moi quelqu'une de ces impressions qui me donnaient un bien-être délicieux' (ii. 95; tr. ii. 364), is almost exactly repeated in 'plaisir d'avoir extrait de moi-même et amené à la lumière quelque chose qui y était caché dans la pénombre' (ii. 95; tr. ii. 364). The attempt to decide between passive, active, solitary, or shared procedures, for the truest methods facilitating subjective expression, is the dilemma that defines the novel. It is here played off in miniature against the shortfall offered by proximity with like-minded others:

Si j'avais passé deux ou trois heures à causer avec Robert de Saint-Loup et qu'il eût admiré ce que je lui avais dit, j'éprouvais une sorte

[34] In 'Proust's Narrative Selves', Malcolm Bowie demonstrates that a further teleology apparent in Saint-Loup's unravelling is that of the narrator's concentration of singularity into his own activities and identity, effected precisely by the spectacle of Saint-Loup's dispersal and his adoption of the modernist 'fragmented' self as a satisfactory identity. Bowie puts forward Saint-Loup's highly literary description of the German bombers in Paris who are compared to Valkyries (iv. 337; tr. vi. 84), as an example of the potential gone missing of Saint-Loup's aesthetic sensibilities (Craig and McGowan (eds.), *Moy Qui Me Voy*, 131–46). Duncan Large has written on Proust's views of friendship in 'Proust on Nietzsche: The Question of Friendship', *The Modern Language Review*, 88 (1993), 612–24.

de remords, de regret, de fatigue de ne pas être resté seul et prêt enfin
à travailler. Mais je me disais qu'on n'est pas intelligent que pour soi-
même, que les plus grands ont désiré d'être appréciés, que je ne
pouvais pas considérer comme perdues des heures où j'avais bâti une
haute idée de moi dans l'esprit de mon ami, je me persuadais facilement que je devais en être heureux. (ii. 95; tr. ii. 364–5)

Whereas initially the boundaries of the narratorial self were
demarcated by a *competitive* critique of Saint-Loup's intellectu-
alism, asserting his own mastery over insight, and formulating
epistemology as the logic of discrimination, here, overriding
an act of judgement, and making an artificial attempt to
prolong a situation, both maintain the differential at the price
of the narrator's integrity. It is the tortured coils of *narration*
which have preoccupied us throughout this book, and which
are succinctly staged by Marcel's self-persuasion at this
moment. For his attempts to tell himself to 'live a little' run
counter to every argument in the novel about the hard solitary
work of retrieving subjective truth. The half-hearted
masochism of this particular spanner in the works of *A la
recherche*'s teleological drive is not at all inwardly directed, but
directed, beyond Saint-Loup, at the *reader*. The heavy sigh of
'Je me persuadais facilement que je devais en être heureux',
because self-persuasion and duty reinforce one another to
deny any trace of a founding, primary, or real pleasure, forces
the responsibility of indulgence outwards towards the reader.
The reader is handed the task of managing the narrator's pleasure. The martyr's greater cause, the disaffected worker's
grumblings, the thwarted artist's self-pity, all combine in this
short clause.

Rejecting the intimacy of friendship as a means of fulfilment,
but doing so ambivalently, is accomplished by means of an elegy
on the impossibility of unmediated communication. Marcel feels
he is incapable of knowing 'la joie par un sentiment qui au lieu
d'accroître les différences qu'il y avait entre mon âme et celle des
autres—comme il y en a entre les âmes de chacun de nous—les
effacerait' (ii. 96; tr. ii. 365). The syntax here inverts a simple
ordering of the clauses, to put widening differences and the
narratorial self before others and the effacement of difference.
The pronoun *les*, referring back to *différences*, is so far removed in
the sentence from its anchoring noun that the effects of the verb

that governs it start to be dangerously applicable to *celles des autres*: the effacement of difference that is so impossible for Marcel starts to twist awkwardly round into the murderous wish to efface otherness. Marcel's extended description of friendship's constraints sounds like an argument for solipsism. Dangerous proximity to others can produce, by contagion, a desire for differentiation that overbalances equally perilously into one-sidedness or separatism.

The final section of Saint-Loup's portraiture withdraws fully from the proximities of friendship to observed character as ekphrasis: 'Quelquefois je me reprochais de prendre ainsi plaisir à considérer mon ami comme une œuvre d'art, c'est-à-dire à regarder le jeu de toutes les parties de son être comme harmonieusement réglé par une idée générale à laquelle elles étaient suspendues' (ii. 96; tr. ii. 366).[35] Unlike the vision of Saint-Loup in the Hôtel hall, the theoretical modelling of spectating here refuses to situate itself firmly either inside or outside its object. The *idée générale* which the narrator elects to see as regulating Saint-Loup's behaviour, the 'souplesse héréditaire des grands chasseurs' (ii. 96; tr. ii. 366), is both *intérieur* and *antérieur* to the young man:

j'y sentais surtout la certitude ou l'illusion qu'avaient eues ces grands seigneurs d'être 'plus que les autres', grâce à quoi ils n'avaient pu léguer à Saint-Loup ce désir de montrer qu'on est 'autant que les autres', cette peur de paraître trop empressé qui lui était en effet vraiment inconnue et qui enlaidit de tant de raideur et de gaucherie la plus sincère amabilité plébéienne. (ii. 96; tr. ii. 366)

Although the narrator makes a comparison with the act of looking at a *paysage* (ambiguously suspended between a 'real' and a represented landscape), to reduce the phenomenological complexity of what takes place in this section of text to vision as epistemology, a straightforward subject/viewer → object/viewed relationship, is to ignore the extraordinary intensity of the integration being attempted. The narrator wants no less than a method of moving between phylogenesis and ontogenesis, buckled securely into an understanding of

[35] I have derived a great deal of benefit from reading *Sight or Cite? Aspects of the Visual in Proust* (forthcoming, Peter Lang), in which Jonathan Murphy discusses the notion of the ekphrastic, or a metalanguage of the experience of viewing.

aristocratic genealogy, together with a metapsychological hypothesis of object relations:

> En revanche par moments ma pensée démêlait en Saint-Loup un être plus général que lui-même, le 'noble', et qui comme un esprit intérieur mouvait ses membres, ordonnait ses gestes et ses actions; alors, à ces moments-là, quoique près de lui, j'étais seul, comme je l'eusse été devant un paysage dont j'aurais compris l'harmonie. Il n'était plus qu'un objet que ma rêverie cherchait à approfondir. (ii. 96; tr. ii. 365)

Robert is here to be no more than an object, but in objectifying him, the narrator finds himself gathering evidence that Saint-Loup's ancestry has had a determining influence on his being, in his 'agilité morale et physique', his *aisance* and his *adresse*. This is no nod to positivistic Naturalism, however. 'La certitude ou l'illusion qu'avaient eues ces grands seigneurs d'être "plus que les autres" ' is a hypothesis without a foundation: certainty having its origins in a history not of facts about events, but speculative projection into a psychological past, which always runs the risk of self-fulfilling mythologizing. Having set up his hypothesis, however, the narrator runs it forward to produce a Saint-Loup whose qualities may be deduced negatively, by what he has *not* inherited: 'ils n'avaient pu léguer à Saint-Loup ce désir de montrer qu'on est "autant que les autres" '. The narrator fuses this speculation on genetic pre-programming, with aesthetic appreciation, conjoining ethics with apprehension. He hooks Saint-Loup up to a mythologized genealogy, but at the same time, splits him off from any autonomous understanding of such a conjunction: 'le jeu de toutes les parties de son être comme harmonieusement réglé par une idée générale à laquelle elles étaient suspendues *mais qu'il ne connaissait pas* et qui par conséquent n'ajoutait rien à ses qualités propres, à cette valeur personnelle d'intelligence et de moralité à quoi il attachait tant de prix' (ii. 96–7; ii. 366; my emphasis).

Moments later, however, the narrator is perfectly capable of giving Saint-Loup his intentionality back. Marcel, we have seen, reproaches himself for divorcing Saint-Loup from his own self-perception, in order to apprehend him as an artwork on the theme of noble descent ('Quelquefois je me reprochais de prendre ainsi plaisir à considérer mon ami comme une œuvre d'art'). When Saint-Loup is said to be 'vraiment pur et désintéressé', precisely because he is a *gentilhomme*, but who then, in fighting his own aristocratic past, is also taking it for granted, a complex exchange of responsibilities is to be seen at work: 'Se croyant l'héritier d'une caste ignorante et égoïste, il cherchait sincèrement à ce qu'ils [the 'jeunes étudiants prétentieux' that Saint-Loup seeks out] lui pardonnassent ces origines aristocratiques qui exerçaient sur eux, au contraire, une séduction et à cause desquelles ils le recherchaient, tout en simulant à son égard la froideur et même l'insolence' (ii. 97; tr. ii. 366). Marcel justifies his lack of warmth towards Saint-Loup as *different from* that of pretentious young students who only simulate coldness to mask snobbery, by protectively facilitating Saint-Loup's self-justificatory wish to compensate the faults of the whole of his caste through his own *aspirations socialistes*.

The various elements of birthright, indifference, snobbery, intellectual interests, effeminacy, that make up the portrait of Saint-Loup, a portrait by turns static and mobile, together with the narratorial account of the developing friendship between the two men, undergo an extraordinarily complicated shuffling and reshuffling in the passage we have just looked at. The famous Proustian mobility of perspective is in the grip here of a self-justificatory motivation that we can define as a bid to hold at a distance that which might render vulnerable the security of a sustainable identity

At this point in the narrative, an example of the pretentious bourgeois is introduced into the series of young men. Bloch is not only a representative of the same class from which the narrator proceeds, but is furthermore a Jew. Kristeva has taken up Bloch's *défense*, looking first at Bloch's genesis from biographical, or in some cases only quasi-biographical, sources.[36] She then looks at his textual genetic origins, showing how Bloch's character grew by taking on aspects at first

---

[36] See *Le Temps sensible* (1994), 52–65. Sources include Léon Brunschvicg, editor of Pascal; Horace Finaly, director of the Banque de Paris; Rustinlor, the former teacher of Jean Santeuil, who uses a Homeric style of speech; Pierre Quillard; Albert Bloch, a professor in Buenos Aires, who signed the *Manifeste des cent quatre* organized by Proust and his friends in support of Dreyfus.

intended for Swann.[37] It is Swann whom the great-uncle (not yet the grandfather) teases by humming airs from Halévy and Scribe's opera, *La Juive*, and Saint-Saëns's *drame lyrique, Samson et Dalila*. Swann is in the first drafts of *Contre Sainte-Beuve*, written in 1909, and at that stage marked with his Jewish origins more strongly than later in the text's evolution. According to Kristeva, Bloch takes on Proust/Swann's 'culpabilité juive' (*Le Temps sensible*, 54). Bloch is 'français de fraîche date' (p. 55): 'il a cru que la meilleure façon de se faire une place dans ce pays de culture est de s'amouracher de Leconte de Lisle, le grand parnassien à la mode, et notamment de ses traductions en prose de l'*Iliade* et de l'*Odyssée*, pour en fabriquer son jargon à lui, Bloch, un jargon homérique' (p. 55). She asserts that: 'Le jargon est la voie obligée de l'étranger en français' (p. 55). Or again, 'On laisse s'exprimer les excentriques, les nouveaux venus, les métèques, qui naturellement en profitent pour exagérer dans cette marge de liberté qu'on leur a consentie'; again, 'porter la mode à son excès lui donne un aplomb époustouflant' (p. 55).

Kristeva sets out in a deliberately jaunty style to champion the underdog Bloch, but her language of the *marginaux* risks missing something else being played out in the text. Proustian 'culpabilité juive' there certainly is, but in the service of a manipulative narratorial experiment in the finely calibrated functioning of differential self-justification: Bloch is to stand as an example of one of the people to whom Saint-Loup 'était amené à faire des avances' (ii. 97; tr. ii. 366). In setting up his experimental study, Proust shows us two kinds of differentiating self-justification. One is imitative, or ironic, and the other is a denial:

Un jour que nous étions assis sur le sable, Saint-Loup et moi, nous entendîmes d'une tente de toile contre laquelle nous étions, sortir des imprécations contre le fourmillement d'Israélites qui infestait Balbec. 'On ne peut pas faire deux pas sans en rencontrer,' disait la voix. 'Je ne suis pas par principe irréductiblement hostile à la nationalité juive, mais ici il y a pléthore.' (ii. 97; tr. ii. 367)

The utterer of the anti-Semitic *imprécations* is immediately afterwards identified as Jewish, by his name ('C'était mon camarade

---

[37] See *Esquisse* XII (i. 681).

Bloch': ii. 97; tr. ii. 367). This metonymic shorthand explanation organizes a series of different sentence types that play a trick on the Jew without acknowledging it. Saint-Loup and the narrator are too close not to hear him, and Bloch is too close to his Semitic origins to escape mockery for his artificial amputation of his caste. Bloch's vulnerable exposure of the integrationist's desire to deny his own ethnic identity is a diversion in two senses. It is both ludicrous and it allows us to ignore the narrative context in which it is placed: that of a narratorial bid to pinpoint differences between himself and similar others (though the narrator is an integrationist in the guise of a social climber, and not as a Jew).

We have already seen Bloch's direct speech giving him away, exposing him as an outsider in the Faubourg (ii. 531; tr. iii. 267). Here, however, in gathering the evidence of proximity's dangers, we see another kind of giveaway: Saint-Loup's somatic symptoms of a generously pre-emptive forgiveness. Legrandin, in loosing his well-disciplined *bête immonde*, gives his snobbery away to a scrutinizing, accusatory narrator (ii. 501; tr. iii. 231). In response to Bloch's social gaffes, Saint-Loup blushes to demonstrate present tolerance, and future pity, if Bloch ever becomes aware of his error:

la gêne que la peur de froisser faisait naître en lui, chaque fois que quelqu'un de ses amis intellectuels commettait une erreur mondaine, faisait une chose ridicule, à laquelle lui, Saint-Loup, n'attachait aucune importance, mais dont il sentait que l'autre aurait rougi si l'on s'en était aperçu. Et c'était Robert qui rougissait comme si ç'avait été lui le coupable, par exemple le jour où Bloch lui promettant d'aller le voir à l'hôtel, ajouta: '. . . dites au "laïft" de les faire taire.' (ii. 97; tr. ii. 367)

The triangulated circuit that we have been seeing has moved in this direction:

dangerous proximity → judgement → differentiation.

Saint-Loup's action, however, *reverses* this movement: he notices a moment of marked difference of like from like, suspends his judgement by an act of will, but the effort of maintaining a tolerant proximity to the other's error itself generates a bodily excess, a blush.

The *colonie juive* at Balbec is a ready-made spectacle of 'un cortège homogène en soi et entièrement dissemblable des gens qui les regardaient passer' (ii. 98; tr. ii. 368: curiously analogous in this to the *petite bande*). It is momentarily entertained as a site of exclusivity, and, as such, similar to the mysteriously exclusive Faubourg Saint-Germain, but is almost immediately dismissed precisely on the grounds of that exclusivity:

De sorte qu'il est probable que ce milieu devait renfermer comme tout autre, peut-être plus que tout autre, beaucoup d'agréments, de qualités et de vertus. Mais pour les éprouver, il eût fallu y pénétrer. *Or, il ne plaisait pas, le sentait, voyait là la preuve d'un antisémitisme contre lequel il faisait front* en une phalange compacte et close où personne d'ailleurs ne songeait à se frayer un chemin. (ii. 98; tr. ii. 368; my emphasis)

Without irony, the narrator has told a parable of pre-emptively circular self-justification, that turns on *or* and *plaisait*. The differences marked by homogeneous groups within what they transform into larger heterogeneous groups lead to a resistance to any full dissolution (assimilation, integration) that is, ironically, maintained by two incompatible indifferences, from the minor group outwards, and the encompassing group towards it. Having a thin skin can lead to growing a protective hide. A standard reading of *A la recherche* accounts for its narrative structure as a succession of exclusivities, into which the narrator desires to penetrate, succeeds after some effort, and then abandons. Not so for Judaic exclusion zones. Bloch as borderline case, in trying to mark his distance from the defensiveness of exclusive introversion, is mercilessly marked out by the narrator through his intellectual errors. Where at Mme de Villeparisis's salon, Marcel tries to accommodate Bloch's excesses, here, he steps back to watch Saint-Loup perform the same function, in order to watch from the outside the dangerously proximate self-justification that threatens at all times to be born of magnanimity:

Mais la peur que Bloch, apprenant un jour qu'on dit Venice et que Ruskin n'était pas lord, crût rétrospectivement que Robert l'avait trouvé ridicule, fit que ce dernier se sentit coupable comme s'il avait manqué de l'indulgence dont il débordait et que la rougeur qui colorerait sans doute un jour le visage de Bloch à la découverte de son erreur, il la sentit par anticipation et réversibilité monter au sien. (ii. 99; tr. ii. 369)

When the narrator triumphs over Bloch by being the oracular revelation that *laïft* is pronounced *lift*, a further differential widening of the frames of reference within which this local experiment in dangerous proximity is taking place implicitly enables the narrator to write a superior because general version of Saint-Loup's indulgence. He absorbs the performances of both the other men into a gnomic pronouncement that demonstrates the capacity of dialectical thinking to kill its component parts in the joy of synthesis:

'Ah! on dit lift.' Et d'un ton sec et hautain: 'Cela n'a d'ailleurs aucune espèce d'importance.' . . . phrase tragique parfois qui la première de toutes s'échappe, si navrante alors, des lèvres de tout homme un peu fier à qui on vient d'enlever la dernière espérance à laquelle il se raccrochait, en lui refusant un service: 'Ah! bien, cela n'a aucune espèce d'importance, je m'arrangerai autrement', l'autre arrangement vers lequel il est sans aucune espèce d'importance d'être rejeté étant quelquefois le suicide. (ii. 99; tr. ii. 369–70)

This bid to take over the position of the high-minded *moralisateur* does not, however, end with the detailed local work of analysing Bloch's speech defects. Another conversation with Bloch is the springboard for a prolonged sequence of reflections on virtue and vice, a digression of four pages from the main narrative. Marcel's friend asks, rhetorically, 'Dis-moi, es-tu snob? Oui, n'est-ce pas?', and prompts a narratorial aside to the reader: ' "la mauvaise éducation" était son défaut, par conséquent le défaut dont il ne s'apercevait pas' (ii. 100; tr. ii. 370). Instead of passing politely over Bloch's bad taste, the narrative is obscured under a series of maxims, particular examples, and character portraits. Far from a leisurely perusal of alternative ethical behaviours inflicted by one's friends, we find, buried in the heart of this amorphous, permissive digression, a statement of such dangerous proximity to the concerns of this novel as a whole that the material that surrounds it begins to take on the aspect of wadding:

Et à la mauvaise habitude de parler de soi et de ses défauts il faut ajouter, *comme faisant bloc avec elle,* cette autre de dénoncer chez les autres des défauts précisément analogues à ceux qu'on a. Or, c'est toujours de ces défauts-là qu'on parle, comme si c'était une manière de parler de soi, détournée, et qui joint au plaisir de s'absoudre celui d'avouer. (ii. 102; tr. ii. 373; my emphasis)

An apparently expansive, humanist exploration of human morality suddenly starts to look queasy, as its boundaries are reached and found to turn back round upon the humanist himself. The would-be moralizer traps himself in an analogy, *comme faisant bloc avec elle*, which draws, not an abstract and secure conclusion, permitting the observer to remain on the sidelines, but a noose around the guilty self, progenitor and deflector of all his own evils.[38] The escapism of the sanctimonious seeker after truth is exposed and deflated: the writing narrator must be as mercilessly critical of himself, as he is of the Blochs and Saint-Loups, even in his sophisticated deferrals and self-improving differentiation from them. All that has gone before in the novel, all that is to come, demands to be reread through the puncture mark of this systematic denunciation and collapse of the architectural edifices of selfhood's security. There is, apparently, no escape. Beyond control and discipline, 'chaque vice, comme chaque profession, exige et développe un savoir spécial qu'on n'est pas fâché d'étaler. L'inverti dépiste les invertis, le couturier invité dans le monde n'a pas encore causé avec vous qu'il a déjà apprécié l'étoffe de votre vêtement' (ii. 102–3; tr. ii. 373). Try as we might, the narrator tells us, there is no avoiding our own narcissistic self-reflections from coming out. Whatever elaborate barriers we put up in the form of a personal moral hygiene, we are sure to give ourselves away. Not only are we bound to give ourselves away as soon as we speak about ourselves, or denounce faults in others, those same faults will be so entrenched that they will entail professional choices

---

[38] The opportunity is irresistible: Bloch the Jewish writer who justifies himself with repeated and overt vulgarity, and Marcel, here, chips off the same *bloc*. And they coincide too wonderfully with Freud's writing pad (and its intermittent cathexis); Saint-Loup, the honourable homosexual gentleman, who fights in the war and never cries 'Wolf', but has inherited the infant name given to Marcel Proust by his mother: too, too close to the nickname by which we know Freud's most significant case-study, the 'Wolf Man'. What precisely *is* the explanation for this uncanny, early-20th-cent., mid-European subtextual *enchaînement* of signifiers? It's all too true to be good: psychoanalysis supplies the glasses, and we are tempted to read through them, and find a satisfying explanation for such a set of coincidences; tempted, perhaps, to reduce self-justificatory behaviour to (hysterical) neurosis. My argument is not, however, that solutions to the problem of self-justification are to be found in any kind of psychological *diagnosis*. Self-justification is the *dynamic*, not just the *problem:* it is through the relentless attempts to find the ends of self-justification that moral thinking in *A la recherche* is plumbed and questioned.

which will mean exposure throughout our working lives. We do not need to profess our own sins, our professions bespeak them for us. Worldly professionalism is not the only regulating force ensuring the confession of vice, 'un dieu spécial est là qui lui cache ou lui promet l'invisibilité de son défaut' (ii. 103; tr. ii. 373): divine agencies intervene upon our best intentions, and cajole our egos into disseminating viciousness as though the rest of the world were blind. The apparently boundless freedom of the maxim-maker, the essay-writer, La Bruyère's, La Rochefoucauld's, or Montaigne's world, stretching away to all horizons with *carte blanche* on the pettiness and baseness of mankind, finds a sinister corrective in this tightly coiled self-reflection: in the midst of formulating the *caractère* of others, we will only ever be articulating our own.

5. ENVOI

Where in *Sodome et Gomorrhe* digressions hold up the narrative by distending it, here digression upholds the narrative integrity by ending itself. A sudden return to the everyday business of characterizing Bloch, with his *défauts de prononciation* and vulgar taste, his accusations of snobbery which give him away, comes as a blessed relief to the narrator, after being swept up into his own aside: 'Bloch était mal élevé, névropathe, snob et appartenant à une famille peu estimée supportait comme au fond des mers les incalculables pressions que faisaient peser sur lui non seulement les chrétiens de la surface, mais les couches superposées des castes juives supérieures à la sienne' (ii. 103; tr. ii., 374). Restratifying his narrative in a vertical hierarchy, the compensatory classificatory system which blinds itself to any excesses, preferring to label them misfits, the narrator can wilfully turn his back on the blind spot he has just glimpsed. The signification of universal guilt slips under such a top-heavy superpositioning, not lost, but stifled. If desire demands proximity, proximity does not always equal what is desired. We saw in the Faubourg evidence of the self-justificatory steps taken with the goal in mind of integration into a hostile environment. Here this activity finds a distressing corollary in terms of self-definition, or the building of one's own *caractère*. For Proust shows how rivalry and competitiveness, which may well be justified for the purposes of camouflage and disguise in the midst of danger, reverses into unjustifiable manipulativeness when used in the midst of like-minded others.

Threaded all the way through the narrative, sometimes in digressions, sometimes into anecdotes, often into the direct speech of other characters, comes, then, a fourth narrative problem, that of like-mindedness, to which the narrator of *A la recherche* pays insistent attention. If self-justification at parties had indeed *been* justified by being the attempt to be assimilated into an external social framework, the difficulties of discrimination find another outlet, and become more clearly a moral problem when we see how attempts are made to distinguish between the narrator's most closely held beliefs and those of similar others. This we might want to write off as one of the peculiar technical innovations of Proust's characterization, but its staging throughout the novel affords moments not only of *A la recherche*'s most comic tone, but of deep moral crisis. For in judging like-minded others critically, hostilely, or disparagingly, the narrator exposes himself to the potential for judgement to reverse upon its producer.

Dangerous proximity is an aspect of self-justification which requires detailed thought about whether relations of similitude are always, in Proust, indicators of a happy reversibility, the ways in which identity as being struggles against identity as sameness. Where Marcel is put into the position of like-mindedness with surrounding others, we see a new kind of pre-emptive self-justification taking place: a rapid mastery of the codes and commonplaces that form either an endo- or an exo-skeleton of the similar other, an imitation of these codes, a phenomenological assessment of the other which pays particular attention to an understanding of proximity and detachment, and finally a double movement, a rejection of the other followed by a compensation for the rejection, in the form of a forgiveness of their imagined faults. This is self-justification as differentiation, and it forces discussion of the interconnection between affective and ethical apprehension in this novel, an uncomfortable splitting of discrimination from incrimination. It is exactly such a discussion that forms the final part of this study.

III

Inwards

5

Under Cover of Mourning: The Ethics of Vulnerability

Il était bien, me disais-je, qu'en me demandant sans cesse ce qu'elle pouvait faire, penser, vouloir, à chaque instant, si elle comptait, si elle allait revenir, je tinsse ouverte cette porte de communication que l'amour avait pratiquée en moi, et sentisse la vie d'une autre submerger, par des écluses ouvertes, le réservoir qui n'aurait pas voulu redevenir stagnant.

(iv. 34; tr. v. 515)

Profonde Albertine que je voyais dormir et qui était morte.

(iv. 624; tr. vi. 450)

I. INTRODUCTION

Let us stop and take a moment or two to consider our discoveries about self-justification in *A la recherche*. After close analysis of different parts of the text, we have put together a portfolio of evidence that self-justificatory activity manifested as linguistic expression is a locus of moral dilemma for the Proustian narrator, whether at the empirical level of *histoire,* or the retrospective levels of *récit* and *narration*, and that he responds to this multi-faceted moral difficulty through keen experimentation, putting different parts of his, or other characters', cognitive or affective apparatus to the test of his own conclusions.

We should further remind ourselves that what we have so far seen is self-justification tested in relation to *external factors* of one kind or another. The narrator tests the security of different kinds of self-expression in the public arena of parties, assessing the possible degrees and types of sincerity, vulnerability, or self-interest permitted in a setting governed by a set of rigid assumptions of value and hierarchy. This interest in working out how public judgements are passed has a difficult side-effect, which we can identify playing itself out through one of the main rhetorical tropes of *A la recherche*. Through listening to the play between externally and internally professed opinion, permitted by the rhetorical trope of digression, we have become attuned to the minute adjustments and the moral dilemmas involved when the narrator thinks about how to pass critical judgement on others. If judgement passed on him is painful, and to be avoided, how can he pass judgement on others? This dilemma leads to bulges in the narrative, which are part of it, but do not contribute to it, tenuously attached and yet separated from the main thrust of the narrative, in which a great deal of raw material is stored, analysed, and abandoned before decisions have to be passed on its suitability for inclusion in a novel project. The inclusiveness of this approach is, once again, based on the fear of exclusion.

If it is at all possible to formulate judgements that are not mere opinions, ideologically motivated, or prompted by self-interest, it ought also to be possible to found them on some kind of stable epistemological footing. In *A la recherche*, however, Proust repeatedly demonstrates that difficult affective knowledge may be screened off, to be exposed—or *known*—under safer conditions. What is known may be either wilfully or involuntarily disowned, mislaid, recovered—and once again evaporate from consciousness. The move between empirical and abstract knowledge, the point at which a thing or an event, a sensation or a decision, finds itself identified, codified, and granted a positive or negative valency, such a move is acutely problematic for the Proustian narrator. To formulate such epistemological judgements simultaneously signifies abandoning the heroic work of intellectual excavation, the accumulation of evidence, the persistent self-doubt and consequent pleasurable anguish. Judgement also threatens to bring with it failure. Commitment seems to force dichotomy upon otherwise multiple outcomes to a knotty problem, whether the epistemological field be sexual, literary, mathematical, or political. Decisiveness does not entirely exclude the threat that an erroneous judgement will demand revision; nor does it do away with chance disaster, or conflict of interests. If anything, securing a perspective invites such conflict. Finally, all the careful work put into identifying how judgements are passed in public, and into juggling discrepant judgements within the confines of a rhetorical trope, can itself come into conflict with the desire or need to discriminate and differentiate between ostensibly like-minded selves, to find points of separation between self and other.

All of these protective and necessary, excessive and evasive manœuvres take place as relational movements between one subjectivity and another, or a group of others; and we now have ample evidence of the ease with which one kind of self-justification can turn into another. As a means of apprehending and sifting material that is external to the narrator, self-justification has shown its manifold uses. A tool for phenomenological interpretation, with a handily inbuilt auto-corrective function that marries acts of critical interpretation to the fine-tuning of social acceptability, thus safeguarding the narrator from either making a fool of himself, or becoming a social pariah, we can see that self-justification needs to be recognized as one of the major components powering Proust's narrative drive.

What we have not yet listened to, however, is the pain of self-justification when it takes place *wholly within* one subjectivity. Self-justification also occurs in *A la recherche* during stretches of it devoid of external props on which to lean, without further aristocrats to impress, or exciting discoveries to be made about human sexuality. The final section of my argument is concerned with the *limits* of self-justification's usefulness for *A la recherche du temps perdu*. It causes us to consider one of the bleakest and most critically resistant parts of the novel: *Albertine disparue*. This chapter concentrates on an attentive reading of the processes of narratorial vulnerability, suffering, and mourning in part of its first chapter, 'Le Chagrin et l'Oubli'. Once we have listened to the movements of this section of text with an ear attuned to the functioning of a new and very particular kind of self-justification, we will be in a better position to rethink both our preconceptions about how suffering works in *A la recherche*, and our conclusions to date on self-justification.

2. *ALBERTINE DISPARUE*

It is easy to forget that many events take place in this section of
the novel which are crucial to the overall structure of *A la
recherche*. Leaving for a moment the opening chapter, which
takes up almost half the text of the current Pléiade edition of
Albertine disparue, we should reacquaint ourselves with its broad
movements. Albertine's departure and death, most of it written
after 1914, swells the text internally by a full further volume
before the account of the First World War and the denouement
of the *Adoration perpétuelle* and the *Bal de têtes*, both the latter in
a well-established condition from 1910 onwards, and it also takes
on a vital responsibility for the novel's overall analysis of, and
experimentation in, transformation.[1] In it is articulated a
massive reorientation of the narratorial engagement with
others, that begins with the introspection and mourning of its
first part, followed by the reactivation of Marcel's desire for
morally slight women: to wit, his frenzy at spotting a woman he
believes to be Mlle d'Éporcheville, and who turns out to be
Gilberte, now adopted daughter of Forcheville. The reorientation is charted as a palindromic reversal out of mourning, blue-
printed in the text as 'quatre étapes' (iv. 139; tr. v. 639 has
instead 'there were three stages') of which three are in
evidence: the identification of Mlle de Forcheville, the second
conversation with Andrée, and the trip to Venice.[2] Submerged
proaieretic strands of *A la recherche*, buried under the mass of
repetitive minutiae of Albertine's sequestration and loss, are

---

[1] See the *Notice* of vol. iv of the 1987–9 Pléiade edn. for a fascinating and
detailed examination of the textual genesis of *Albertine disparue* (iv. 993–1038). This
explains the clear embedding of an episode detailing the love and loss of a 'greatest love' figure, as well as an investigation of lesbianism, from the earliest projects
for the novel; the major drafting of an episode of mourning between 1914 and 1915;
and the unresolvable authorial and editorial crisis over whether the long or the
excised version of *Albertine disparue* is the 'right' one. Christie McDonald analyses
the different effects produced by the two 'versions' of *Albertine disparue* left in
Proust's lifetime, speculating that the instability of this text reflects an uneasy authorial desire to quash the potentially limitless irruption of the pain of mourning while
yet producing that pain as fundamental to the novel's project: *The Proustian Fabric*
(1991), 132–53.
[2] It is tempting to suggest that the missing fourth *étape* is the reconfiguration
of Saint-Loup's identity, a discovery of his homosexuality, but strictly speaking this
falls subsequent to the mourning of Albertine.

here brought forward, reactivated, and developed: the publication of Marcel's childhood article by *Le Figaro* (iv. 148–51; tr. v. 649–54); the acceptance of Gilberte by the Guermantes after Swann's death (iv. 153–67 and 171; tr. v. 657–64 and 678); Andrée's marriage to Octave (in a proleptic digression, iv. 184–7; tr. v. 693); Venice (ch. 3, iv. 203–35; tr. 'Sojourn in Venice', v. 715–54); the marriage of Legrandin's nephew to Jupien's niece (iv. 236; v. 756); a visit to Tansonville and the coming together of Marcel's imagined two ways (iv. 268; tr. vi. 3). It is this reactivation, this illusion of events taking on a life of their own, and displaying their autonomy from the mental life of the narrator, their glorious inbreeding, and regeneration of themselves under new guises, which supplies the narrator's indifferent acceptance of things-as-they-are, his detachment from the production of allegorical flesh for his own psychological processes, which had hitherto marked his dealings with external reality.[3]

Perhaps most importantly, in *Albertine disparue*, revelations by women about their own and each other's sexual desires, whether heterosexual or homosexual, take on a significant status. Gilberte tells the narrator that she had desired him from their very first meeting (iv. 269; tr. vi. 4). Andrée visits Marcel three times in the course of this section.[4] She makes a different and contradictory form of confession or revelation about Albertine each time, and ends by suggesting that Albertine had left Marcel not out of sexual frustration, but because her hand was being forced by social considerations, pressure from her

---

[3] This so-called external reality, it must not be forgotten, is a textual reality. Episodes like the publication of a piece of juvenilia, the piece on the *clochers* at Martinville, in *Le Figaro*, operate both at the level of narrative development, and bring into focus the textual genesis of *A la recherche*. The *Figaro* publication is one of the oldest ideas *for* the novel, as well as the oldest piece of textual production *in* the novel. The projected visit to Venice, a text which never stopped evolving and reshaping itself, is another montage of idea-scraps dating from 1910–11 onwards. The obsession with the *femme de chambre de Mme Putbus*, of which only traces remain, is also an idea dating from the prehistory of the novel, but in contrast to the reactivation of the *Figaro* text, and the palimpsest feltwork of the Venice sequence, the residua of the Putbus affair shows how originally concrete ideas can turn into scaffolding for the novel project, and are finally either buried, become implicit armature for it, or are excised and dismantled.

[4] The first visit ends the first chapter of *Albertine disparue*, iv. 126; tr. v. 623. Then iv. 175; tr. v. 683; and iv. 193; tr. v. 703.

aunt to marry Octave and become respectable. Autonomous female desire appears for the first time in a form that has not been diverted through the narrator's jealous interpretation, with the onset of narratorial sexual indifference: 'Leur immobilité viendra de notre indifférence qui les livrera au jugement de l'esprit' (iii. 574; tr. v. 67), Marcel had once apostrophized, on girls. Now indifference arrives, but instead of judgement, arises splendid, candid, autonomous female sexuality.

As a fully functioning and integrated part of *A la recherche*, *Albertine disparue* has, however, disappeared strangely from critical view. One strategy in commentary has been to look at the less starved and evacuated territories of it, such as the 'Séjour à Venise'.[5] But even in commentaries whose arguments would seem to demand an assessment of its contents, the text itself is all but ignored, especially those parts of it which describe the flight and death of Albertine, and subsequent mourning for her. In *Love's Knowledge*, Martha Nussbaum names as a kind of affective cataleptic impression Proust's theory that other people are knowable through subjective suffering, but argues that all the suffering of *Albertine disparue* is contained in 'Mademoiselle Albertine est partie!'.[6] She says, at the end of her essay, that 'to make room for love stories, philosophy must be more literary, more closely allied to stories, and more respectful of mystery and open-endedness' (p. 284). Yet by concentrating her reading upon a single line from Proust's text, Nussbaum's account curiously avoids the dreadful prolongation of the governance of suffering, the sheer length of the account (some 140 pages) and its contamination of all the writing that proceeds from this shocking line.

Emmanuel Lévinas seems to be about to offer us some of that 'mystery and open-endedness', when he reads the Marcel–Albertine relation, against the grain of its apparent failure, as Proust's brilliant representation of the way in which responsibility for the Other manifests itself:

---

[5] See e.g. Peter Collier, *Proust and Venice* (1989), and Bowie, *Freud, Proust and Lacan* (1987). In the 1987 Mauriac and Wolff edn. of *Albertine disparue*, claimed to be the final state of the manuscript seen in the author's lifetime, only two parts of the text remain: the opening chapter and that describing the trip to Venice.

[6] *Love's Knowledge* (1990), 261.

Quand elle n'est plus là pour défendre son absence, quand les évidences abondent pour ne plus laisser place au doute, ce doute subsiste intégralement. Le néant d'Albertine découvre son altérité totale. La mort c'est la mort d'autrui contrairement à la philosophie contemporaine attachée à la mort solitaire de soi. Celle-là seule se place aux carrefours de la recherche du temps perdu. Mais la mort quotidienne et de tous les instants d'autrui qui se retire en lui-même, ne jette pas les êtres dans l'incommunicable solitude, c'est elle précisément qui nourrit l'amour. Eros dans sa pureté ontologique qui ne tient pas à une participation à un troisième terme,—goûts, intérêts communs, connaturalité des âmes,—mais relation directe avec ce qui se donne en se refusant, avec autrui en tant qu'autrui, avec le mystère.[7]

But Lévinas is bracketing *A la recherche* off into a vacuum without readers, characters, stories, or conflicts. His notion of ontological purity, dramatized as the erotic relation founded in a (daily) death of the Other, disregards the uncomfortable moral questions that are raised by duration and change, in favour of an atemporal, silent mystery. The process of mourning narrated in *Albertine disparue*, makes, on the contrary, insistent demands to be heard. Pain is unspeakable in this section of text—but it goes on speaking. Lévinas does not address the linguistic difficulties of asking a psychological state like mourning to give a morally justifiable account of itself. And he ignores one of the most important points about mourning, both in clinical psychological accounts of this peculiar state, and as it is portrayed in *Albertine disparue*, which is that mourning is a state whose stasis is imaginary and that it ineluctably comes to an end.[8] This, too, might cause some moral disquiet in the reader.

A notable exception to this shying away from the text of *Albertine disparue* is Richard Terdiman, who uses a reading of *La Fugitive* (he is using the 1954 Pléiade edition, revised by the 1987–9 edition) to support his thesis about authorial disenfranchisement in the nineteenth- to twentieth-century development

---

[7] Emmanuel Lévinas, 'L'Autre dans Proust', *Deucalion*, 2 (1947), 117–23.

[8] See Colin Murray Parkes, *Bereavement* (1996); John Bowlby, *Attachment and Loss* (1969). Bowlby's work draws on psychoanalysis, ethology, sociology, and anthropology to study the effects of separation. He reminds us that affective numbness, or apparent indifference in those undergoing the difficulties of separation, is evidence of self-protective attempts to keep pain in abeyance.

of the French novel.[9] Terdiman shows how total immersion in a traumatic mental state in *La Fugitive* is conveyed through grammatical slippages such as an unexpected use of the present tense, or the summarizing of whole temporal periods under *parfois*.[10] He gets over the difficulties of the text's incoherences by giving them a name: 'synthetic narration', a much over-used term in his account, raising the suspicion that it is a convenient catch-all for discrepancy.[11] Terdiman's assertion that Proust's narrative technique is *synthetic* is itself a critical synthesis of the text with which we are presented. It orders and attributes meaning to a text whose workings are relentlessly disordered, disjunctive, and unrecuperable, and thus functions as a shield hovering between the vulnerable disarray of Marcel's mourning and a readerly desire for controlled understanding of it. Something troubling has happened to *Albertine disparue*. It has been disowned by the collective memory of this novel. We do not want to know about what takes place in the sombre outback that occupies the textual space between Marcel's panicky sequestration of his beloved, and his dulled registering of the fact that the two ways were only ever one.

3. ANTE-MORTEM

Proust's representation of death in *A la recherche* consists almost wholly in mourning. When thanatology in relation to *A la recherche* is considered, indeed, it is usually in relation to the death of the narrator's grandmother. Even as commentators assert that her death is what they are looking at, however, we realize that they are reading Marcel's involuntary resurrection of her: there are very few instances of deathbed readings. The grandmother's death is actually presented by means of a series of clipped, crisp sentences, devoid of explicit pathos or pleas for sympathy on the part of the narrator:

Tout d'un coup ma grand-mère se dressa à demi, fit un effort violent, comme quelqu'un qui défend sa vie. Françoise ne put résister à cette vue et éclata en sanglots. Me rappelant ce que le médecin avait dit, je

---

9 *The Dialectics of Isolation* (1976), 224.   10 Ibid. 204–5; 214.
11 Ibid. 202, 203, 204, 205, as well as in other places.

voulus la faire sortir de la chambre. A ce moment, ma grand-mère ouvrit les yeux. Je me précipitai sur Françoise pour cacher ses pleurs, pendant que mes parents parleraient à la malade. Le bruit de l'oxygène s'était tu, le médecin s'éloigna du lit. Ma grand-mère était morte. (ii. 640; tr. iii. 397)

It is as a function of simplicity that the terror of death is communicated, by the unembellished physiological steps an organism may be seen to pass through as it expires. And when Marcel re-encounters her death as her resurrection by memory, the mourning process is formally contained, as we have seen, within the confines of a chapter, and staged in terms of a rather elegant mortuary aesthetic peculiar to involuntary memory. The pain of mourning is transmitted, for the grandmother at least, as the pleasure of mournful writing. The involuntary nature of the process of mourning narrated as a consequence of Albertine's death is, as we shall hear, diammetrically opposed to the controlled, pictorial quality of the first *intermittence du cœur* scene.

The narrative experiment we are about to confront, which has so spectacularly fallen out of our overall understanding of *A la recherche*, is nothing less than a sustained forcefeeding of the agonies and emptiness of another's absence back into the syntax of a text elsewhere so astonishingly proficient at amplifying plenitude, and multiplying the already complex. Here, what we must come to terms with is the acute pain of exposure to narratorial pain, the relentless, repetitive, skittering lexicon of nullity and despair. In my exploration of the remote textual wasteland that follows upon the news that Albertine is dead, I want to show, following the order that has been imposed by the *récit*, the faltering steps taken by Marcel in the name of recovery, the ways in which he tries to justify to himself the loss of Albertine.

4. READING MOURNING: THE DEATH OF ALBERTINE

This series of textual effects harbours surprises that are not straightforwardly concomitant with the surprises of the storytelling. One such is that we are never allowed to forget that Marcel's mourning consists in the textual revisiting and reordering of that mourning. For him, the surprise has been and gone once the act of relating it to a reader is under way. The irony of the absence that refuses to make sense, refuses to justify itself, is doubled by the irony of having to tell it again. Albertine's departure and death in a riding accident are explicitly preplotted into the narrative, which twitches with incessant bi-directional movement: narratorial dread of the unknown, overlaid by narratorial revisiting of an event, in order to write about it. There is a peculiar relationship in *A la recherche*, especially evident at the end of *La Prisonnière*, between *prolepsis*, the deliberate staging of anticipation which emphasizes tragic inevitability, and *paralepsis*, narratorial knowing that flies in the face of normative expectations about what he should know. Bearing down upon the inexorability of Albertine's escape is all the self-directed mockery and loathing of the narratorial goad: 'si la vie n'apporte pas de changements à nos amours, c'est nous-mêmes qui voudrons en apporter ou en feindre et parler de séparation, tant nous sentons que tous les amours et toutes choses évoluent rapidement vers l'adieu' (iii. 855; tr. v. 402). Think of the narrator's emotional reaction at the sight of his first aeroplane, which makes the horse he is riding swerve (iii. 417; tr. iv. 495), or a split-second reflection on the possibility of being jealous of a beloved after her death (iii. 594; tr. v. 91). There is the sight of Albertine asleep: 'Ce fut une morte en effet que je vis . . . ses draps, roulés comme un suaire autour de son corps, avaient pris, avec leurs beaux plis, une rigidité de pierre' (iii. 862; tr. v. 411). There is even the *explicit* premonition of Albertine's death in a riding accident:

'Je vous en prie, ma petite chérie, pas de haute voltige comme vous avez fait l'autre jour. Pensez, Albertine, s'il vous arrivait un accident!' Je ne lui souhaitais naturellement aucun mal. Mais quel plaisir si avec ses chevaux elle avait eu la bonne idée de partir je ne sais où, où elle se serait plu, et de ne plus jamais revenir à la maison![12] (iii. 627; v. 130)

Albertine's departure, like Isabel Archer's return to Rome, is one of European literature's truly great surprises: the crash-

---

[12] Other premonitory moments are to be found: 'Comme on fait à la veille d'une mort prématurée, je dressais le compte des plaisirs dont me privait le point final qu'Albertine mettait à ma liberté' (iii. 674; tr. v. 185). See also iii. 900, tr. v. 458; iii. 902, tr. v. 459; iii. 904, tr. v. 461.

ingly predictable, rendered by the gaggle of fellow characters who swarm to the edge of her absence and look uncomfortably after her.[13] While the heroine of James's novel ends it by exiting from it, however, Albertine's self-ejection from this novel, which revolves around expulsion, sucks all the air out with it and leaves behind nothing in the collapsed lung of the narrative but Marcel.

Another of the textual effects that dramatize vulnerability is more difficult to locate, since it consists, very precisely, in the unverifiability of pain. Marcel experiences shock *as the disbelieving attempt at consolation*, jumping straight from despair about an uncontrollable situation (Albertine's flight) to perfect assurance, and instant comprehension of the new situation (her death). Affective pain seems not to take place at all, or finds itself unsymbolized in the text. It relies on a readerly act of faith. The immediate aftermath of the telegram informing Marcel that Albertine is dead shifts from an attempt to verbalize his realization that she will not return: 'Mais ne m'étais-je pas dit plusieurs fois qu'elle ne reviendrait peut-être pas?' (iv. 58; tr. v. 544), to a description of a purely physical reaction:

Instinctivement je passai ma main sur mon cou, sur mes lèvres qui se voyaient embrassés par elle depuis qu'elle était partie, et qui ne le seraient jamais plus; je passai ma main sur eux, comme maman m'avait caressé à la mort de ma grand-mère en me disant: 'Mon pauvre petit, ta grand-mère qui t'aimait tant ne t'embrassera plus.' Toute ma vie à venir se trouvait arrachée de mon cœur. (iv. 59; tr. v. 544–5)

Ma main transforms into *Maman*, as he offers himself the remembered consolation at a previous death, of his mother's assumption of the role of his grandmother. The instinctively sexual act of touching himself, presenting himself with tangible evidence of Albertine's absence, fuses with an equally primitive need for a maternal consolation. If pain is unverifiable, it is also unspeakable. When Marcel says 'Toute ma vie à venir se trouvait

---

[13] *The Portrait of a Lady*, by Henry James (1881). Isabel's self-immolation takes place textually as the paragraph break after 'She had not known where to turn; but she knew now. There was a very straight path.' The next begins, 'Two days later Caspar Goodwood knocked at the door of the house in Wimpole Street ...' (p. 591).

arrachée de mon cœur', we know this to be a fabrication of the truth, which is that his life *has* continued, in some form. The part of pain that is uncommunicable seems to be its insistent, yet invisible, clutch on duration, symbolizable only in concentrate form.

The third textual effect that relentlessly forces itself upon us is the collapse of the narratorial function. Two telegrams from Albertine arrive after the news of her death. The first encourages Marcel to invite Andrée as her replacement. The second asks to be able to return to him: 'Car tout le temps j'avais imaginé dans l'absurde ses intentions qui n'avaient été que de revenir auprès de moi et que quelqu'un de désintéressé dans la chose, un homme sans imagination, le négociateur d'un traité de paix, le marchand qui examine une transaction, eussent mieux jugées que moi' (iv. 59–60; tr. v. 546). We find that we cannot gauge whether Marcel's bitterness is an instantaneous response, or whether it is a retrospective judgement of his own lack of judgement. It is one of the unreadabilities of *Albertine disparue* that Marcel the protagonist and Marcel the writing narrator become, not simply pleasurably intertwined, but glutinously indistinguishable. The moment of self-directed contempt at his own inability to stand detached from the pain he either is still undergoing, or has already gone through, also stands in for its own infinite recurrence; and for the dimly perceived recognition from within the coils of personal agony that the subjective perspective mutates eventually into the detached external perspective.

The self-justificatory ability to see ahead clearly, to imitate detachment ahead of time, however, is absolutely without purchase upon the *process* that will be necessary before that detachment is attained:

Pour que la mort d'Albertine eût pu supprimer mes souffrances, il eût fallu que le choc l'eût tuée non seulement en Touraine, mais en moi. Jamais elle n'y avait été plus vivante. Pour entrer en nous, un être a été obligé de prendre la forme, de se plier au cadre du temps; ne nous apparaissant que par minutes successives, il n'a jamais pu nous livrer de lui qu'un seul aspect à la fois, nous débiter de lui qu'une seule photographie. Grande faiblesse sans doute pour un être, de consister en une simple collection de moments; grande force aussi; il relève de la mémoire, et la mémoire d'un moment n'est pas instruite de tout ce qui s'est passé depuis; ce moment qu'elle a enregistré dure encore, vit encore, et avec lui l'être qui s'y profilait. Et puis cet émiettement ne fait pas seulement vivre la mort, il la multiplie. Pour me consoler, ce n'est pas une, c'est d'innombrables Albertine que j'aurais dû oublier. (iv. 60; tr. v. 546–7)

The dead endure, not because of their remarkably memorable personalities, but because their identities are grafted onto every single instant of time we have spent with them, each successive timeframe a separate, self-contained photographic image, functioning independently of all the others. Like a nightmare folktale army that reproduces itself as it is mown down, like the Hydra with its regrowing heads, or Macbeth's vision of the procession of kings, no amount of forgetting will erase all the images.[14]

Our fourth slow-dawning realization is that this experience, more than any of the others undergone by Marcel, partakes automatically of a universality none of his elaborate plotting or staging could have prepared for him, or he for it. The relation between writing and experiencing narrator, which as we have seen collapses into itself, also reverses: instead of keeping a tight grip on the possible outcomes of narrative, and being able to account sometimes perilously, but always brilliantly, for his own trials and misfortunes, the narrative at this point is taken over by the banal vastness of universal pain, that redundant knowledge that we all suffer in the same way. The death of Albertine is figured only *in absentia*. It is evacuated from direct representation (in strict accordance with first-person narrative coherence, since Marcel was not there to observe it with his own eyes), and signified by a simple telegram. The death is never questioned, and there is no public response to it, no funeral, no commentary by any of her friends or family. It is the fact, not the facts, of her death that suffices: the signifying detail, 'Albertine n'est plus' (iv. 58; tr. v. 544) ends all other significance. All the threads of Albertine's fictional existence, and its secondary fictionalization by Marcel in his suspicious imaginings, are tied to the full stop of the telegram. But the full stop of Albertine's insignificant death is a false ending. From

---

[14] William Shakespeare, *The Tragedy of Macbeth*, in *The Complete Oxford Shakespeare*, ed. Stanley Wells and Gary Taylor, 4 vols. (1987), iii. 1307–34: 4. 1. 85–139.

that full stop proceed a new set of narrative threads, those of mourning, whose movements, taut, or coiled upon themselves, broken and reknotted, offer us a literary representation of the mind in a state of grief. We are by now used to Marcel's astonishing capacity for adopting and adapting models of mind which enable him to negotiate, assimilate, and dissect external and internal data. But in entering a study of the state of mourning, our expectations might be different. The extreme trauma of losing an intimate other is itself, beyond any textual representation, a universal experience; and the telling of death is the most reiterable and reiterated accompaniment of death. The frequent efforts made by Marcel to erect his singular vision into a general law in this novel, most often through careful narrative preparation and triumphant anagnorisis (the *madeleine* episode and its ultimate complement, an elaborate restaging of its import on a bigger scale) are made redundant by the very content of the plotting used here. Albertine's death and Marcel's attendant suffering, as events which contain enough internal power to generate their own resonance, pathos, and signification as catastrophe even prior to textualization, are also events which transmit themselves intact, inexplicable because effectively needing no explanation. Yet explanation, a superabundance of it, is exactly what we find, plugging the aching gap between loss and the recovery from loss.

Memories we might expect, in a novel about retracing the past, and here, of course they are, explicitly figured as internal explosions: 'je me détournais violemment, sous la décharge douloureuse d'un des mille souvenirs invisibles qui à tout moment éclataient autour de moi dans l'ombre' (iv. 61; tr. v. 547). But there is something odd about these memories. When Françoise opens the curtains, a 'rayon de soleil ancien qui m'avait fait paraître belle la façade neuve de Bricqueville l'Orgueilleuse' (iv. 61; tr. v. 547) introduces the action of light as a catalyst to memory which is reiterated over several pages of text: 'Ce n'était plus assez de fermer les rideaux, je tâchais de boucher les yeux et les oreilles de ma mémoire' (iv. 62; tr. v. 548). The very act of trying to close down his memory enables it to function, reminding him of the 'bande orangée du couchant', and the 'invisibles oiseaux', 'l'humidité des feuilles' and 'la montée et la descente des routes en dos d'âne' (iv. 62; v.

548–9). The remembered objects grip him: 'Mais déjà ces sensations m'avait ressaisi, ramené assez loin du moment actuel, afin
qu'eût tout le recul, tout l'élan nécessaire pour me frapper de
nouveau, l'idée qu'Albertine était morte' (iv. 62; tr. v. 549). He
craves total darkness, but is reminded of the light by 'la partie
vitrée' (iv. 63; tr. v. 550) of the door, and 'une étoile vue à côté
de l'arbre de la cour' (iv. 63; tr. v. 550). Daytime, sunshine, and
moonlight signify the onslaught of memories: 'la pureté
naturelle d'un rayon de lune au milieu des lumières artificielles
de Paris, . . . en faisant rentrer un instant pour mon imagination la ville dans la nature' (iv. 63–4; tr. v. 551) opens up a
memory of a countryside walk with Albertine. The dawn
reminds him of the summer in Balbec spent taking each other
home in the small hours. Yet what is so odd is the sense that
Marcel is merely going through the motions. Here, we might
find ourselves thinking, is his big chance, the one event that no
one can take away from him, the description of pure loss, of
grief and pain, those eminently literary subjects. And the narrator seems indifferent to the full sparkle and play of the array of
pain's vocabulary available to him.

There is an explanation for this tired-looking rehearsal of
the processes of pain given in the text, and it centres very
precisely upon the function of indifference in the workings of
mourning. This play of light and dark and its effect upon the
functioning of memory, Marcel tells us, is less vital to our
understanding of suffering than is the ceaseless intercutting of
suffering with the anticipation of future indifference. The
unavoidable arrival of forgetfulness is meshed into the analysis
which suffering induces:

Je n'avais plus qu'un espoir pour l'avenir—espoir bien plus déchirant
qu'une crainte—, c'était d'oublier Albertine. Je savais que je l'ou-
blierais un jour, j'avais bien oublié Gilberte, Mme de Guermantes,
j'avais bien oublié ma grand-mère. Et c'est notre plus juste et plus
cruel châtiment de l'oubli si total, paisible comme ceux des
cimetières, par quoi nous nous sommes détachés de ceux que nous
n'aimons plus, que nous entrevoyions ce même oubli comme
inévitable à l'égard de ceux que nous aimons encore. A vrai dire nous
savons qu'il est un état non douloureux, un état d'indifférence. Mais
ne pouvant penser à la fois à ce que j'étais et à ce que je serais, je
pensais avec désespoir à tout ce tégument de caresses, de baisers, de

sommeils amis, dont il faudrait bientôt me laisser dépouiller pour jamais. (iv. 64; tr. v. 551)

Perhaps the increasing difficulties of reconciling the discrepancies between our expectations and the textual realities of Marcel's mourning have to do with an unexpected *continuity* between our previous expectations of Proust's mode of storytelling, and the narration of mourning's atemporal flux. In another novel, the loss of a recognizable time-scale would itself constitute a convention by which to recognize trauma or instability,[15] but in *A la recherche*, temporal fluidity, repetition, flashback, and an incommensurability between narrative space devoted to an event, and normative expectations of such an event's duration based on the convention of *vraisemblance*, have been established as the very medium of narration.

Shifts between incommensurable tenses might then perhaps be read as attempts at self-justification in the mode of reassurance: 'Sans doute ces nuits si courtes durent peu. L'hiver finirait par revenir, où je n'aurais plus à craindre le souvenir des promenades avec elle jusqu'à l'aube. … Mais les premières gelées ne me rapporteraient-elles pas, conservé dans leur glace, le germe de mes premiers désirs … ?' (iv. 65; tr. v. 552–3). Reassurance is undone even as it is attempted: tenses sought as immobilizers of time in one or other state fail as explanations of another's death or recovery from it, in that they give way to one another during the process of reflection upon them. This seems a satisfactory explanation: temporal fluidity and slippage does not strike us as unusual in a novel whose opening line leaves us floundering about for a beginning, and reassuring ourselves that the narrative's slipperiness here is a reflection of slippery mental processes, in which self-justification is part of healing, goes a long way to accounting for it.

But worse is to come. The text is not behaving at all as it should. Where is the black armband, the lyrical evocation of Albertine's lost loveliness? Of all the emotions to be experienced in the wake of the death of a beloved other, jealousy seems perhaps the most obscene and shameless, the most inexplicably promiscuous of the opportunistic degradations visited

---

[15] In Alain Robbe-Grillet's *La Jalousie* (1957), for example. See Ann Jefferson, *The Nouveau Roman and the Poetics of Fiction* (1980), 133–43.

upon the suffering self, and the most in need of some kind of justification.

Even before the sequence of Aimé's successive forays to Balbec and Touraine to investigate Albertine's lesbianism, a justification of post-mortem jealousy is offered, as being a function of selfhood's multiplication in different temporal orders:

> Puisque rien qu'en pensant à elle, je la ressuscitais, ses trahisons ne pouvaient jamais être celles d'une morte, l'instant où elle les avait commises devenant l'instant actuel, non pas seulement pour Albertine mais pour celui de mes moi subitement évoqué qui la contemplait. De sorte qu'aucun anachronisme ne pouvait jamais séparer le couple indissoluble où à chaque coupable nouvelle s'appariait aussitôt un jaloux lamentable et toujours contemporain. (iv. 72; tr. v. 560)

But just as jealousy disseminates its way into the very bloodstream of evocation, its pernicious presence has side-effects on the coherence of attempts to account for it. Some time after her death, Marcel remembers a stray oddity of Albertine's behaviour: 'Tout d'un coup c'était un souvenir que je n'avais pas revu depuis bien longtemps. . . . comme on parlait de son peignoir de douche, Albertine avait rougi' (iv. 73; tr. v. 561). The decision to investigate the secrets potentially gathered behind this minute memory passes from rational to obsessional, through a self-justificatory displacement and redefinition of how the imagination is constituted:

> Comme la constitution de l'imagination, restée rudimentaire, simpliste (n'ayant pas passé par les innombrables transformations qui remédient aux modèles primitifs des inventions humaines, à peine reconnaissables, qu'il s'agisse de baromètre, de ballon, de téléphone, etc., dans leurs perfectionnements ultérieurs), ne nous permet de voir que fort peu de choses à la fois, ce souvenir de l'établissement de douches occupait tout le champ de ma vision intérieure. (iv. 73; tr. v. 562)

If we can accept that post-mortem jealousy might be part of the breaking down of introjected Gestalt images of the beloved, a way of forgetting by degrading and recycling the past, this reshuffling of *l'imagination*'s constitution, in other parts of the novel Marcel's favoured mental category, imposes a new incoherence that we must swallow. *Imagination* has suddenly taken on a new personification and responsibility, that of crude apologist for jealousy's antics. Where no externally justifiable reason may be given for jealousy, an abstract noun, with its capacious and slippery definitional contours, is enlisted to cover the deficit.

The semi-allegorization of *imagination* as independent agency, rather than component of an individual's psychological profile, conceals a multitude of more dubious possible explanations for post-mortem jealousy. Nothing characterizes this section of text so much as a narratorial *indifference* to the sustained coherence of the explanatory metaphors, paradigms, or allegories that are ceaselessly being put forward. They are abandoned as soon as uttered, contravened by the next reference made to them. A moment later, Marcel sees investigation as a duty, enforced by his own continued doubts: 'j'aurais dû depuis bien longtemps me livrer à des enquêtes' (iv. 74; tr. v. 563). When he adds: 'On eût dit qu'il n'y avait rien eu d'autre dans toute la vie d'Albertine' (iv. 74; situated earlier in the translation, v. 562), a revision of the slightly earlier 'ce souvenir de l'établissement de douches occupait tout le champ de ma vision intérieure' (iv. 73; tr. v. 562) redistributes degrees of attachment to the object, inserting a layer of observational detachment, *On eût dit*, which, while it reinflects the earlier over-involvement, also introduces its own temporal confusion. What is so hard to read here is not that Marcel should be in pain, but that pain should *take the form of jealousy*, and that our hitherto reliably ironic, detached narrator should have lost control, to the extent of lying blatantly to us.

The action of deciding to send Aimé on an investigative quest has as a concomitant feature a moment of impropriety in the form of a spectacularly bigoted appraisal of the man, based on class stereotyping:

il appartenait à cette catégorie de gens du peuple soucieux de leur intérêt, fidèles à ceux qu'ils servent, indifférents à toute espèce de morale et dont—parce que si nous les payons bien, dans leur obéissance à notre volonté, ils suppriment tout ce qui l'entraverait car ils se montrent aussi incapables d'indiscrétion, de mollesse ou d'improbité que dépourvus de scrupules—nous disons: 'Ce sont de braves gens.' (iv. 74; tr. v. 563)

Just as Marcel had attributed mercenary motives to the Bontemps (iv. 5; tr. v. 479), and just as he and Saint-Loup had discussed the economic bases to sexual bargaining (iv. 55–6; tr. v. 540–1), here a social analysis exceeds limits we might hope to place upon it (those of tolerance, or appreciation), and reveals itself as virulent snobbery.

Its secondary function, however, is to throw the permissiveness of context into relief: Marcel's snobbery may itself come under the governance of mourning, if it is relabelled as an unwitting expediency born of uncontrollable grieving. Marcel, in being abandoned, abandons himself to the state of abandonment, turning the narration of self into devastation told as moral unravelling.

The action of sending Aimé returns Albertine to him as though by an accidental sighting of an unposed photograph:

l'idée de cette question que j'aurais voulu, qu'il me semblait que j'allais lui poser, ayant amené Albertine à mon côté, non grâce à un effort de résurrection mais comme par le hasard d'une de ces rencontres qui—comme cela se passe dans les photographies qui ne sont pas 'posées', dans les instantanés—laissent toujours la personne plus vivante, en même temps que j'imaginais notre conversation, j'en sentais l'impossibilité; je venais d'aborder par une nouvelle face cette idée qu'Albertine était morte, Albertine qui m'inspirait cette tendresse qu'on a pour les absentes dont la vue ne vient pas rectifier l'image embellie, inspirant aussi la tristesse que cette absence fût éternelle et que la pauvre petite fût privée à jamais de la douceur de la vie. Et aussitôt, par un brusque déplacement, de la torture de la jalousie je passais au désespoir de la séparation. (iv. 74–5; tr. v. 563–4)

His action motivates a transition from jealousy to tenderness, together with a series of revisions of Albertine's status and value. Yet even as this revision is accomplished, an analysis which contradicts and subverts it is produced: 'mon chagrin se rapportait, non à ce qu'Albertine avait été pour moi, mais à ce que mon cœur, désireux de participer aux émotions les plus générales de l'amour, m'avait peu à peu persuadé qu'elle était' (iv. 75; tr. v. 564).

At every stage of the transitions of mourning, detached, observational, or cynical analysis is generated which seeks to capture, but which annihilates, the previous stage. And if the preceding sequence of revisions about Albertine's worth have facilitated a moment of tenderness towards her ('la pauvre petite'), that tenderness further mutates into self-pity:

Et j'avais alors, avec une grande pitié d'elle, la honte de lui survivre. Il me semblait, en effet, dans les heures où je souffrais le moins, que je bénéficiais en quelque sorte de sa mort, car une femme est d'une plus grande utilité pour notre vie, si elle y est, au lieu d'un élément de bonheur, un instrument de chagrin, et il n'y en a pas une seule dont la possession soit aussi précieuse que celle des vérités qu'elle nous découvre en nous faisant souffrir. Dans ces moments-là, rapprochant la mort de ma grand-mère et celle d'Albertine, il me semblait que ma vie était souillée d'un double assassinat que seule la lâcheté du monde pouvait me pardonner. (iv. 78; tr. v. 567)

The over-compensatory auto-accusation which combines Albertine's death with an incommensurable partner death, the grandmother's, functions doubly. It is both an enactment of the hyperbole governed by suffering, a means of managing distress by expressing it as excessive guilt—but also an evasion of any kind of actual responsibility for Albertine's life.

When this moment of guilt is followed by a series of summative and austere sentences disposing aphoristically of romantic love as an illusion and a euphemism for the desire to possess and control the other, duplicity of their foundation opens onto two kinds of reading. Here are four of the statements consequent upon Marcel's self-blame:

[i] On désire être compris parce qu'on désire être aimé, et on désire être aimé parce qu'on aime. La compréhension des autres est indifférente et leur amour importun. (iv. 78; tr. v. 568)

[ii] Ma joie d'avoir possédé un peu de l'intelligence d'Albertine et de son cœur ne venait pas de leur valeur intrinsèque, mais de ce que cette possession était un degré de plus dans la possession totale d'Albertine, possession qui avait été mon but et ma chimère depuis le premier jour où je l'avais vue. (iv. 78; tr. v. 568)

[iii] Quand nous parlons de la 'gentillesse' d'une femme, nous ne faisons peut-être que projeter hors de nous le plaisir que nous éprouvons à la voir. (iv. 78; tr. v. 568)

[iv] Ce qui explique par ailleurs que les hommes ne disent jamais d'une femme qui ne les trompe pas: 'Elle est si gentille,' et le disent si souvent d'une femme par qui ils sont trompés. (iv. 78; tr. v. 568)

Auto-accusation is self-justificatory to the extent that it posits an exaggerated, unviable interpretation of an individual's actions

in the hope that an audience will reinterpret and reduce the scale
of the exaggeration, dividing self-blame into a minor misdemeanour and pity for the individual's self-inflicted suffering.
Self-blame, in other words, is a persuasive trope whose rhetorical identification tag is hyperbole, but it is risky to the extent
that an audience cannot be relied upon to respond with pity. It
must be staged or couched within a context which already facilitates empathy. The 'erreur de localisation consécutive à
certains accidents mais tenace' (iv. 79; tr. v. 568) by which
Albertine as being, lover, text, is transferred inwards, inside the
narrator, diminished and evaporated by the narration of grief,
is a movement that leaves no trace of itself behind: the insecure
footing of an ambivalence both psychological and textual can
never be fully interpreted. The two kinds of reading that I
mentioned earlier are, then, simply that Marcel's telling of his
own sadness is the absolute truth and an absolute fabrication of
the truth. From a paucity of events flails a tattered collage, a
makeshift response. In it, the *moi* is simultaneously represented
both as an imaginary site into which Albertine has been introjected, and as a rapidly dwindling and shrinking site of possible
symbolization:

Tous ces instants si doux que rien ne me rendrait jamais, je ne peux
même pas dire que ce que me faisait éprouver leur perte fût du
désespoir. Pour être désespéré, cette vie qui ne pourra plus être que
malheureuse, il faut encore y tenir. J'étais désespéré à Balbec quand
j'avais vu se lever le jour et que j'avais compris que plus un seul ne
pourrait être heureux pour moi. J'étais resté aussi égoïste depuis lors,
mais le moi auquel j'étais attaché maintenant, le moi qui constituait
ces vives réserves qui mettent en jeu l'instinct de conservation, ce moi
n'était plus dans la vie; quand je pensais à mes forces, à ma puissance
vitale, à ce que j'avais de meilleur, je pensais à certain trésor que j'avais
possédé (que j'avais été seul à posséder puisque les autres ne
pouvaient connaître exactement le sentiment, caché en moi, qu'il
m'avait inspiré) et que personne ne pouvait plus m'enlever puisque je
ne le possédais plus. Et à vrai dire je ne l'avais jamais possédé que
parce que j'avais voulu me figurer que je le possédais. Je n'avais pas
commis seulement l'imprudence, en regardant Albertine avec mes
lèvres et en la logeant dans mon cœur, de la faire vivre au-dedans de
moi, ni cette autre imprudence de mêler un amour familial au plaisir
des sens. J'avais voulu aussi me persuader que nos rapports étaient
l'amour, que nous pratiquions mutuellement les rapports appelés

amour, parce qu'elle me rendait docilement les baisers que je lui donnais. Et pour avoir pris l'habitude de le croire, je n'avais pas perdu seulement une femme que j'aimais, mais une femme qui m'aimait, ma sœur, mon enfant, ma tendre maîtresse. (iv. 80; tr. v. 569–70)

I have quoted at such length because of the startling degree to which self is proposed as the precise location of relentless self-exposure and self-cannibalization. That is, rather than discharge a secret, explain an action, or offer a confession, Marcel as narratorial identity is lost from view and in his place a listless but insistent despoiling of selfhood's accoutrements is doggedly undertaken. The degradation of Albertine's image is being gradually taken over by the narratorial self, and we no longer know whether the recessive pain that is so clearly being staged as a courtroom drama, with the narrator as accused and accuser, condemning himself over and over again, is somehow a pleasurable self-flagellation or a serious portrayal of self-immolation. Where are the boundaries? Where is our comforting narratorial agency; we want his capacious, fleet-footed multiplicity back.

Here more clearly than anywhere else in the novel, we hear the struggle to apprehend the epistemology of alterity, through the very attempt to account for the termination of another's alterity. It is a struggle, however, that can only take a portion of the past into account, cannot bear to feed into it the possibility of future difference:

En perdant la vie je n'aurais pas perdu grand-chose; je n'aurais plus perdu qu'une forme vide, le cadre vide d'un chef-d'œuvre. Indifférent à ce que je pouvais désormais y faire entrer, mais heureux et fier de penser à ce qu'il avait contenu, je m'appuyais au souvenir de ces heures si douces, et ce soutien moral me communiquait un bien-être que l'approche même de la mort n'aurait pas rompu. (iv. 81; tr. v. 570–1)

While a multiplicity of logics may be used to explain animate processes, the death of Albertine reduces logical alternatives to two. The *rythme binaire* of the jealous imagination which had seemed so rigorous and so deluded throughout *La Prisonnière* is reduced still further, to a nonsensical algorithm, by the death of the beloved other: no longer Albertine loves me/Albertine is a lesbian, but Albertine is dead/I must go on living. The forensic investigation of the terms of endearment which had built such towering constructions of insecurity is not so much proven to be methodologically suspect by Albertine's death, as left suddenly purposeless, evacuated of meaning. Signification is simply withdrawn; intention, desire, pursuit, and orientation instantaneously rendered pointless:

Tout cela qui n'était pour moi que souvenir avait été pour elle action, action précipitée, comme celle d'une tragédie, vers une mort rapide. Les êtres ont un développement en nous, mais un autre hors de nous . . . et qui ne laissent pas d'avoir des réactions l'un sur l'autre. J'avais eu beau, en cherchant à connaître Albertine, puis à la posséder tout entière, n'obéir qu'au besoin de réduire par l'éxpérience à des éléments mesquinement semblables à ceux de notre moi, le mystère de tout être, je ne l'avais pu sans influer à mon tour sur la vie d'Albertine. (iv. 81; tr. v. 571)

The death of the beloved other has a significant remainder. Psychological investigation can no longer be apprehended as the epistemological pursuit of the singular self's signification. The deviations that alterity might have been thought to cause a securely bounded self to undertake, skilful feints and swerves which yet preserve it intact, impact upon that otherness, and cause it to deviate as well; while 'otherness', in return, traverses and inflects self. Marcel has had an effect on Albertine, and she on him:

Si bien que cette longue plainte de l'âme qui croit vivre enfermée en elle-même n'est un monologue qu'en apparence, puisque les échos de la réalité la font dévier, et que telle vie est comme un essai de psychologie subjective spontanément poursuivi, mais qui fournit à quelque distance son 'action' au roman purement réaliste, d'une autre réalité, d'une autre existence, dont à leur tour les péripéties viennent infléchir la courbe et changer la direction de l'essai psychologique. (iv. 82; tr. v. 571–2)

Here displaced onto a piece of textual taxonomy, classifying the 'longue plainte de l'âme' as a dramatic monologue, an essay on psychology, or a realist novel, is a cautious acknowledgement that external factors may overlap, conflict with, and cause deviations in subjective apprehension. The *monologue* is seen as a hybrid, permeable, and malleable account of self, and not a focused and independent announcement of personal needs, desires, and goals. It is a tentative postulation that amounts to an entire revaluation of conceptual priorities for Marcel. The nature of self-justification can no longer be conceived, Marcel realizes, as a contestatory struggle that seeks to safeguard a reassuringly known quota of interests, motivations, talents, or ideals, but an unmitigated exposure to cross-currents of alterity which inflect and reshape a wholly permeable and vulnerable *moi.*

Yet even as Marcel seems to accept that otherness passes through and inflects his own sense of self, he is busily pursuing new sets of explanations that will recontain the enormity of Albertine's death. Even now, at a moment of possible acceptance of either her death or her autonomy, we find him speculating on causality, necessity, plausibility. Intense moments of psychological and interpersonal revelation have *no permanent purchase* upon his continually unravelling cognition of the state of mourning. After all, it didn't *have* to be Albertine: 'ç'aurait pu ne pas être elle que j'eusse aimée, que c'eût pu être une autre' (iv. 83; tr. v. 573). He takes a physiological standpoint to assess the possible connections to be drawn between Gilberte and Albertine, but their physical types are opposites; so he immediately abandons this hypothesis in favour of another kind of theory of similarity:

pourtant elles avaient la même étoffe de santé, et dans les même joues sensuelles toutes les deux un regard dont on saisissait difficilement la signification. . . . Je pouvais presque croire que la personnalité sensuelle et volontaire de Gilberte avait émigré dans le corps d'Albertine, un peu différent il est vrai, mais présentant, maintenant que j'y réfléchissais après coup, des analogies profondes. (iv. 83–4; tr. v. 574)

It is as though, bent on producing plausibility for his current disorientation, he were reaching for Frazer's principles of primitive magical effect: 'First, that like produces like, or that an effect resembles its cause; and second, that things which have once been in contact with each other continue to act on each other at a distance after the physical contact has been severed. The former principle may be called the Law of Similarity, the latter the Law of Contact or Contagion'.[16]

---

[16] James Frazer, *The Golden Bough* (1993), 11.

The pursuit of explanatory analogies between Albertine and Gilberte seemingly cannot be abandoned. We find ourselves plunged into a series of partial repetitions, and hesitant expositions of possible chronologies, attempting to demonstrate the connectedness of the two women:

[i] Je pouvais presque croire que l'obscure personnalité, la sensualité, la nature volontaire et rusée de Gilberte étaient revenues me tenter, incarnées cette fois dans le corps d'Albertine, tout autre et non pourtant sans analogies. (iv. 84; tr. v. 574)

[ii] Pour Albertine, grâce à une vie toute différente ensemble et où n'avait pu se glisser, dans un bloc de pensées où une douloureuse préoccupation maintenait une cohésion permanente, aucune fissure de distraction et d'oubli, son corps vivant n'avait point, comme celui de Gilberte, cessé un jour d'être celui où je trouvais ce que je reconnaissais après coup être pour moi (et qui n'eût pas été pour d'autres) les attraits féminins. (iv. 84; tr. v. 574)

[iii] A l'aide de Gilberte j'aurais pu aussi peu me figurer Albertine et que je l'aimerais, que le souvenir de la sonate de Vinteuil ne m'eût permis de me figurer son septuor. (iv. 84; tr. v. 574)

[iv] cette femme unique, nous savons bien que c'eût été une autre qui l'eût été pour nous, si nous avions été dans une autre ville que celle où nous l'avons rencontrée ... Unique, croyons-nous? elle est innombrable. Et pourtant elle est compacte, indestructible devant nos yeux qui l'aiment, irremplaçable pendant très longtemps par une autre. C'est que cette femme n'a fait que susciter par des sortes d'appels magiques mille éléments de tendresse existant en nous à l'état fragmentaire et qu'elle a assemblés, unis, effaçant toute lacune entre eux, c'est nous-même qui en lui donnant ses traits avons fourni toute la matière solide de la personne aimée. (iv. 85; tr. v. 575).

Reaching after firm positions from which to ascertain control or dominance over the necessity of Albertine, her representation is shuffled from the concrete to the essential. The plethora of possible explanatory paradigms is put forward not as a reasoned construction, but as a permanently variable assortment of logical fragments, each abandoned in favour of a further momentary theoretical stasis: from coagulation, to magic, to unpredictability, to fragmentation, to psychological projection, to habit, to aberrant causalities, to economic forces, no single discourse can supply the truth of loving Albertine. The unstable leafing through this series of discourses external to his own past ultimately comes to rest, though not on a particular representation of femininity or causality. Contingency and unverifiability have been displaced onto a model of self as a set of anxieties, *a permanently fruitful source of predetermined failure*, failure inscribed as a series of fortuitous abandonments:

> Or à partir d'un certain âge nos amours, nos maîtresses sont filles de notre angoisse; notre passé, et les lésions physiques où il s'est inscrit, déterminent notre avenir. Pour Albertine en particulier, qu'il ne fût pas nécessaire que ce fût elle que j'aimasse était, même sans ces amours voisines, inscrit dans l'histoire de mon amour pour elle, c'est-à-dire pour elle et ses amies. (iv. 86; tr. v. 577)

He has ample evidence to sustain this dark vision of predetermination. By recalling the *jeunes filles*, it is a simple matter to put forward the proposition that: 'l'amour avait été alternatif et par conséquent, en somme, il n'y en avait eu qu'un à la fois' (iv. 87; tr. v. 578). By stepping back into the past out of which the uniqueness of Albertine had been constructed, he can benefit from the confusion and arbitrariness of a whole set of female units, rather than focus on the one for which he had ultimately taken responsibility. For every choice he did not make, another opportunity for failure. He remembers little arguments with some of the girls:

> Celle qui ferait les premiers pas me rendrait le calme, c'est l'autre que j'aimerais si elle restait brouillée. . . . Or il arrivait que persuadé que l'une ou l'autre au moins allait revenir à moi, aucune des deux pendant quelque temps ne le faisait. Mon angoisse était donc double, et double mon amour. . . . *C'est le lot d'un certain âge, qui peut venir très tôt, qu'on soit rendu moins amoureux par un être que par un abandon*, où de cet être on finisse par ne plus savoir qu'une chose, sa figure étant obscurcie, son âme inexistante, votre préférence toute récente et inexpliquée: c'est qu'on aurait besoin pour ne plus souffrir qu'il vous fît dire: 'Me recevriez-vous?' *Ma séparation d'avec Albertine, le jour où Françoise m'avait dit: 'Mademoiselle Albertine est partie,' était comme une allégorie de tant d'autres séparations.* Car bien souvent, pour que nous découvrions que nous sommes amoureux, peut-être même pour que nous le devenions, il faut qu'arrive le jour de la séparation. (iv. 87–8; tr. v. 578–9; my emphasis)

This deeply satisfactory and richly evidenced justification to himself of innumerable half-remembered separations, a multitude of minute abandonments within his own past, provides him with an unassailable configuration of predetermination that is entirely predicated on aligning previously independent factors by means of one kind of resemblance, that of separation.

Its unassailability also sets up a pathway to generalization: 'Mensonges, erreurs, en deçà de la réalité profonde que nous n'apercevions pas, vérité au-delà, vérité de nos caractères dont les lois essentielles nous échappaient et demandent le Temps pour se révéler, vérité de nos destins aussi' (iv. 89; tr. v. 580). The mournful tone of this lament has the formal quality of an elegy, with its strong repetition of *vérité*, and its evocation of and dependence on abstract nouns making it a literary sentence type. Yet its paucity of referentiality, even if only a reference to the Marcel–Albertine story, exercises a strangely anaesthetizing effect, deadening the rawness of the narrative. These 'successful', overarching sentences, which we might be tempted to extract from *Albertine disparue* as evidence of Proust's ability to write about painful affective and psychological states, are also, and surprisingly, what is most foreign, most borrowed about that writing, because most completely finished.

There follows a fantasy about Albertine's death. Its tone shadows that of the elegy to truth. This time it is the quavering repetition of *peut-être* which lends the sentence its specially heightened quality of hopeless appeal, or wish. Here again we are confronted with a reliance on the codifications and clichés of death, and with our everyday stock of commonplaces about it:

peut-être, dans ces dernières lueurs si rapides mais que l'anxiété du moment divise jusqu'à l'infini, elle avait peut-être bien revu notre dernière promenade, et dans cet instant où tout nous abandonne et où on se crée une foi, comme les athées deviennent chrétiens sur le champ de bataille, elle avait peut-être appelé au secours l'ami si souvent maudit mais si respecté par elle, qui lui-même—car toutes les religions se ressemblent—avait la cruauté de souhaiter qu'elle eût eu aussi le temps de se reconnaître, de lui donner sa dernière pensée, de se confesser enfin à lui, de mourir en lui. (iv. 89–90; tr. v. 581)

The reconstruction of Albertine's last moments relies on several clichés, one the experience of time just before death; two, that a conversion takes place at the moment before the Maker is met. The third cliché refers to Marcel himself, as much-cursed but ultimately much-revered lover. Marcel takes this iconic instantiation of the Lover, and displaces it onto that of the Confessor, or administrator of the last rites. Both these versions of Albertine's last conscious moments thus postulate Marcel in the best possible light. They feed, by association, a fantasy of the good self, dutifully reactivating the pain of loss as a proof of remembrance: 'Peut-être si elle l'avait su, eût-elle été touchée de voir que son ami ne l'oubliait pas, maintenant que sa vie à elle était finie, et elle eût été sensible à des choses qui auparavant l'eussent laissée indifférente' (iv. 92; tr. v. 583). This is a vision of pity mixed inextricably with self-pity. It raises Marcel and his assiduous mourning to the level of martyrdom. The wish that Albertine should pity him at seeing how well he mourns her triggers its own opposite, however: he remembers that he has forgotten his grandmother:

j'étais effrayé de penser que si les morts vivent quelque part, ma grand-mère connaissait aussi bien mon oubli qu'Albertine mon souvenir. Et tout compte fait, même pour une même morte, est-on sûr que la joie qu'on aurait d'apprendre qu'elle sait certaines choses balancerait l'effroi de penser qu'elle les sait *toutes*? et si sanglant que soit le sacrifice, ne renoncerions-nous pas quelquefois à les garder après leur mort comme amis, de peur de les avoir aussi pour juges? (iv. 92; tr. v. 584)

Suddenly a wholly different view of death appears. Having concentrated in fantasy on the conventionally proper desire to see the dead person again, and the wish to be remembered by her, Marcel makes a discovery. His wish is also a hypothesis, and if he tests it using another dead and much-loved figure, he finds that a host of side-effects not at first clear from the seeming purity and innocence of the wish come into force: the dead might know that we not only remember them—but that we forget them. The wish that the dead in general might be able to react to remembrance offered them by the living needs to be refined, and have some of the dead screened out of it.

Intervening upon these self-generating fantasies comes the return of Marcel's investigative prowess: Aimé's letter from Balbec offers the narrative of mourning its most substantial external object. It is, like all the letters and telegrams by which new shocks are introduced into the text, copied in full. Unlike the previous letters, however, it is given a short interpretative introduction by Marcel, telling us that the casual insertion of it into the narrative was unimaginably painful, and that its bald reprinting here can convey nothing of what he had felt:

une souffrance inattendue, la plus cruelle que j'eusse ressentie encore, et qui formait avec ces images, avec l'image, hélas! d'Albertine elle-même, une sorte de précipité comme on dit en chimie, où tout était indivisible et dont le texte de la lettre d'Aimé, que j'ai séparé d'une façon toute conventionnelle, ne peut donner aucunement l'idée, puisque chacun des mots qui la composent était aussitôt transformé, coloré à jamais par la souffrance qu'il venait d'exciter. (iv. 96; tr. v. 588–9)

This pre-emptive announcement of a subjective interpretation, which reserves for itself the highest notch on the pain scale is, at one level, perfectly legitimate. Marcel's is the narrative we are following, and it is in some sense predictable that the letter from Aimé, which we deduce will contain confirmation of Albertine's 'deviant' sexual practices, should have the most severe effect on him, and that he will lay claim to such an effect. But it expresses, by being situated prior to the transcription of the letter, the very difficulties of writing about the subjective state of suffering from a subjective viewpoint. Since *each* of the shocks he has experienced has been described as the most shocking experience, he is always in danger of hyperbole. The hurried assurance that *this* is the worst, followed by the thrusting of the letter into the text enacts both a pre-emptive anxiety about being believed, and a risky strategy of self-exposure, or playing his trump card first, by offering unassailable proof of suffering.

What makes this risk seem most like brinkmanship is that Marcel cannot resist a critique of Aimé's style. When the *maître d'hôtel* writes about a possible eyewitness 'qui se rappelle très bien (Mlle A.)' (iv. 96; tr. v. 589), Marcel intervenes upon his own previous statement that he would cite the letter separately: 'Aimé qui avait un certain commencement de culture, voulait mettre Mlle A. en italique ou entre guillemets' (iv. 96; tr. v. 589). We can hardly help but be surprised by the crudeness of the interpolation when he goes on: 'les fautes des gens du peuple consistant seulement très souvent à interchanger—comme a fait d'ailleurs la langue française—des termes qui au cours des siècles ont pris réciproquement la place l'un de l'autre' (iv. 96;

tr. v. 589). We might seek to explain it either as the remark of a
writer returning to an experience which no longer pains him,
or as a nervous tic, a remainder of a habitual response to incor-
rect syntactic usage. But at another level it also throws into
doubt, if not the sincerity of Marcel's suffering, then certainly
the means by which it is expressed. There is an undecidable
tension between a full account of suffering in narrative form
which might be described as fuller, and more authentic for
including relaxed moments, moments when the acuteness of
pain is off duty, so to speak, and an aesthetic disruption, in
which a certain *reading* pleasure (which we can term
Schadenfreude) is interrupted and confused by a discursive intrusion in another rather less vulnerable voice. This is self-justification straying from its appointed task as processer of
mourning, into the territory of literary criticism, from a mode
which does not bear the weight of such keen scrutiny, that of
soft pain; and it wrestles with what is monological about monologue, splitting into different, incommensurable versions of
itself, in search of control over unimportant items, because it
cannot control the larger issue.

The letter gives allusive details of Albertine's activities, carefully avoiding names, staying vague, but suggestive: 'Comme
m'a dit cette personne, vous pensez bien que si elles n'avaient
fait qu'enfiler des perles elles ne m'auraient pas donné dix
francs de pourboire' (iv. 97; tr. v. 589). Aimé reports the speech
of his witness, but does not use the grammatical conventions of
reported speech, rather running together frame and content
of her words without demarcating speech marks or a change of
tense from present to past. This gives the letter a confidential
and gossipy tone, which goes against the grain of Aimé's
attempt to use a high and formal register for his information.
The allusiveness which suggests a great deal is also, however,
inexplicit and open to misinterpretation: 'la personne avec qui
j'ai parlé savait ce que cela voulait dire' (iv. 97; tr. v. 590) tells
Marcel very little, but suggests that knowledge has a secret,
arcane significance, transmissible only by code. Yet the witness,
the attendant at the baths, turns out not to be so reliable: 'Cette
personne n'a pu me donner d'autres détails ne se rappelant pas
très bien, "ce qui est facile à comprendre après si longtemps" '
(iv. 97; tr. v. 590). Furthermore Aimé ends the letter by running

together a different kind of string of incompatibles. Referring to Albertine's death thus: 'Il est vrai qui si jeune c'est un grand malheur pour elle et pour les siens' (iv. 97; tr. v. 590), he continues with a reference to his own situation in Balbec as a 'petit voyage que Monsieur m'a ainsi procuré', informing Marcel that 'le temps est on ne peut plus favorable' (iv. 97; tr. v. 590). The result is another ironic understatement: Aimé shows that he has missed the significance of Albertine's death to Marcel by thinking all in the same breath about her death and what he calls his holiday.

Armed with his dubiously researched and presented evidence, Marcel insistently reminds us that he, unlike the agent of his jealous investigation, Aimé, is not asking run-of-the-mill questions of detail about Albertine's sexual behaviour, but seeking answers to the far more high-minded question of the nature of Albertine's essence:

il faut se rappeler que les questions que je me posais à l'égard d'Albertine n'étaient pas des questions accessoires, indifférentes, des questions de détail, les seules *en réalité* que nous nous posions à l'égard de tous les êtres qui ne sont pas nous, ce qui nous permet de cheminer, revêtus d'une pensée imperméable, au milieu de la souffrance, du mensonge, du vice et de la mort. Non, pour Albertine c'était une question d'essence: en son fond qu'était-elle, à quoi pensait-elle, qu'aimait-elle, me mentait-elle, ma vie avec elle avait-elle été aussi lamentable que celle de Swann avec Odette? (iv. 97–8; tr. v. 590; my emphasis)

Yet even as he makes the distinction between Aimé's gossip and the altogether more sophisticated degree and kind of knowledge he himself requires, he reminds himself that the everyday questions of detail are '*les seules en réalité que nous nous posions* à l'égard de tous les êtres qui ne sont pas nous'. And although the detail of his own questions is presented as 'essential', one of those questions is a competitive and petty one which effaces Albertine altogether: it is whether he had it better than Swann.

The effect of Aimé's letter is to introduce, not much-needed information, but a systematic degradation of Albertine's desires. Far more important than knowledge, here, is the continued need for mastery: 'le besoin de savoir ayant toujours été surpassé, dans mon amour pour Albertine, par le besoin de lui montrer que je savais' (iv. 100; tr. v. 593). But in the absence of any full confession of sin by Albertine herself, refutation of the charges found against her are the only available route for his self-justificatory neediness: 'dans ce fouillis où les souvenirs ne s'éclairent qu'un à un—je découvris, comme un ouvrier l'objet qui pourra servir à ce qu'il veut faire, une parole de ma grand-mère', who had said of the *doucheuse*, 'C'est une femme qui doit avoir la maladie du mensonge' (iv. 101; tr. v. 595). Spurred by this reassuring memory, the freewheeling of Marcel's excessively sensitized explanatory machinery can trot through its circular paces once again: 'On peut venir prendre des douches avec des amies sans penser à mal pour cela'; 'Peut-être, pour se vanter, la doucheuse exagérait-elle le pourboire'; 'ainsi je cherchais, et je réussis peu à peu, à me défaire de la douloureuse certitude que je m'étais donné tant de mal à acquérir' (iv. 102; tr. v. 595).

Aimé's first investigative results mark a transition, as I have said, to the degradation of Albertine's memory and her desires. This is a qualification, however, whose moral undertone is an ambivalent one. The sequence which follows shows that degra-dation is to be taken in many senses at once: as the natural decay of memory, its supplementation by fresh experiences, but also as a gradual abdication of mourning, Marcel's abandoning of the state of abandonment. That we have sought to charac-terize mourning as in some sense wanton in this section of text fuses exactly with the conception of the exit from mourning as a shady ethical area, fraught with diplomatic minefields. The self-justificatory imagination that has sought for so long to find an adequate explanation for Albertine's otherness, sexuality, and disappearance, with so few materials, that has poached upon its own resources in a relentless effort to find a scapegoat, a reason, a redemption, gradually starts to disintegrate alto-gether. Its own incoherences, which have fed it seemingly inter-minably, now start to re-emerge as incoherences which signify difference, detachment, recovery, irony, and acceptance.

Albertine's absence in life, for example, can now start to seem analogous to her absence in death: 'Quand notre maîtresse est vivante, une grande partie des pensées qui forment ce que nous appelons notre amour nous viennent pendant les heures où elle n'est pas à côté de nous. Ainsi l'on prend l'habitude d'avoir pour objet de sa rêverie un être absent. . . . Aussi la mort ne change-t-elle pas grand-chose' (iv. 104; tr. v. 598). Marcel's retrospective jealousy itself is seen to crumble and collapse, as a side-effect of Aimé's over-implication in his researches: when Aimé beds the *blanchisseuse* in Touraine in order to extract information from her, he becomes not only complicit but bound up in his own investigation:

> Et elle m'a dit: (Si vous aviez vu comme elle frétillait, cette demoiselle, elle me disait: (Ah! tu me mets aux anges) et elle était si énervée qu'elle ne pouvait s'empêcher de me mordre.) J'ai vu encore la trace sur le bras de la petite blanchisseuse. Et je comprends le plaisir de Mlle Albertine car cette petite-là est vraiment très habile. (iv. 106; tr. v. 600)

And with this degree of collapse, even via the one remove of the substitute investigator, of detective work into sexual opportunity, Marcel's jealousy is exhausted. Repetition no longer signifies either pattern-making, or exacerbation:

> Sans doute je me disais: 'Pourquoi me tourmenter? Celle qui a eu du plaisir avec la blanchisseuse n'est plus rien, *donc n'était pas une personne dont les actions gardent de la valeur.* Elle ne se dit pas que je sais. Mais elle ne se dit pas non plus que je ne sais pas, puisqu'elle ne se dit rien.' (iv. 109; tr. v. 604; my emphasis)

Albertine still exists as fragments of memory, yet these are fragments not as shards but as keepsakes: 'ce fut surtout ce fractionnement d'Albertine en de nombreuses parts, en de nombreuses Albertines, qui était son seul mode d'existence en moi' (iv. 110; tr. v. 605). They are visual freezeframes of her as 'bonne, ou intelligente, ou sérieuse, ou même aimant plus que tout les sports' (iv. 110; tr. v. 605). In forgetting that he has forgotten the other Albertines, as he had earlier forgotten the *heures ennuyeuses* spent frustrated by her, the thesis of the multiple versions of the *moi* can make a triumphant reappearance. Exactly the same materials, those photographic instants of Albertine alive, or Albertine fantasized, rotate through the poaching, pilfering processes of self-justificatory raids upon them, through the ceaseless return to and pawing over of the past in the hope of its delivering up some sort of explanation, and become the material basis *for* recovery from the past:

> Et ce fractionnement, n'était-il pas au fond juste qu'il me calmât? Car s'il n'était pas en lui-même quelque chose de réel, s'il tenait à la forme

successive des heures où elle m'était apparue, forme qui restait celle
de ma mémoire, comme la courbure des projections de ma lanterne
magique tenait à la courbure des verres colorés, ne représentait-il pas
à sa manière une vérité bien objective celle-là, à savoir que chacun de
nous n'est pas un, mais contient de nombreuses personnes qui n'ont
pas toutes la même valeur morale, et que si l'Albertine vicieuse avait
existé, cela n'empêchait pas qu'il y en eût d'autres. (iv. 110; tr. v. 605)

A revision which reinstates multiplicity and variety as an interpretation of what we have just heard as impoverished, repetitive, jealous, and incoherent pushes against already strained
readerly expectations. It seems a desperate kind of moral rela-
tivism, a late-coming forgiveness or permissiveness, a broad-
mindedness that goes against the rigour and parsimony of the
preceding hundred pages, and the incoherences and abandonment of narrative control with which we have been assailed and
which we have found ourselves trying so hard to account for.

When this magnanimity is followed by a flagrant flouting of
the rules that have governed the signification of the *cloison* in
all other parts of the text, not once, but twice in quick succession, it operates as a final breach of the contract that has been
established with the patient reader. The *cloison* which had
served as the limit marker of access to dangerous knowledge,
the saddening but necessary imposition of a difference
between what we desire, and what it would be far too dangerous
for our frail animate organisms to know, is, at the further end
of Marcel's revisitation of past mourning, thoroughly torn
down:

[i] Alors je ne fus plus seul; je sentis disparaître cette cloison qui nous
séparait. Du moment que cette Albertine bonne était revenue, j'avais
retrouvé la seule personne à qui je pusse demander l'antidote des
souffrances qu'Albertine me causait. (iv. 110–11; tr. v. 605)

[ii] Pour être persuadé de son innocence il me suffisait de l'embrasser, et je le pouvais maintenant qu'était tombée la cloison qui
nous séparait, pareille à celle impalpable et résistante qui après une
brouille s'élève entre deux amoureux et contre laquelle se briseraient
les baisers. (iv. 111; tr. v. 606)

The triumphant return of Good Albertine, as a fantasy reconstruction which finally dispenses with any acceptance of responsibility for her troubled last months, and her ultimate lonely
death, kills her again with its overwhelming flooding of the

textual means by which the barrier between self and other is healthily maintained. For this vision of unmediated acceptance, and tolerance, this abdication of the proprieties of secular earthbound mourning, this loss of the tone of rigorously explored psychological fissuring, in favour of a sickly transcendentalism, far from commemorating Albertine, and enshrining her in a glaze of pathos, infinitely retrievable as a sad absence, cannibalizes her as most malleable, least different from the narratorial ego, accomplishes the work of mourning by rendering her absolutely indifferent.

5. CONCLUSION

Mourning is an internal, introspective, unknowable process, which comes to an end. From an external perspective, the process seems to take on the characteristics of stasis, a state that can only be known once it is over. In other words, it cannot be known, since the ultimate coming to rest of mourning is as a memory of itself. The living process of mourning is not known, but rather inhabited by those who pass through it. Freud reminds us at the beginning of 'Mourning and Melancholia' that: 'Although mourning involves grave departures from the normal attitude to life, it never occurs to us to regard it as a pathological condition and to refer it to medical treatment. We rely on its being overcome after a certain lapse of time, and we look upon any interference with it as useless or even harmful.'[17] A state which is a process, it mutates imperceptibly into recovery. Mourning begins with an ending, and functions on the shifting cusp of two incomprehensibilities: ungraspable by the suffering self until it comes to an end, it is also incomprehensible to its observers. If mourning is precipitated by loss, it is defined by resistance: an internal resistance to its ending, the guilty fear of indifference to the dead by recovering from their loss, and an external resistance to its perpetuation, the fear of its contagion.

Reading 'Le Chagrin et l'Oubli' similarly necessitates beginning with an ending, the double loss of Albertine, first as

[17] *SE* xiv. 239–58 (pp. 243–4).

escapee, then as dead other. The contingent intrusion of her accidental death precipitates a new kind of self-justification from the narrator, to which the reader cannot but bear witness. This self-justification is a helpless, vulnerable, self-accusatory, and self-cannibalistic generation of linguistic attempts to frame, discard, repeat, reorder, possess, and ultimately become indifferent to the lost object. The time of mourning in *Albertine disparue* is both reversed time (it is a temporality that begins with an ending), and borrowed time (it is time audited by another, here the reader). But to the extent that auditing encourages a double meaning, both as listening and judging, the borrowed time of mourning is a licence taken by the narrator which puts the reader at a loose end, turns her into the timekeeper prepared, but also forced by the loss of future-directed narrative progression, to wait on the end of Marcel's grief.

Proust's writing about the mourning of Albertine emphasizes forgetting as loss. This is forgetting not as magical, poetic, retrievable, and poignantly ironic, but as unstoppable, inexorably bound towards its own successful completion, leaving behind not the melancholy and pleasingly aesthetic fetishes of dust and ashes, yew and headstone, but vacancy, emptiness, nothing. The play in language has all gone, there are none of the anecdotal digressions which swell the text without defeating it. Repetition now signifies the inability of poets, prose-writers, and ordinary men and women to do anything but repeat aimlessly their inadequate psychological responses to unjustifiable events. Pain cannot be seen anywhere in this text on mourning, it is not locatable in a visible wound or even in the events that we are told are, or it is implied must be, the cause of pain.

How, then, is pain transmitted? What is it? We expect a sharpness, or a dull ache, or a verifiable source, and this, of course, we can assert must be supplied by Albertine's departure, then her death, and the few material objects and events which encrust themselves around, or drape themselves over, these two principal pivots of the text. Yet as the text extends itself further away from these events, but without seemingly being able to abandon them, and more and more cut off from the sources of itself, unable to revivify the shock of the original, subsiding into dull, blank, white noise, the unjustifiability of Albertine's death mutates softly into the unjustifiability of Marcel's suffering, into a critical whispering campaign of doubts about his sincerity in mourning her so long, in maintaining his jealousy so dutifully, in fetishizing her, in parading his feelings around so much in the same way that we have seen them paraded thinly disguised as other characters' weaknesses, foibles, moral scruffiness. The narrator doth protest too much: perhaps, like his innumerable digressions, this mourning *sounds like* a way of avoiding the truth, a justification by obfuscation for never having loved at all. He has cried wolf too often, been too often falsely modest about not loving his grandmother enough, failing to be a dutiful grandson: we demand proofs for the authenticity of his pain, a justification for its duration. Why does the mourning of Albertine not have a place yet in the vision of the novel? Because it is dull and slow, not excruciating and witty and ironic and flattering to read. In the opening of *Albertine disparue*, Proust does not test our ability to keep up with the lightning strikes of his lacerating character assassinations, but our ability not to meet the indifference of mourning with the indifference of boredom at it.

I argued earlier in this book that the figure of the *cloison* in *A la recherche* is a metaphor for narratorial hermeneutic activity. It is a mnemonic for the discovery (or rediscovery) of—and resistance to—dangerous or unwanted knowledge. The use to which it is put in *A la recherche* indicates that we should privilege auditory modes of epistemological enquiry over visual ones. If we apply Proust's analytical tool to the process of reading mourning in *A la recherche*, and figure ourselves as listeners, we find ourselves struggling to negotiate the self-protective screens we also, and far more automatically than his narrator, throw up in our timid and aggressive toiling through everyday interpretation and vice. Looking at the uses of self-justification in *A la recherche* affords us, for the most part, a pleasurable opportunity to tease out evasion and blindness, whether in the text's semantic self-contradictions, or in the narratorial self and all his discrepant modes. When the direction of the reading excludes any kind of analysis of the reader herself, permitting a one-way critical gaze which is based on the assumption that texts give away, or give up, their secret identities to unremitting scrutiny, the reader may rest assured of her capacity for detachment. Listening to mourning in *A la recherche*, however, opens us to the insatiability of the narratorial self in pain. Pre-empting any single interpretation by writing a text which is itself a patchwork of interpretations, and presenting suffering with a clarity which itself is conditioned by that suffering, under the governance of grief and evasion, Proust turns any lurking desire to summarize, marginalize, even deride the content of the text into the *reader's* province. The death of Albertine and its surrounding interpretations, the unacknowledged still centre of this great novel, is written out of accounts of the book, precisely because it forces us to confront our own desires for entertainment, for irony, and for detachment from pain in ourselves, and challenges us to account for the novel's flagrant unjustifiabilities.

Proust tests where we might be inclined to locate the fringes, the limits, of our readerly responsibility, by provoking all the consequences of tolerant listening. He invites us to submit our critical patience to his narrator's agony, and dares our sceptical scrutiny to intervene with its rationalizing, classificatory accountancy upon the state of mourning, as it is represented in a literary text. His bargain with finitude shows, as if it were a residue, though it is the most important component of self-justification, the desolation of our attempts at any kind of purely ethical response to a suffering other: not the bad faith of the attempt, but its impossibility. We do not require murderers, psychopaths, and earthquake victims to prove to us the need for compassion, and the equal but agonizingly opposite demand for indifferent appraisal, even hostile judgement. Proust gives us, in narrative form, an account of why it matters to listen to self-justification, and he supplies his own desperately painful dialectical opposition. It matters, not because nothing else matters, but because nothing ever matters completely.

Conclusion: Self-Justification, Judgement, Indifference

> I was flung from the chariot but, my limbs being still entangled in the reins, my living flesh was dragged along, while my muscles were held fast by the stump. Part of my body was pulled away, and part was left impaled. There were ominous cracks from breaking bones, and there you might have seen me, utterly prostrated, breathing out my life, no part of my body recognizable, but all one gaping wound.[1]
>
> (Ovid, *Metamorphoses*, 15)

Proust formulates his criteria for reading at many points. 'En réalité, chaque lecteur est quand il lit le propre lecteur de soi-même' (iv. 489; tr. vi. 273) is the famous Proustian disclaimer, the fictional book-balancing moment that hands the baton from writerly intention to readerly activity.[2] The impression produced on the reader is described, in the excited words of the narrator, as his first article is published in *Le Figaro*: 'C'est une Vénus collective, dont on n'a qu'un membre mutilé si l'on s'en tient à la pensée de l'auteur, car elle ne se réalise complète que dans l'esprit de ses lecteurs. En eux elle s'achève' (iv. 150; tr. v. 651–2). But into that declaration is sewn all the intensity of the desire for an absolute justification by a faceless public, a secular judgement which would approve and endorse the first-person implicatedness in what he describes, which would agree that 'toute impression est double, à demi engainée dans l'objet, prolongée en nous-même par une autre moitié que seul nous pourrions connaître' (iv. 470; tr. vi. 248). Proust's narrator, even

---

[1] Hippolytus tells Egeria of his own death in a riding accident; Ovid, *Metamorphoses*, book 15, tr. M. M. Innes (1955), 348.

[2] These recommendations on reading appear both in the novel, and in the preface to the translation attributed to Proust, but largely carried out by Marie Nordlinger, of Ruskin's *Sesame and Lilies*, 'Sur la lecture' (1905), publ. in *CSB* 160–94, as 'Journées de lecture'.

as he announces his indifference to his own impending death, and to the reception of his work, will not abandon the erotics of influence, the desire to be the intrusive disseminator, and not the quiet persuader.

I started this study by pointing out that there are moments early on in the text where the narrator, ambiguously double-voiced, tells his reader the source of the novel he is finally undertaking at the end of *A la recherche*: that source is, of course, the narratorial self. Underwriting the announcement is the credibility problem of involuntary memory, which is unverifiable, but which, apparently, demands extraordinary sacrifices when it makes its rare appearances, rather like Giotto's depiction of all-consuming Envy, all but consumed by her serpent.

This early moment, which opens the vast question of finding a firm foundation for subjective judgements, is matched, at the very end of the novel, by an extraordinarily similar statement: 'Je savais très bien que mon cerveau était un riche bassin minier, où il y avait une étendue immense et fort diverse de gisements précieux' (iv. 614; tr. vi. 437). While the first utterance, in the present tense, looks towards serious-minded future attempts to find a solution to the problem of subjectivity, the second is couched in the past tense of acquired knowledge. Subjectivity has passed from being a subject of vulnerable curiosity to the subject of detached speculation, but that passage, the process of arrival and the direction that it takes, itself carries subjectivity in different guises, in repetitions, and in reversals of itself across a vast textual distance.

The movement by which we can describe change in *A la recherche* is as an exchange. The thin-skinnedness of Marcel's *pre-emptive* attempts at self-protection give way across the body of the text to the thin skin of his affective *vulnerability*. Indifference shifts from being perceived as external hostility, to being understood as the ghastly, amoral cohabitant of the tremulous, desiring self. That overarching exchange mechanism is easy to state, more difficult to account for. My study maps five of the stages of the passage, the hard work to which self-justification is put in *A la recherche*, and we can give them names: they are integration, accommodation, deprivation, discrimination, and vulnerability. These five faces of self-justification articulate separable but interconnected fields of enquiry, and, taken together, chart the *tropisme* of self-justification's inward turn in this text. Looking at self-justification's different kinds of activity in this vast novel takes us to parts of it that are often avoided by critics, and unearths the hidden mechanisms by which the text functions: Proust has given us, written into the novel itself, the best instrument with which to read it.

He shows how self-justification works across the span of large textual distances, at parties, and in digressions. Party-going prompts self-justification as different strategies for self-preservation: disguise, imitation, rivalrous jockeying, close analysis, and then practice of the linguistic codes by which social systems are sustained. He shows us that digressions are spaces within which to hold together otherwise morally or psychologically incommensurable material, the high-minded but also desperate attempt to manage the self-justification manifested by others; and he takes to awe-inspiring lengths the extraordinary elasticity of digressiveness, always organized by its inevitable ending. Proust has supplied a cognitive device with which to dramatize the two-way reversibility of self-justification, that functions with wonderful flexibility at both a metaphorical and a concrete level, the permeable partition of the *cloison*. He takes this reversibility and throws it at his own processes of characterization, showing us how dangerous proximity can be, as it overbalances into the desire to discriminate. And finally, he takes his own narrative experimentation in self-justification to its limits, and demonstrates that though it is a tolerable spectacle when an outwardly directed activity, propped up by desires that are readily comprehensible to watching others, because flattering the sensibilities or the analytic prowess of others, it becomes absolutely intolerable when inwardly directed, helpless, uncontrollable.

Wanting to fit in, holding discrepant materials together, clinging to props, wanting to be different, and accepting absolute failure, are the simply couched parts of a powerful piece of cognitive apparatus, which at times puts all these seemingly disparate activities into play at once, at others dwells on, or is motivated by, only one. To look at *A la recherche* in terms of this set of moving parts is to see the text operating with cogency even in its contradictions, to see how rigorously each of these parts is tested by and against each of the others.

Proust has given us a cross-referenced moral and psychological manual by which to see how, for example, the desire for assimilation learns to imitate indifference for acceptance's sake, but glimpses that imitation might be limiting, and so strives for discrimination. The desire to protect and disguise personal interests will strive to be magnanimous to other instances of the same desire, but may reach a saturation point at which judgement and rejection take place. The desire to cling to protective props will watch them being stripped away in agitation, then in despair, and finally become indifferent to them, or perish. The refusal to accept unjustifiable events like the death of others will become indifferent to unjustifiability— and *thereby* perish. The movement of self-justification that appeals outwards, then turns in upon itself, there to succumb to its own workings and be transformed into indifference, is the simple vector of complex Proustian plotting. None of its stages can be skipped, each is as full as the last, and each predicts the following.

I have used the term *Schadenfreude* several times in the course of trying to describe particular ironic or rueful narratorial tones, but perhaps it is now appropriate to draw together its various tensions. *Schadenfreude* is the counterbalance to Sartre's brilliantly expressed criteria for judgement in my Introduction: it describes the instant of abandoning moral responsibility for another, the shrugging off of their right to a continued hearing, in exchange for the self-hugging pleasure of the spectacle of suffering. It is a transitional moment in which judgement shifts from an active to a passive form in the self, and not, as Sartre would like to see it, the other way round. It is a mental mechanism for putting otherness out of one's mind, and also into another temporality, into the past of unfulfilled potential. One's own helplessness in the face of another's problem is expertly translated into blame, rejection, judgement, and quickly stifled glee. Above all, *Schadenfreude* is the name for a way of regulating the incomings and outgoings of vulnerability, sidestepping the pain of metamorphosis for the illusory gratification of a moment's immobilization, a split second's control over death.

Yet Proust has shown us uncompromisingly, passionately, that self-justification is the unstable sand on which recuperative hope for personal moral improvement is based. The question is of redemption and change, and whether immorality is assimilable to a fixed identity or personality, whether a locatable self is responsible for his or her actions. And the Janus-faced first-person narrator builds himself into this complex equation, by being both the subject of his text, and subject to its writing. We cannot quite dispense with the knowledge that this is a first-person text, that all of the characterization that we witness, while fictionalized, comes from a controlling narratorial source. Redemption or its possibility turns out to depend on Marcel's powers as a narrator. And so we cannot rid ourselves of the knowledge, however repellent, that *all* of the grandiose moral speculations, psychological explanations, and justifications in the novel come from one mind, and can be returned to it, refuted, and denounced as utterly subjective whimsy. Proust will not allow us to forget this threat, and this is why he is a great writer.

This is a very new vision of his novel. Its rigours are those that Proust has stayed with, followed to their logical and unremittingly complex and troubling ends. His is a novel which takes the first-person narrative genre into the infinitely troubling sphere of vulnerability that shades into irresponsibility. Proust shows us that none of us is excluded from self-justification; that we are all its expert practitioners; that compassion necessarily fails as we make the discovery that compassion harbours the very same indifference for which suffering others need compensation. The analysis and experimentation in self-justification reveal to us terrifying indifference, which must be defeated for compassion to take place, but which is so necessary if we are to understand and judge unjustifiability correctly. We must, says Proust, take self-justification seriously as evidence of suffering, of doubt, of the fragility of our self-esteem, and of real victimization, a genuine cry for help, and it will trouble us endlessly that these pleas and cries which demand real compassion, pity, and empathy *look exactly like* whingeing, complaint, the attempt to garner unjustifiable exonerations and redemptions. *Touché*. Moral responsibility is reinflected in Proust's novel to become a process by which even the most careful precaution over judging might yet result in rejection, expulsion, and victimization, and which cannot fully rule out the possibility of unjustifiability wearing the same decorative mask, of crying wolf with the loudest of real victims.

The grand central issue of self-justificatory activity is its dependence on the resistance offered by indifference. Its victory and downfall are that we simply cannot tell the difference between crying wolf and crying for mercy. That single undecidability is the moral fulcrum of the issue: and it must force us to do battle with our desire to scapegoat, to reject and exclude, to triumph in our indifference every time we meet vulnerability. For the 'we' who judge, are, of course, exactly the same as the first-person narrator caught *in medias res* with all his unresolvable hermeneutic problems. Marcel finally understands that indifference is not all that he can expect to meet in a world beyond his own mental horizons, but that it nevertheless inhabits the workings of his own consciousness. Yet we who stand in a circle around him and shake our heads sadly at his prostration, who think ourselves on the far side of this lesson, are also more truly and more blindly those whose lovers die for lack of love, who cling tenaciously to the beliefs that destroy us, who make incoherent moral decisions, who condemn in others exactly what it is we do ourselves, and who lose by giving away on a daily basis the esteem, the status, the possessions by which we think we are defined.

Appendix I

A Table of Proustian Parties

Du côté de chez Swann [Paris]	(These 3 events are attended by Swann.) La soirée Verdurin (i. 197–246) Un dîner Verdurin (i. 247–62) La soirée Saint-Euverte (i. 317–47)
A l'ombre des jeunes filles en fleurs [Paris]	(Henceforth, events are attended by the narrator.) Le dîner avec le marquis de Norpois (i. 443–68) Le déjeuner avec Bergotte (i. 536–63) Le salon de Mme Swann (i. 581–96)
A l'ombre des jeunes filles en fleurs [Balbec]	Le dîner chez M. Bloch (ii. 126–34) Dîners à Rivebelle (ii. 165–76)
Le Côté de Guermantes I [Paris]	*Le Salon de Mme de Villeparisis (ii. 481–592)
Le Côté de Guermantes II, ch. 2 [Paris]	Soirée chez Mme de Villeparisis (ii. 666–77) Le soir de l'amitié (ii. 688–708) *Dîner chez les Guermantes (ii. 709–839)
Sodome et Gomorrhe II, ch. 1 [Paris]	*Soirée chez la princesse de Guermantes (iii. 34–122)
Sodome et Gomorrhe II, ch. 2 [Balbec]	Soirée à La Raspelière (iii. 291–368)
La Prisonnière [Paris]	Les Verdurin se brouillent avec M. de Charlus (iii. 730–830)
Albertine disparue	————
Le Temps retrouvé [Paris]	Chez les Verdurin (iv. 344–72) Matinée chez la princesse de Guermantes (including, from iv. 496, Le Bal de Têtes, iv. 433–609)

*Indicates those parties I look at more closely.

Appendix II

A Table of Digressions in *A la recherche du temps perdu*

The following table of digressions is in no sense complete. It has been compiled partly by reference to Pierre Bayard's 'Table des principales "digressions" de la *recherche*' but mainly in contradistinction to Bayard's terms.[1] As Bayard of course explains, the project of compiling a complete digressions table from the new Pléiade edition of *A la recherche du temps perdu* is a Herculean and, in the final instance, perhaps pointless task. What is far more important is to notice the variety of definitions of digression that such a table generates. The question of the ending of a digression, necessary for it to be so defined at all, is difficult and treacherous. The endings of digressions always take place, and are sometimes flagged with phrases such as 'pour en revenir à'. Sharply delineated returns to narrative order, or dovetailed, interlocking reattachments are not always, however, explicitly signalled.[2] The length of digression in *A la recherche* is entirely elastic, sometimes a few words in a sentence, sometimes running to pages of supplementary conversation, anecdote, or remembrance. Digressions within digressions are common. Their content raises the issue of whether particular *subjects* are to be defined as digressive. A digressive subject might well become a mainstream subject over the reception time of a novel.

What is deemed to be digressive does not always depend on isolatable rhetorical flags, but may be a gradual associative drift. Digressions may appear because of additions to typescripts or manuscripts: as a rhetorical feature of Proust's prose style, they have a privileged relationship with the celebrated genesis of the text, in *cahiers*, *carnets*, and with *paperoles* attached to various proof stages. Were a study of Proust's digressions ever to be perfected, the project would involve an amalgamation of both the findings and the methodology of Alison Winton's *Proust's Additions*,[3] an exact line by line delineation of all Proust's

---

[1] See *Le Hors-Sujet*, pp. 185–8   [2] Ibid. 20, n. 6.

[3] *Proust's Additions* is by far the best way to source the genetic development of supplementary text in *A la recherche* written after 1914, the outbreak of the First

digressions, a thoroughgoing assessment of the *Esquisses* published with the new Pléiade edition, Bayard's list of principal digressions, and the table given here, which combines some cataloguing with a hermeneutics of digression in a form loosely akin to Barthes's term, *lexies*.[4]

Digressiveness also has a privileged relationship with the novel's investigation of composite, superposed, parallel, and reversible temporalities and temporal sequencing: the phrase *par anticipation*, which often signals proleptic digressions, engages a temporal, not only a spatial model of narrative. Digressiveness of a proleptic kind builds time, or overtime, into the text. Here, then, in neatened and digestible form, are just some of Proust's digressions, to be read or consulted as the reader chooses.

VOLUME I

i. 32

Grand-mère's sisters mentioned digressively in sentence.

i. 185–375
Un amour de Swann

Little justification in text for this strange, heterogeneous intrusion into Marcel's own story. Raises issue of safe definition of digressions: Swann's story is used to justify Marcel's experience (iv. 494–5). Does the novel's reception history, which focuses on *Du côté de chez Swann* as exemplary of entire novel cycle, modify our understanding of what constitutes a digression? Compare *Le Hors-Sujet*, p. 103. What justification there is for the third-person narrative insertion appears as the term *association*:[5] 'C'est ainsi

World War, and Proust's change of editor from Bernard Grasset to Gaston Gallimard (between Aug. and Oct. 1916). Winton's work is a mine of information about the moral and aesthetic side-effects of such supplementation. It is not easy to use the new Pléiade edition to reconstruct the construction of *A la recherche*, but patient perusal of the overall introduction, as well as the *Chronologie*, and the *Introductions*, and *Esquisses, notices, notes et variantes* sections at the end of each volume, do yield rewards. Anthony Pugh provides a good introduction to the genesis of the Proustian text in *The Birth of 'A la recherche du temps perdu'* (1987).

    4 See Roland Barthes, *S/Z* (1970), 20.
    5 *Association* in Proustian stylistics can signify either metaphorical and substitutive associations, or metonymical and contiguous ones, the latter underpinning the former as Genette and de Man, followed by Culler, have been at pains to demonstrate, all themselves indebted to the linguistic model of mental functioning proposed by Roman Jakobson. See Roman Jakobson and Morris Halle, 'Two Aspects of Language and Two Types of Aphasic Disturbances', *Fundamentals of Language* (1956).

que je restais souvent jusqu'au matin à songer
au temps de Combray, à mes tristes soirées
sans sommeil, à tant de jours aussi dont l'image m'avait été plus récemment rendue par
la saveur—ce qu'on aurait appelé à Combray
le "parfum"—d'une tasse de thé, et *par association de souvenirs* à ce que, bien des années
après avoir quitté cette petite ville, j'avais
appris, au sujet d'un amour que Swann avait
eu avant ma naissance, avec cette précision
dans les détails plus facile à obtenir quelquefois pour la vie de personnes mortes il y a des
siècles que pour celles de nos meilleurs amis'
(i. 183–4; my emphasis).

i. 238–40
On *chic*

Swann's silent possession of it, Odette's
unselfconscious betrayal of her lack of it.
Digression within *Un Amour de Swann*; plays
out in miniature a question of *taste* directly
analogous to the questions of exclusionary
judgement in the Faubourg Saint-Germain.

i. 317–20
Valets at *soirée
Sainte-Euverte*

Relation between *digressiveness* and novelistic *description*. Valets described by Swann
who is 'dans un état de mélancolique *indifférence* à toutes les choses qui ne touchaient
pas Odette'; 'c'est la vie mondaine tout
entière, maintenant qu'il en était détaché,
qui se présentait à lui comme une *suite de
tableaux*' (i. 317; my emphasis).

i. 423–5
'cette réponse de mon
père demande
quelques mots
d'explication . . .'
(i. 423)

Opening of *A l'ombre*. Omniscient or retrospective narratorial intervention to justify
transformation perceived by Marcel's father
in Swann's character. Raises issue of split
between narratorial voices (paralepsis);
relation between *retrospection* and *justification*
of narratorial decisions through their explanation to a readership. Digression within
which space is provided to orchestrate
enactment of vital Proustian questions: what
is the relation between experience and
essence; are changes imposed from without
permanent or superficial; what relation do
they have to subjective desires to appropriate and incorporate change?

i. 425	Mother's shock when she finally notices that her niece wears make-up. Relation of digression to *exemplarity*: anecdote intended to exemplify narratorial blindness to Swann's vanity. Digression as opportunity to offer analogical, explanatory supplementation; enactment of narrator's behaviour which conveniently shifts focus away from his own failure to see or read Swann clearly.
i. 451–5 Norpois's diplomatic language	Direct speech on *le roi Théodose* included in full, though it contributes nothing to plot teleology. Digression as *performative opportunity to pastiche* Norpois, to play out Norpois's language as an experiment in the difficulty of safely identifying literary worth in language, *in demarcating what is properly literary*. Marcel founds the dilemma thus: 'je ne saisissais pas l'esprit ou la sottise, l'éloquence ou l'enflure qu'il trouvait dans une réplique ou dans un discours et l'absence de toute raison perceptible pour quoi ceci était mal et ceci bien, faisait que cette sorte de littérature m'était plus mystérieuse, me semblait plus obscure qu'aucune' (i. 450).

VOLUME II

ii. 5–6	On travel and railway stations.
ii. 14	Prolepsis. Digression that leads from a consideration of Mme de Sévigné to Elstir to Dostoevsky: gives away in advance one of novel's major aesthetic tenets. Digression as method of seeding ideas for future development.
ii. 100–3 'la variété des défauts n'est pas moins admirable que la similitude des vertus' (ii. 100)	Famous digression on vice and virtue. Prompted by Bloch's accusation that Marcel is a snob. Digression opportunity for speculation, triggered by subjective experience and justifying narrator in relation to that experience. (See Chapter 4.)
ii. 212–14	On shifting belief systems; relative unimportance of 'l'Albertine réelle' to 'entretien

intérieur' she provokes in narrator: *triggered* by failure to meet Albertine. Contains *secondary* digressive anecdote on love. Ending: 'Il fallait rejoindre Elstir.' Example of digressive dalliance sharply wrested back onto narrative course.

ii. 310–15 'A l'âge où les Noms . . .' (ii. 310)	*Rêverie* on names. Digression as reminder of textual genesis. The significance of the Name emerges in writing from the post-*CSB* period, 1909–11. See *Esquisse* VIII (ii. 1051–63), Cahier 66 (N. a. fr. 18316); and *Esquisse* VII (ii. 1048–51), Cahier 13 (N. a. fr. 16653).
ii. 369–437 *Doncières*	Digressions *within* proairetic sequence that is itself an *excursion*: ii. 374–7, on the absence of sound, and deafness; ii. 384–8, on sleep; ii. 408–16, on military strategy (addition after 1914 to Grasset galleys); ii. 427–31, on the prince de Borodino; ii. 431–2, on the *Demoiselles du téléphone*.[6]
ii. 481–6, 491–3	Mme de Villeparisis's *déchéance mondaine*.
ii. 560–3 Morel's first appearance	Digression from account of Mme de Villeparisis's *salon*. Morel brings Oncle Adolphe's photographs to narrator: 'dernières images de cette vie de vieux viveur qu'il séparait, par une cloison étanche, de sa vie de famille' (ii. 561). Separation Oncle Adolphe installs between his private sexual life and his familial obligations signified by term *cloison*, or permeable partition (see Chapter 3). Morel causes narrator to justify himself over issue of keeping photographs of relations in his bedroom. Morel is the subject of many future digressions.
ii. 712–15	On Elstir's paintings. Digression from narrative account of the Guermantes *dîner*.
ii. 730–73	On the superiority of the Guermantes over other Saint-Germain families such as the

---

[6] See *S/Z*, 25–6: the *proaïrétique*, one of his five narrative codes (pp. 25–7), it specifies plot actions, or praxis.

Courvoisiers (during *récit* of Guermantes *dîner*): genealogy, aesthetic capacities, enhanced sense of irony, ability to appear open-minded while remaining more exclusive than any other Faubourg family, on the nature of that exclusivity, characterized by style rather than birth, although determined and underpinned by caste (see Chapter 1).

ii. 820–1   *Rêverie* on rue de Saintrailles provoked by chance mention of the name by duc de Guermantes. Ellipsis signals textual fade-out.

ii. 829–32   Digression on genealogies.

VOLUME III

iii. 3–33   Digression as *exordium* to *Sodome et Gomorrhe.*
Sodome et Gomorrhe, ch. 1,   But by *delaying* the account of how the
'Première apparition   narrator discovers homosexuality ('si
des hommes-femmes'   importante en elle-même que j'ai jusqu'ici, jusqu'au moment de pouvoir lui donner la place et l'étendue voulues, différé de la rapporter': iii. 3), Proust has, structurally, made this the centrepoint of the entire novel.

iii. 34–120   The *soirée* breaks down into myriad digres-
soirée chez la   sions. It may be analysed according to its
princesse de Guermantes   bipartite teleology: (i) Marcel's presentation to prince de Guermantes, (ii) Swann's final appearance in novel/the account of Swann's conversation with prince de Guermantes about the latter's conversion to *Dreyfusisme.* Party structure then represents a series of *impediments* to Swann's final judgement of himself (see Chapter 1). A selection of these painfully digressive interruptions are given below.

iii. 41–2   On medicine.

iii. 43   On homosexuality: Vaugoubert. Opens: 'Les proportions de cet ouvrage ne me permettent pas d'expliquer ici ...' Yet those proportions do admit a digression on how Vaugoubert's homosexuality affects his professionalism; and on strategic coupling which makes his wife compensate for her husband's *tare* by adopting masculine characteristics (iii. 46–7).

iii. 51–2
'laissez-moi, monsieur l'auteur, vous faire perdre une minute de plus pour vous dire qu'il est fâcheux que, jeune comme vous l'étiez (ou comme était votre héros s'il n'est pas vous), vous eussiez déjà si peu de mémoire' (iii. 51)

Famous self-reflexive and self-justificatory digression on memory.[7] Contains conversation with imaginary reader. Digression which behaves as *generic catachresis*. The narrator replies to the reader, justifying his amnesia: 'Une mémoire sans défaillance n'est pas un très puissant excitateur à étudier les phénomènes de mémoire' (iii. 52).[8] Representation of *ideal reader* is being promoted and included within the body of the narrative, not as formal or playful acknowledgement of 'fictiveness of fiction', but as a pre-emptive attempt to appropriate reader response. In seeming to apologise in advance for readerly boredom, the narrator is extending the boundary of public self-justificatory activity to include, pre-emptively, the phantom reader of an account not yet written, characterizing his own ideal of a reader *as that which would reject, very precisely, his advances.*[9]

---

[7] Beckett notices this methodological justification. See *Proust*, p. 29.

[8] In dialogic novels of the 18th cent. such as *Jacques le Fataliste*, or *Le Neveu de Rameau*, this transgression of the *vraisemblable* is so abundant as to constitute a narrative norm. In the 19th cen., however, in apparently stably third-person novels such as Stendhal's *Le Rouge et le Noir* (1831; Garnier, 1960), the self-reflexive narratorial voice draws attention to its function as technical device transgressive of the 'Realist' novel, partly because of its comparative rarity. Proust, in a first-person novel, has here punctured the conventional edifice by which *first-person* narrative is sustained, namely that the *je* figure is unaware of the outcome to his own story.

[9] This is the reverse side of a reading coinage so successfully (if idealistically) articulated in the 1905 text subsequently published as the preface to Proust and Marie Nordlinger's translation of Ruskin's *Sesame and Lilies*, and there entitled 'Sur la lecture' (now 'Journées de lecture', *CSB* 160–94): 'Nous sentons très bien que notre sagesse commence où celle de l'auteur finit, et nous voudrions qu'il nous donnât des réponses, quand tout ce qu'il peut faire est de nous donner des désirs' (p. 176). It is too little pointed out that the optimistic 'Sur la lecture' vision, which makes participants of readers, and texts *scriptible* (to borrow another of Barthes's terms from *S/Z*, 10), is fundamentally damaged by its revision here *within* the text

iii. 56–7	'Hubert Robert' fountain (ekphrasis: narrator goes to see 'for himself' a fountain represented in form of painting by Robert, then re-represented in textual form). Plot digression: Marcel diverted while seeking out Swann. Late addition to definitive text (much reworked, to be found in *Cahier* 52, N. a. fr. 16692, see n. 1, iii. 1359–60). Digressiveness rejoins questions of novelistic genesis, and formal representation.
iii. 98–100	Charlus on Mme de Sainte-Euverte.
iii. 192–3	Digression on doctors after *danse contre seins* scene at the casino. Contains secondary anecdotal digression on the *enflure* of a grand-duc's eye. Textual enactment of *evasion* of reaction to Cottard's revelation.
iii. 199–200 Self-justificatory mechanism: digression as means of introducing *internal narrative coherence.*	Momentary detachment and narratorial self-reflexivity, comparing narrator's life with Swann's: 'Au fond si je veux y penser, l'hypothèse qui me fit peu à peu construire tout le caractère d'Albertine et interpréter douloureusement chaque moment d'une vie que je ne pouvais pas contrôler tout entière, ce fut le souvenir, l'idée fixe du caractère de Mme Swann, tel qu'on m'avait raconté qu'il était. Ces récits contribuèrent à faire que dans l'avenir mon imagination faisait le jeu de supposer qu'Albertine aurait pu, au lieu d'être une jeune fille bonne, avoir la même immoralité, la même faculté de tromperie qu'une ancienne grue, et je pensais à toutes les souffrances qui m'auraient attendu dans ce cas si j'avais jamais dû l'aimer' (iii. 199–200). Digression that *holds text together.* Simultaneous loosening and securing of narrative stays. Justification of narrator's experience by comparison with narrative of another's.

of *A la recherche*. The mechanism by which text gives itself up to readerly pleasure is not a neutral one, nor does it operate in one direction only, from the author to the reader. Its side-effect is a pre-emptive narratorial fantasm of readerly judgement *as* rejection.

Staged aside which doubles as vital plotting moment. Two-way narrative switch: simultaneously proleptic and retrospective, refers to comparison internal to the text's own past, and pre-empts future outcome of the text. But by apparently *misinterpreting* the available data, the narratorial agency thrusts interpretative responsibility onto the reader. At an *in medias res* moment of apparent openness, confession, and self-understanding, full knowledge is still yet to come. Such trading on the recessive and recidivist opportunities afforded by digression is fundamental to understanding Proustian self-justification.

iii. 254–7 Charlus's first meeting with Morel	Digression as *chance encounter*, reliant on narrative device of *petit train* and its series of stations. Begun and ended with Albertine's request for forgiveness, after causing a jealous reaction in Marcel over their meeting with Saint-Loup.
iii. 259–368 La Raspelière	Salon providing an opportunity unmatched anywhere else in the novel for the sustained examination of linguistic tics.
iii. 280–4	Brichot's etymologies (I).
iii. 299–300 'les mères profanées'	On the entrances of homosexuals into rooms. Ends with a famous digressive musing: 'Mais laissons ici ce qui mériterait un chapitre à part: les mères profanées' (iii. 300). The chapter on desecrated mothers is, in effect, a *promised* digression that does not take place.[10]
iii. 301–3 on Morel (*sa bassesse*)	Digression as late addition.[11] Includes narratorial disclaimer: 'Mais comme j'avais

---

[10] Baudry suggests that 'Ce chapitre, il le dissimula en le dispersant dans son œuvre' (*Proust, Freud et l'autre*, 43). The theme of the desecration of the parental image, of course, intrudes at many points in this novel (most famous is the Montjouvain incident: i. 157–61), and is also apparent in articles composed before *A la recherche* took shape (see Introduction).

[11] See *Proust's Additions*, ii. 120: not in N. a. fr. 16712 (*Sodome et Gomorrhe* manuscript, *5ième cahier*), but in separately typed page, in N. a. fr. 16740 (typescript of *5ième cahier*) and margin thereof, and N. a. fr. 16766 (proofs).

en moi un peu de ma grand-mère et me plaisais à la diversité des hommes sans rien attendre d'eux ou leur en vouloir, je négligeai sa bassesse, je me plus à sa gaieté' (iii. 303). See Chapter 4.

iii. 310–12 *la dureté des invertis*	Homosexuality and dangerous proximity: 'un inverti qui ne lui plaisait pas n'était pas seulement une caricature de lui-même, c'était aussi un rival désigné' (iii. 312). See Chapter 4.
iii. 316–17	Brichot's etymologies (II: *Pont-à-Couleuvre*).
iii. 318–19	Digression as mental drift: 'je pensais à une conversation . . .' with mother over Albertine.
iii. 320	Digression as hair-splitting. 'Le mot "cheveu" au singulier': parenthetical digression on linguistic trends, exemplified by Mme de Cambremer.
iii. 321–3; 324	Brichot's etymologies (III), with secondary digressive interruption by the 'philosophe norvégien'.
iii. 327–9	Brichot's etymologies (IV). Actively requested by narrator to prevent *supplice* of Saniette. Digression as manipulated intervention with moral purpose: attempt at social control.
iii. 369	*Chasseur louche* tells Marcel the story of his sister who defecates in hotel bedroom cupboards. Despite Marcel's fatigue, the *chasseur*'s direct speech is included *in toto*. Framed by Marcel's fatigue and his reflections on sleep and narcotics, the *chasseur*'s babble functions doubly as (implicit) self-justificatory proof of Marcel's exceptional tolerance of external reality.
iii. 370–4 replacement for var. *a* (see iii. 1551–6)	Digression on sleep and narcotics. Late addition, includes a discussion fused from a conversation with, and a book by, Bergson. See iii. 1556 n. 1. In Sept. 1920, Bergson and Proust had a conversation about sleep and narcotics. The Bergson text to which Proust

also seems to be responding is entitled 'Le Rêve', a 1901 paper reprinted in *L'Énergie spirituelle* (1919). Bergson argues that dream materials are constituted by real sensations, apprehended by the sleeper, turned into dream *form* by the engine of unconscious memory. Proust, however, attributes to Bergson, and then argues against, an idea not in his paper; namely that narcotics dissolve not everyday memory, but memorized Greek quotations.

Variant *a* of iii. 369–74 Excised dream of resurrected grandmother, iii. 1553–4: 'peut-être aussi avant de mourir, quand ceux ont vécu le plus détachés d'eux-mêmes voudraient un instant retenir ce corps qu'ils sentent se dérober sous eux, avait-elle compris la duperie qu'avait été pour elle sa vie de sacrifice, et peut-être mon égoïsme cessant tout à coup de lui être caché par les sophismes de son cœur lui était-il apparu dans son immensité' (iii. 1553).

Excised digression on sleep and dreams. At corrected typescript stage, Proust introduced a break in the manuscript now seen as the divide between chapters 2 and 3. The final few pages of chapter 2 and the first few of chapter 3 were entirely suppressed by qui Proust and replaced by the current discourse on sleep. These excised pages, from *Cahiers* V and VI of the manuscript, repr. iii. 1551–6 as variant *a*, contain a long and fascinating account of one of Marcel's dreams after the death of his grandmother. The dream begins with the idea that the grandmother is 'dans la *chambre contiguë*, moi je travaillais à ma table et je me disais: "Enfin elle va me voir travailler, elle qui l'a tant désiré . . . " ' (iii. 1552; my emphasis). It goes on to describe how the grandmother enters the room, only to tell Marcel guiltily that she must leave the next day. The dream scene switches to a railway station: 'Dans toutes les directions j'entendais siffler des trains qui partaient' (iii. 1553). He sees his dishevelled, distressed grandmother hurrying along the platform. He begins to attribute reasons for her distress to himself, imagining her belated realization that she has sacrificed her life for an ungrateful boy she still loves. The grandmother is finally bundled *brutalement* into a carriage by a railway employee (iii. 1554). The dream is also partly to be found in *Cahiers* 48 and 50, which form the groundwork of the first 'Intermittence du cœur' section of the published text.[12]

iii. 394 On driving.

iii. 395–400
Opportunistic digression, riding on the narrative of Marcel's *sorties* by car. Linguistic sadism and artistic integrity

Opens: 'un des clients du chauffeur était M. de Charlus . . .'. Tells exemplary story ('Je raconte un de ces repas . . .', iii. 395) of the linguistic sadism that Morel facilitates: 'mon rêve, ce serait de trouver une jeune fille bien pure, de m'en faire aimer et de lui prendre sa virginité' (iii. 396). But the pleasures of linguistic bad behaviour are not confined to Morel's direct speech. Charlus says to Morel, 'vous semblez ne pas apercevoir le côté *médiumnimique* de la chose' (iii. 396; my emphasis). *Médiumnimique*, an adjective that describes spiritual communion with the dead, is subsequently redefined by Proust to refer to a channel of communication connecting sadism and musicality: 'l'idée que Morel "plaquerait" sans remords une jeune fille violée lui avait fait brusquement goûter un plaisir complet. Dès lors ses sens étaient apaisés pour quelque temps et le sadique (lui, vraiment *médiumnimique*) qui s'était substitué pendant quelques instants à M. de Charlus avait fui et rendu la parole au vrai M. de Charlus, plein de raffinement artistique . . .' (iii. 398). Proust has here himself perverted a definition for his own purposes. By allowing sadism to be tinged with ideas about the afterlife, and sensitivity to music, he suffuses these areas of human activity with each other's attributes.

iii. 414–15 Self-justificatory digression on Marcel's egalitarianism. Ends with maternal disapproval that he should take this as far as eating with his chauffeurs. Digression *as*

---

[12] See *Notice*, iii. 1225–33; and *Esquisses* XII and XIII, iii. 1030–48. See also Ch. 3 of this book.

	rhetorical trope of excess or licence enacts an aside *about* licentious behaviour.
iii. 416–17	Digression on riding: space for overdetermined Proustian autobiographical topoi: chauffeurs connected with Morel; horseriding, both narratorial *évasion* from Albertine, but also pre-emptively signifying her flight into mortality; (*Phèdre* intertext); Elstir's pictorial *paysages* experienced as 'real' *paysages*; first sighting of aeroplane (topos for death).
iii. 417–22	Reflections on Morel and immorality.
iii. 427–50	Morel and Charlus: disguise and revelation of homosexuality (conversation with Brichot on Balzac and Chateaubriand: iii. 437). Narrative digressive to the point of unravelling, though section is stitched together thematically, as variations on the theme of the relationship between Morel and Charlus.
iii. 450–61 *duel fictif*	The 'devises des livres' (iii. 453; see also iii. 427) intended by Charlus for Morel. Inscriptions as proscriptions.
iii. 461–515 *Les stations du petit train* 'C'était bien Morel qu'il avait devant lui, mais comme si les mystères païens et les enchantements existait encore, c'était plutôt l'ombre de Morel, Morel embaumé, pas même Morel ressuscité comme Lazare, une apparition de Morel, un fantôme de Morel, Morel revenant ou évoqué dans cette chambre (où partout les murs et les divans répétaient des	Freud's metaphors for the mental transport system by which his patients 'freely' associated come straight from the lexical field of the rail network: *Linie, Verkettung, Zug,* and *Knotenpunkt.* The Proustian narrative vehicle for structuring and including digressions is the coastal Balbec train with its opportunities for digressive anecdote at every stop. The memories evoked by *petit train* stops are often a pretext for digressions on Morel's morality. The proliferating strands of Morel's habits colonize the text. The narrative sometimes cannot hold even its *digressive* direction. Before the *Maineville* digression, we find a series of feints and evasions: 'Avant d'en parler ...' (iii. 462); 'que je vais raconter dans un instant' (iii. 462); 'Il y en eut d'autres, mais je me contente ici, au fur et à mesure que le tortillard s'arrête ..., de noter

emblèmes de sorcel- lerie)' (iii. 466)	ce que la petite plage ou la garnison m'évo- quent' (iii. 463); 'Mais avant de dire en quoi Maineville a quelque rapport dans ma mémoire avec Morel et M. de Charlus, il me faut noter la disproportion (que j'aurai plus tard à approfondir) . . .' (iii. 463). The narra- tor's desire and ability to organize his *récit* seems thrown into disarray by Morel's 'vie . . . tellement enténébrée' (ii. 463). The Maineville memory (iii. 461–8) is the story of Charlus spying on a literally framed Morel, tricked into a bedroom tableau with three women. At the heart of the digression, through Charlus's perspective, Morel's name reproduces itself crazily. Free indirect speech functions here as a moment of frenzy, permitted within a digression, but discontin- uous with any idea of a main narrative.
iii. 481 [Digressive note on Morel's name]	When Mme de Cambremer deliberately avoids the narrator's brusque questions about who the baron knows 'de très mal', she says ' "Moreau, Morille, Morue, je ne sais plus. Aucun rapport, bien entendu, avec Morel, le violoniste," ajouta-t-elle en rougissant' (iii. 481). This deliberate amne- sia about Morel's 'bad' name deforms it into names that are even more apposite for an onomastics of Morel's *caractère*, since the first bears etymological traces of the Black Nightshade; the second, an edible fungus (Morchella); while the third refers to the fish, cod, which in slang idiom means 'whore' (1849). Just as Morel is summed up by his name, so that name swims freely and associatively throughout *Sodome et Gomorrhe*: as a narrative character, he is a vehicle for issues of morality, and his name functions as a mnemonic for questions of what consti- tutes good or bad character.
iii. 484–6	Brichot's etymologies (V).
iii. 486–93	Digression on Bloch, which turns into a digression on Charlus's conflation of

	Judaism with sadism. Both digressions are importations of direct speech.
iii. 499–501	Digression triggered by Albertine's revelation that she knows Mlle Vinteuil and her lesbian lover. Albertine unwittingly departs from the norms of her affair with Marcel, and this throws the narrative itself off course for a full two volumes, *La Prisonnière* and *Albertine disparue*.
iii. 525	Evocation of the curé de Combray. Digression as regression to earlier part of narrative.
iii. 543–6	Digression on duchesse de Guermantes's linguistic *côté terrien et quasi paysan*.
iii. 548–51	Digression on Dreyfus Affair.
iii. 553–63 Chance meeting	Proairetic digression, about Morel's marriage to Jupien's niece. Charlus hears Jupien's niece say to Morel 'je vous paierai le thé', and gives Morel a 'leçon de distinction', which is itself intercepted and taken over by the pleasure Charlus derives from his own anger: he 'aimait à froisser et se grisait de sa propre colère' (iii. 553). Contains famously undecidable authorial/narratorial self-justification: 'Avant de revenir à la boutique de Jupien, l'auteur tient à dire combien il serait contristé que le lecteur s'offusquât de peintures si étranges' (iii. 555–6). This important digression also contains an analysis of Morel's procedures of self-justification: 'Dès que la personne ne lui causait plus de plaisir, ou même, par exemple, si l'obligation de faire face aux promesses faites lui causait du déplaisir, elle devenait aussitôt de la part de Morel l'objet d'une antipathie qu'il justifiait à ses propres yeux, et qui, après quelques troubles neurasthéniques, lui permettait de se prouver à soi-même, une fois l'euphorie reconquise de son système nerveux, qu'il était, en considérant même les choses d'un point de vue purement vertueux, dégagé de

toute obligation' (iii. 561).

iii. 573–5 'vous m'avez ouvert un monde d'idées'	Digression triggered by Albertine's direct speech. On the *jeunes filles* and indifference: 'Leur immobilité viendra de notre indifférence qui les livrera au jugement de l'esprit. . . . De sorte que du faux jugement de l'intelligence, laquelle n'entre en jeu que quand on cesse de s'intéresser, sortiront définis des caractères stables de jeunes filles' (iii. 574).[13]
iii. 628–33	On sleep.
iii. 633–5	On street cries in Paris.
iii. 636–7	Albertine's digression: erotic speech on desirable food.
iii. 664–8	On Wagner.
iii. 668–70	On Morel. Triggered by digression on Wagner, by 'un brusque crochet' (iii. 668). This *crochet* is an example of metonymic *frayage*.
iii. 683–5	Amplificatory digression on *le mensonge*.
iii. 686	Morel and madness.
iii. 696–7	Albertine and *le mensonge*.
iii. 698–702	Digression as chance encounter, facilitated by *hearing*. Marcel overhears Morel: 'j'entendis des sanglots' (iii. 698).
iii. 709–22	Digression as chance encounter: Charlus. See Chapter 2.
iii. 735–9	Digression on Charlus's methods and motivations for seeking power over others (importation of direct speech). Begins 'Celui-ci . . .': cued and justified by prior narrative interest in Mme Verdurin's interest in Charlus. At iii. 739, the same gesture is reversed, 'celle-ci . . .' returns us to Mme Verdurin.

[13] Compare Sartre's comments in *L'Être et le néant*, pp. 398–9, given in the Introduction. Judgement comes when indifference has stopped being a property of the object (the undifferentiated mass of *jeunes filles*) and has become a property of the subject who no longer desires. But the narrator calls this a '*faux* jugement de l'intelligence'.

iii. 739–42

Digression on how Mme Verdurin has benefited from the Dreyfus Affair. 'Pour en revenir à' (iii. 742), the common sign of the end of a digression, or moment of self-conscious reorientation of the narrative, returns us to the subject of Charlus. Digression includes a further reference to an imaginary or ideal reader, staged as direct narratorial speech: ' "Je ne sais si je vous ai dit . . .," pourrais-je demander au lecteur comme à un ami à qui on ne se rappelle plus, après tant d'entretiens, si on a pensé ou trouvé l'occasion de le mettre au courant d'une certaine chose' (iii. 739–40). The conditional tense, the simile introduced by 'comme', the suggestion that news is passed on if opportunities are provided or taken, all contribute to a disingenuous seductiveness, which seeks justification for digressiveness under the screen of disseminating newsworthy information, even as it ironizes the worth of the news being transmitted.

iii. 765–9
'chemin de traverse, de raccourci'

Digression on revelation; digression as narrative connective tissue: Marcel explains that Mlle Vinteuil's lover is the decipherer of Vinteuil's 'indéchiffrables notations' (iii. 765). Moral speculation justifying contravention of conventional morality (through adultery, homosexuality, sadism, parental desecration) through atonement in the service of Art. The *motif proche* for the Bourgeois gathering at the Verdurins' salon 'résidait dans les relations qui existaient entre M. de Charlus et Morel' (iii. 768), and 'la cause plus lointaine' is 'une jeune fille entretenant avec Mlle Vinteuil des relations parallèles à celles de Charlie et du baron' (iii. 768). These maligned relationships have been a 'sorte de chemin de traverse, de raccourci, grâce auquel le monde allait rejoindre ces œuvres sans le détour, sinon d'une incompréhension qui persisterait longtemps, du moins d'une ignorance totale qui eût pu durer des années' (iii. 768).

iii. 773–6   Mme de Mortemart and Mme de Valcourt: the intrigue of party invitations.

iii. 794–5   Digression from Charlus's expulsion into—somewhat astonishing—narratorial self-assessment: 'Je tenais de ma grand-mère d'être dénué d'amour-propre à un degré qui ferait aisément manquer de dignité' (iii. 794). Self-justificatory assertions of moral probity take the form of sympathy for the suffering other, but do not translate into preventive action to save Charlus.

iii. 799–812   Digression as plot device: Brichot uses conversation as delaying tactic keeping Charlus in place until his scapegoating by Mme Verdurin. Charlus discourses on homosexuality (*réputations injustifiées*, iii. 800) with the narrator and Brichot. Charlus's exposure of Odette's promiscuity (iii. 803).

iii. 815   Proleptic digression: Morel's behaviour with Jupien's niece, after the Verdurin execution.

iii. 821–3   Proleptic digression: Charlus's heuristic methods for discovering the reasons for his rejection by Morel.

iii. 825–7   Proleptic digression: Charlus's moral improvement due to his illness. But even in the act of converting Charlus's wilfulness to helplessness, a final dig at hysteria crowns the narrator's argument: 'les nerveux, irrités à tout propos contre des ennemis imaginaires et inoffensifs, deviennent au contraire inoffensifs dès que quelqu'un prend contre eux l'offensive, et qu'on les calme mieux en leur jetant de l'eau froide à la figure qu'en tâchant de leur démontrer l'inanité de leurs griefs' (iii. 826).

iii. 829   Digression on 'private' language.

iii. 876–89   Digression structured by speculation on 'deux hypothèses': whether music is more 'real' than literary works (the plenitude offered by art, iii. 876) versus the 'néant': art's uselessness (iii. 883). Contains literary conversation with Albertine.

VOLUME IV

iv. 108–9

Digression as mania: Marcel's obsessive fantasy about Albertine's sexual pleasure feeds itself from recollections of Elstir's *paysage touffu*; an *étude frémissante* depicting Leda and the swan (Jupiter) combines with the blanchisseuse's phrase: 'Tu me mets aux anges'.

iv. 123–4

Digression as textual drift. 'Freely' associative thought: 'Le titre de la mélodie de Fauré, *Le Secret*, m'avait mené au *Secret du roi* du duc de Broglie, le nom de Broglie à celui de Chaumont' (iv. 123). Governed by jealous rigour, the strict logic that always returns the thinker to the same problem; iii. 1083–4 n.1, shows subtextual tracery of connnections based on the principle of contiguity. The surface chain, from this perspective, offers simply the nodal points articulating a denser, rhizomic, *réseau* that teems underneath.[14]

iv. 153–62

Digression as supplying lost narrative information, retrospectively: narrator's *naming error* (de Forcheville/de l'Orgeville) reminds him of hearing Swann's story; *digression* tells us how Gilberte obliterates her father's name and, ironically, thereby becomes acceptable to the Guermantes.

iv. 184–7

Proleptic digression: on Andrée's future husband, Octave 'dans les choux', who has become 'un homme de génie'. Marcel interrupts the narration of Andrée's final, most appalling revelation about Albertine, to speculate on another form of revelation:

---

[14] Compare Derrida's work on the disseminatory capacity of signification in language, in *La Dissémination*, or Deleuze's *Proust et les signes*.

that genius might reside in perfect adaptation to surrounding conditions.

iv. 195–6   Digression as marginal addition to the manuscript of *Albertine disparue*. Narratorial self-justification in the mode of misogyny. Four steps: (i) description of situation-type (intellectual male bewitched by 'femmes insensibles et inférieures'); (ii) focus on intellectual's implied 'special' need for suffering; (iii) justification of this suffering (given the intense engagement of intellectuals with their environment, the intellectual fears that the renunciation of sustaining habit, even if that habit is destructive, will do him more harm); (iv) compensation for such suffering: 'Tout cela crée en face de l'intellectuel sensible, un univers tout en profondeurs que sa jalousie voudrait sonder et *qui ne sont pas sans intéresser son intelligence*' (iv. 196; my emphasis). Does suffering sustained by misogyny, as well as by intellectual interest in the workings of one's own mind, remain authentic suffering? This is one of the painful questions addressed in Chapter 5.

iv. 202–35   Venice: journeys within narratives, as part of *proairetic* sequences, are justifiable digressions in relation to plot teleology. Strikingly, the long-awaited and assumed-to-be revelatory trip to Venice with his mother, is described in very few pages, and is only retrospectively aesthetically illuminating for Marcel.[15]

iv. 247–8   Digression as parenthesis: on the 'valeur d'un titre de noblesse'. Excellent example of the way in which the text at this point has *nothing to say*. Digression as opportunity for self-justification meets digression as helpless

[15] The narratives of the two trips to Balbec, less prized by Marcel because a less exotic location, in fact occupy half of *A l'ombre* (ii. 3–306) and a large section of *Sodome et Gomorrhe* (begun and ended by *Les Intermittences du cœur* I and II: iii. 148–515), and contain many of the novel's most important incidents.

	indifference. Text drifts haplessly and mournfully from tired statement to repetition of oft-formulated law. See Chapter 5.
iv. 264–6	*Retrospective* digression on transformation of Saint-Loup.
iv. 281–3	*Anticipatory* digression on transformation of Saint-Loup.
iv. 340–1	Saint-Loup on the *bataille napoléonienne*.
iv. 346–7 *fécondation orale*	Digression on Morel's calumnious articles decrying Charlus's *germanisme*. Specifies Morel's imitative talents: from oral mimic of Bergotte, he has become a *pasticheur*. 'Elle ne produit, d'ailleurs, que des fleurs stériles' (iv. 347). Narrator quick to assert that publication capitalizing on wilful exposure of another's vulnerability produces not truth, but shifting grounds of moral judgement, when his own narrative depends on exposure.
iv. 359–60	Optimistic narratorial speculation that checks and balances may be written into the moral codes of homosexuality: compensatory moral and psychological mechanisms prevent excess and degeneration. Darwinian cross-fertilization appropriated to stave off the massive slide into moral turpitude adumbrated in this section of the narrative.[16]
iv. 360–8	Series of digressions within digressions: Charlus's brilliant perception of Norpois's linguistic tics, and his own *germanophilie* patiently listened to, then impatiently dismissed by the narrator (iv. 366), who includes further anecdotes and a digression on Odette.

[16] See *Proust entre deux siècles*, 138. Proust's knowledge about the fertilization of flowers by insects came from Amédée Coutance's preface to a French translation of Darwin's *The Different Forms of Flowers on Plants of the Same Species* (1877), trans. Edouard Heckel as *Des différentes formes de fleurs dans les plantes de la même espèce* (1878). Coutance's preface summarizes another of Darwin's texts, also translated by E. Heckel as *Des effets de la fécondation croisée et de la fécondation directe dans le règne végétal* (1877).

iv. 368–72	Brichot's rise to journalistic fame.
iv. 382–8	Prolepsis: Morel shows narrator threatening letter from Charlus.
iv. 401–2	Bloch's language.
iv. 437–43	Digression as chance encounter: degenerate Charlus. Apogee of chance meetings. Moral and sexual degeneration in *A la recherche* is signalled as desire to confess: 'il était en proie presque chaque jour à des crises de dépression mentale, caractérisée non pas positivement par de la divagation, mais par *la confession à haute voix, devant des tiers dont il oubliait la présence ou la sévérité*, d'opinions qu'il avait l'habitude de cacher' (iv. 443; my emphasis).
iv. 572–6; 590–2	Digression from the *Bal de têtes* to the story of la Berma (despite her reported death, iv. 41). Digression as text in state of suspended evolution.
iv. 609–10	Digression as *evasion*: 'Que celui qui pourrait écrire un tel livre serait heureux, pensais-je, quel labeur devant lui! . . . Mais *pour en revenir à moi-même*, je pensais plus modestement à mon livre'. The shifts that take place in this passage between an imaginary writer and his project, and the writer the narrator hopes to be, together with his suggestions as to how he hopes to be read, which end with a proviso clause, is a perfect example of how self-justification in this novel functions in relation to an audience, real or anticipated. The conditional tense in which the narrator tells us he does not want praise or blame also tells us that he is anticipating exactly these two reactions.

Appendix III

Cloison Instances in *A la recherche du temps perdu*

Swann (1913)	*Jeunes Filles* (1919)	*Guermantes* (1920)	*Sodome* (1922)	*La Prisonnière* (1922)	*Albertine disparue* (1925)	*Le Temps retrouvé* (1927)
i. 167 Walks by the Vivonne: ...j'ai vu d'un bleu clair et cru, tirant sur le violet, d'apparence cloisonnée et de goût japonais.	i. 497 Tea with Gilberte: ... elle extrayait pour moi du monument écroulé tout un pan verni et cloisonné de fruits écarlates, dans le goût oriental. i. 623 Odette's salon: ...l'hiver, le printemps, l'été, ne sont pas séparés par des cloisons aussi hermétiques que tend à le croire le boulevardier ...	ii. 335 Mme de Guermantes at the Opéra: ... protégé par une cloison, enfermé dans un vase, au milieu des flots de la vie de tous. ii. 339 At the Opéra: ... comme dans des petits salons suspendus dont une cloison eût été enlevée ...	iii. 9 Jupien's *boutique.* J'avisai alors la boutique à louer séparée seulement de celle de Jupien par une cloison extrêmement mince. iii. 28 *Autofécondation,* the vanilla plant: ... chez elle, l'organe mâle est séparé de l'organe femelle	iii. 521 Marcel's bathroom (Paris): Les cloisons qui séparaient nos deux cabinets de toilette ... étaient si minces que nous pouvions parler tout en nous lavant chacun dans le nôtre ... iii. 537 Marcel's bedroom in Paris: Le soleil venait jusqu'à mon lit et traversait la cloison transparente de mon corps aminci ...	iv. 110 Post-mortem forgiveness of Albertine: ...je sentis disparaître cette cloison qui nous séparait. iv. 111 Posthumous forgiveness of Albertine: Pour être persuadé de son innocence, il me suffisait de l'embrasser, et je le pouvais maintenant qu'était tombée la cloison qui nous séparait ...	iv. 286 Post-mortem revision of Albertine's sexuality: Elle avait peut-être vécu près de l'amie de Mlle Vinteuil et d'Andrée, séparée par une cloison étanche d'elles qui croyaient qu'elle 'n'en était pas' ....

ii. 29 Balbec: grandmother's unconditional love:	ii. 30 Balbec:	ii. 343 At the Opéra: Le marquis De Palancy's monocle:	ii. 561 Morel's first appearance: Oncle Adolphe's photographs:	iii. 159 (x 3) Balbec: involuntary resurrection of grandmother:	iii. 160 Balbec: involuntary resurrection of grandmother:	iii. 667 Listening to Wagner:
... 'mon lit est adossé au tien, la cloison est très mince'.	... le dialogue rythmé de mes trois coups auquel la cloison pénétrée de tendresse et de joie, devenue harmonieuse, immatérielle ...	... paraissait ne pas plus voir le public de l'orchestre qu'un poisson qui passe, ignorant de la foule des visiteurs curieux, derrière la cloison vitrée d'un aquarium.	... cette vie de vieux viveur qu'il séparait, par une cloison étanche, de sa vie de famille ...	... ce qui était contre moi c'était cette cloison qui servait jadis entre nous deux de messager matinal, cette cloison ... Je n'osais pas approcher de cette cloison ...	Et je ne demandais rien de plus à Dieu, s'il existe un paradis, que d'y pouvoir frapper contre cette cloison les trois petits coups ...	Séparé de Wagner par la cloison sonore, je l'entendais exulter ...

Table (*continued*):

Swann (1913)	Jeunes Filles (1919)	Guermantes (1920)	Sodome (1922)	La Prisonnière (1922)	Albertine disparue (1925)	Le Temps retrouvé (1927)
	ii. 39 Balbec: Mme de Villeparisis: … mettaient si bien, entre elle et le monde extérieur auquel il eût fallu s'adapter, la cloison de ses habitudes …	ii. 578 Saint-Loup: love's blindness: … de l'autre côté de la cloison à travers laquelle ces conversations ne passeront pas. …	iii. 430 Jealousy of Albertine: … en revanche, quand j'étais là, une simple cloison, qui eût pu à la rigueur dissimuler une trahison m'était insupportable …			
	ii. 145 Balbec: grandmother's silence: … j'avais beau attendre qu'elle frappât contre la cloison ces petits coups qui me diraient d'entrer lui dire bonsoir, je n'entendais rien …	ii. 667 (x 2) Jupien's *boutique*: … séparés de la boutique de Jupien que par une cloison fort mince … Jupien y mettrait son charbon, ferait abattre la cloison et aurait une seule et vaste boutique.	iii. 501 Balbec: after Albertine's revelation: Je m'assis près de la fenêtre, réprimant mes sanglots pour que ma mère, qui n'était séparée de moi que par une mince cloison, ne m'entendît pas.			

ii. 691
Friendship:
. . . serments
d'amitié qui, nés
dans les cloisons
de cette heure,
restant enfermés
en elle . . .

iii. 502
Balbec:
decision to
imprison
Albertine:
. . . pour ne pas
éveiller ma mère,
de qui nous
n'étions séparés
que par cette
cloison . . .

Bibliography

This bibliography is by no means exhaustive. It gives readers references to all works cited, as well as to works of special interest on Proust, and to works of general theoretical interest. The place of publication is Paris unless specified otherwise.

PRIMARY PRINTED SOURCES: WORKS BY MARCEL PROUST

A la recherche du temps perdu, ed. J.-Y. Tadié and others, 4 vols. (Gallimard, Bibliothèque de la Pléiade, 1987–9).

i. *Du côté de chez Swann*; *A l'ombre des jeunes filles en fleurs*, 'Autour de Mme Swann'; *Esquisses, Introductions, Notices, Notes et variantes, Résumé, Table de concordance*, ed. J.-Y. Tadié, with the collaboration of F. Callu, F. Goujon, E. Nicole, P.-L. Rey, B. Rogers, and J. Yoshida (1987).

ii. *A l'ombre des jeunes filles en fleurs*, 'Nom de pays: le pays'; *Le Côté de Guermantes*; *Esquisses, Notices, Notes et variantes, Résumé, Table de concordance*, ed. J.-Y. Tadié, with the collaboration of D. Kaotipaya, T. Laget, P.-L. Rey, and B. Rogers (1988).

iii. *Sodome et Gomorrhe*; *La Prisonnière*; *Esquisses, Notices, Notes et variantes, Résumé, Table de concordance*, ed. J.-Y. Tadié, with the collaboration of A. Compagnon and P.-E. Robert (1988).

iv. *Albertine disparue*; *Le Temps retrouvé*; *Esquisses, Notices, Notes et variantes, Résumé, Table de concordance, Note bibliographique, Index des noms de personnes, Index des noms de lieux, Index des œuvres littéraires et artistiques*, ed. J.-Y. Tadié, with the collaboration of Y. Baudelle, A. Chevalier, E. Nicole, P.-L. Rey, P.-E. Robert, J. Robichez, and B. Rogers (1989).

Albertine disparue (édition originale de la dernière version revue par l'auteur), ed. N. Mauriac and É. Wolff (Grasset, 1987).

Contre Sainte-Beuve précédé de *Pastiches et mélanges* et suivi de *Essais et articles*, ed. P. Clarac and Y. Sandre (Gallimard, Bibliothèque de la Pléiade, 1971).

Correspondance de Marcel Proust (1880–1922), ed. P. Kolb, 21 vols. (Plon, 1970–93).

Jean Santeuil précédé de *Les Plaisirs et les jours*, ed. P. Clarac and Y. Sandre (Gallimard, Bibliothèque de la Pléiade, 1971).

Le Carnet de 1908, ed. P. Kolb (Gallimard, 1976).
L'Indifférent, ed. P. Kolb (Gallimard, 1978).
Marcel Proust: Lettres retrouvées, ed. P. Kolb (Plon, 1966).

WORKS CITED

ABRAHAM, NICOLAS, and MARIA TOROK, *Cryptonymie: Le Verbier de l'homme aux loups*, précéde de *Fors*, Jacques Derrida (Aubier-Flammarion, 1976).
—— *L'Écorce et le noyau* (Aubier-Flammarion, 1978).
ADORNO, THEODOR, W., 'Petits commentaires de Proust', *Notes sur la littérature* (1958), tr. Sibylle Muller (Flammarion, 1984), 141–52.
AESCHYLUS, *The Oresteia: Agamemnon, The Libation Bearers, The Eumenides*, tr. Robert Fagles (Harmondsworth: Penguin, 1975; repr. 1979).
ARISTOTLE, *Poetics*, tr. Malcolm Heath (Harmondsworth: Penguin, 1996).
AUGUSTINE, *Confessions* (Oxford: Oxford University Press, 1991).
AUSTIN, J. L., 'A Plea for Excuses', *Philosophical Papers* (Oxford: Clarendon Press, 1961), 123–52.
BAKHTIN, M. M., *The Dialogic Imagination: Four Essays* ed. Michael Holquist, tr. Caryl Emerson and Michael Holquist (Austin, Tex.: University of Texas Press, 1981).
BARTHES, ROLAND, *La Chambre claire: Note sur la photographie* (Cahiers du cinéma, Gallimard, Éditions du Seuil, 1980).
—— *Le Bruissement de la langue: Essais critiques IV* (Éditions du Seuil, 1984).
—— 'Proust et les noms', in *To Honour Roman Jakobson* (The Hague: Mouton, 1967); repr. in *Le Degré zéro de l'écriture* suivi de *Nouveaux Essais critiques* (Éditions du Seuil, 1972), 121–34.
—— *Roland Barthes* (Éditions du Seuil, 1975).
—— *Sade, Fourier, Loyola* (Éditions du Seuil, 1971).
—— *S/Z* (Éditions du Seuil, 1970).
—— and JEAN MONTALBETTI, 'Proust' (à Combray et à Paris), *Un homme, une ville* (France-Culture, Paris, 20 and 27 Oct. 1978 and 3 Nov. 1978), released as *Un homme, une ville: Marcel Proust à Paris par Roland Barthes* (audiocassette, Cassettes Radio France, 1978).
BAUDRY, JEAN-LOUIS, *Proust, Freud et l'autre* (Éditions de Minuit, 1984).
BAYARD, PIERRE, *Le Hors-sujet: Proust et la digression* (Éditions de Minuit, 1996).
BECKETT, SAMUEL, *Proust and Three Dialogues with Georges Duthuit* (1931 and 1949; London: John Calder, 1965).
—— *The Unnamable* (London: Calder, 1956; repr. Picador, 1979).
BENJAMIN, WALTER, 'The Image of Proust', *Illuminations: Essays and*

Reflections, ed. Hannah Arendt, tr. Harry Zohn (London: Cape, 1968), 203–17.

BERGSON, HENRI, *L'Énergie spirituelle* (1919; 32nd edn. Presses Universitaires de France, 1944).

BERRY, DAVID, 'The Technique of Literary Digression in the Fiction of Diderot', *Studies on Voltaire and the Eighteenth Century*, 118 (1974), 115–272.

BERSANI, LEO, *Marcel Proust: The Fictions of Life and of Art* (Oxford: Oxford University Press, 1965).

—— *The Culture of Redemption* (Cambridge, Mass.: Harvard University Press, 1990).

BLANCHOT, MAURICE, 'L'Expérience de Proust', *Le Livre à venir* (Gallimard, 1959), 18–34.

BOWIE, MALCOLM, *Freud, Proust and Lacan: Theory as Fiction* (Cambridge: Cambridge University Press, 1987).

—— 'Proust's Narrative Selves', in George Craig and Margaret McGowan (eds.), *Moy Qui Me Voy: The Writer and the Self from Montaigne to Leiris* (Oxford: Clarendon Press, 1989), 131–46.

BOWLBY, JOHN, *Attachment and Loss*, 3 vols. (London: The Hogarth Press and the Institute for Psychoanalysis, 1969; repr. Pimlico, 1997).

BROOKS, PETER, *Reading for the Plot: Design and Intention in Narrative* (Cambridge, Mass.: Harvard University Press, 1984).

BRUNET, ÉTIENNE, *Le Vocabulaire de Proust*, 3 vols. (Geneva: Slatkine-Champion, 1983).

CASAUBON, ISAAC, *Theophrasti Notationes* (1592; repr. De Harsy, 1617).

CHAMBERS, ROSS, 'Gossip and the Novel: Knowing Narrative and Narrative Knowing in Balzac, Madame de Lafayette and Proust', *Australian Journal of French Studies*, 23 (1986), 212–33.

COCKING, J. M., *Proust: Collected Essays on the Writer and his Art* (Cambridge: Cambridge University Press, 1982).

COLLIER, PETER, *Proust and Venice* (Cambridge: Cambridge University Press, 1989).

COMPAGNON, ANTOINE, *Proust entre deux siècles* (Éditions du Seuil, 1989).

CONRAD, JOSEPH, *The Nigger of the 'Narcissus'* (1897; preface, 1914: London: Dent, 1945; repr. 1956).

CRAIG, GEORGE, and MARGARET McGOWAN (eds.), *Moy Qui Me Voy: The Writer and the Self from Montaigne to Leiris* (Oxford: Clarendon Press, 1989).

CRITCHLEY, SIMON, *The Ethics of Deconstruction: Derrida and Levinas* (Oxford: Blackwell, 1992).

CULLER, JONATHAN, 'Apostrophe', *diacritics*, 7 (1977), 59–69.

—— *The Pursuit of Signs: Semiotics, Literature, Deconstruction* (London: Routledge & Kegan Paul, 1981).

CUTLER, MAXINE G., '*L'Esprit des Guermantes*: Is it Witty?', in Maxine G. Cutler (ed.), *Voltaire, the Enlightenment and the Comic Mode* (New York: Peter Lang, 1990), 27–52.

DARWIN, CHARLES, *The Different Forms of Flowers on Plants of the Same Species* (1877; repr. New York: Appleton, 1897).

DELEUZE, GILLES, *Proust et les signes* (8th edn. Presses Universitaires de France, 1964; 1993).

—— 'Zola et la fêlure', *Logique du sens* (Éditions de Minuit, 1969), 373–86.

DE MAN, PAUL, *Allegories of Reading: Figural Language in Rousseau, Nietzsche, Rilke, and Proust* (New Haven: Yale University Press, 1979).

—— 'Autobiography as De-Facement', *MLN* 94 (1979), 919–30.

DERRIDA, JACQUES, *De la grammatologie* (Éditions de Minuit, 1967).

—— *La Dissémination* (Éditions du Seuil, 1972).

—— *L'Écriture et la différence* (Éditions du Seuil, 1967).

DESCARTES, RENÉ, *Œuvres*, ed. Charles Adam and Paul Tannery, 11 vols. (Vrin, 1996).

DESCOMBES, VINCENT, *Proust: Philosophie du roman* (Éditions de Minuit, 1987).

DIDEROT, DENIS, *Jacques le fataliste*, *Le Neveu de Rameau*, in *Œuvres* (Gallimard, 1969).

DOUBROVSKY, SERGE, *La Place de la madeleine: Écriture et fantasme chez Proust* (Mercure de France, 1974).

EISENBUCH, JULIE, *The World of Ted Serios: 'Thoughtographies', Studies of an Extraordinary Mind* (2nd edn. Jefferson, NC: McFarland, 1989).

ELLISON, DAVID R., 'The Self in/as Writing', *The Reading of Proust* (Baltimore: Johns Hopkins University Press, 1984), 133–85.

EMPIRICUS, SEXTUS, *Outlines of Pyrrhonism*, tr. R. G. Bury (New York: Prometheus Books, 1990).

FEUILLERAT, ALBERT, *Comment Proust a composé son roman* (New Haven: Yale University Press, 1934).

FINN, MICHAEL R., *Proust, the Body and Literary Form* (Cambridge: Cambridge University Press, 1999).

FLAUBERT, GUSTAVE, *Madame Bovary* (1856, Flammarion, 1979).

FORRESTER, JOHN, *The Seductions of Psychoanalysis: Freud, Lacan and Derrida* (Cambridge: Cambridge University Press, 1990).

FOSTER, DENNIS, *Confession and Complicity in Narrative* (Cambridge: Cambridge University Press, 1987).

FOUCAULT, MICHEL, *Histoire de la folie à l'âge classique* suivi de *Mon corps, ce papier, ce feu* et *La Folie, l'absence d'œuvre* (2nd edn. 1st publ. Plon, 1961; Gallimard, 1972).

—— *Histoire de la sexualité*, 3 vols. (Gallimard, 1976; 1984), i. *La Volonté de savoir* (1976).

FRAISSE, LUC, *Proust au miroir de sa correspondance* (SEDES, 1996).

FRAZER, JAMES, *The Golden Bough: A Study in Magic and Religion* (1890–1915, 12 vols. 2nd edn.: abridged, Ware: Wordsworth Editions, 1993, with 1922 preface).

FREUD, SIGMUND, *The Standard Edition of the Complete Psychological Works of Sigmund Freud*, tr. under the general editorship of James Strachey, 24 vols. (London: The Hogarth Press and the Institute of Psycho-Analysis, 1953–74).

—— *The Interpretation of Dreams*, SE, iv–v (1900).

—— *Three Essays on the Theory of Sexuality*, SE, vii. 125–243 (1905).

—— 'Formulations on the Two Principles of Mental Functioning', SE, xii. 215–26 (1911).

—— *Totem and Taboo*, SE, xiii. 1–161 (1912–13).

—— 'Instincts and their Vicissitudes', SE, xiv. 111–40 (1915).

—— 'The Unconscious', SE, xiv. 161–215 (1915).

—— 'Mourning and Melancholia', SE, xiv. 239–58 (1917 [1915]).

—— 'From the History of an Infantile Neurosis', SE, xvii. 3–122 ('Wolf Man': 1918 [1914]).

—— *Beyond the Pleasure Principle*, SE, xviii. 3–64 (1920).

—— *The Ego and the Id*, SE, xix. 3–66 (1923).

—— 'A Note upon the "Mystic Writing Pad"', SE, xix. 227–32 (1925 [1924]).

—— 'Negation', SE, xix. 235–39 (1925).

—— *New Introductory Lectures*, SE, xxii. (1933 [1932]).

—— *An Outline of Psycho-Analysis*, SE, xxiii. 141–207 (1940 [1938]).

—— 'Splitting of the Ego in the Process of Defence', SE, xxiii. 273–78 (1940 [1938]).

—— 'A Project for a Scientific Psychology', *The Origins of Psycho-Analysis*, SE, i. 283–359 (1950 [1895]).

FROMENTIN, EUGÈNE, *Dominique* (1863), in *Œuvres complètes* (Gallimard, 1984).

GALLAND, ANTOINE, *Les Mille et Une Nuits* (1704–17; 4th edn. 8 vols. The Hague: Husson, 1714–28).

GAUBERT, SERGE, 'Le Jeu de l'Alphabet', in Gérard Genette and Tzvetan Todorov (eds.), *Recherche de Proust* (Éditions du Seuil, 1980), 68–87.

—— *Proust ou le roman de la différence: L'Individu et le monde social de 'Jean Santeuil' à 'la recherche'* (Lyon: Presses Universitaires de Lyon, 1980).

GENETTE, GÉRARD, 'Discours du récit', *Figures III* (Éditions du Seuil, 1972), 65–273.

—— 'Métonymie chez Proust', *Figures III* (Éditions du Seuil, 1972), 41–63.

—— 'Proust et le langage indirect', *Figures II* (Éditions du Seuil, 1969), 223–94.

—— 'Proust palimpseste', *Figures I* (Éditions du Seuil, 1966), 39–67.

—— and Tzvetan Todorov (eds.), *Recherche de Proust* (Éditions du Seuil, 1980).

GIDE, ANDRÉ, *L'Immoraliste* (1902); *La Porte étroite* (1909); *La Symphonie pastorale* (1919), in *Romans, récits et soties, œuvres lyriques* (Gallimard, 1958).

GIRARD, RENÉ, *La Violence et le sacré* (Grasset, 1972).

—— *Le Bouc émissaire* (Grasset, 1982).

—— *Mensonge romantique et vérité romanesque* (Grasset, 1961).

GOETHE, *Rameaus Neffe: Ein Dialog von Diderot* (Leipzig: Göschen, 1805).

GOSSE, PHILIP HENRY, *Omphalos: An Attempt to Untie the Geological Knot* (London: John Van Voorst, 1857).

GRAY, MARGARET E., *Postmodern Proust* (Philadelphia: University of Pennsylvania Press, 1992).

GRIFFITHS, ERIC, *The Printed Voice of Victorian Poetry* (Oxford: Clarendon Press, 1989).

HECKEL, EDOUARD, *Des différentes formes de fleurs dans les plantes de la même espèce* (Reinwald, 1878).

—— *Des effets de la fécondation croisée et de la fécondation directe dans le règne végétal* (Reinwald, 1877).

HEGEL, G. W. F., *Phenomenology of Spirit* (1807), tr. A. V. Miller (Oxford: Oxford University Press, 1977).

HODSON, LEIGHTON (ed.), *Marcel Proust: The Critical Heritage* (London and New York: Routledge, 1989).

HUGHES, EDWARD, 'The Mapping of Homosexuality in Proust's *Recherche*', *Paragraph*, 18 (1995), 148–62.

HUGO, VICTOR, *Les Feuilles d'automne* [1831] et *Les Chants du crépuscule*, [1835] (Garnier-Flammarion, 1970).

JAKOBSON, ROMAN, and MORRIS HALLE, *Fundamentals of Language* (The Hague: Mouton, 1956; repr. 1971).

JAMES, HENRY, *The Portrait of a Lady* (1881; Harmondsworth: Penguin, 1963; repr. 1972).

JAY, PAUL, *Being in the Text: Self-Representation from Wordsworth to Roland Barthes* (Ithaca, NY: Cornell University Press, 1984).

JEFFERSON, ANN, 'The Missing "I": *La jalousie*', *The Nouveau Roman and the Poetics of Fiction* (Cambridge: Cambridge University Press, 1980), 133–43.

KIERKEGAARD, SØREN, *The Concept of Irony with Constant Reference to Socrates* (1841), tr. Lee M. Capel (London: Collins, 1966).

KOSOFSKY SEDGWICK, EVE, *Epistemology of the Closet* (New York and London: Harvester Wheatsheaf, 1991).

KRAILSHEIMER, A. J., *Studies in Self-Interest: From Descartes to La Bruyère* (Oxford: Clarendon Press, 1962).

KRISTEVA, JULIA, *La Révolution du langage poétique* (Éditions du Seuil, 1974).

—— *Le Temps sensible: Proust et l'expérience littéraire* (Gallimard, 1994).

LA BRUYÈRE, JEAN DE, *Les Caractères de Théophraste traduits du Grec avec Les Mœurs de ce siècle* (1688), in *Œuvres de La Bruyère*, ed. M. G. Servois, 3 vols. (Hachette, 1865).

LACAN, JACQUES, *Le Séminaire*, vii.: *L'éthique de la psychanalyse* (Éditions du Seuil, 1986).

—— *Le Séminaire*, xi.: *Les quatre concepts fondamentaux de la psychanalyse* (1964; Éditions du Seuil, 1973).

—— 'Le stade du miroir comme formateur de la fonction du Je' (1949), *Écrits* I (Éditions du Seuil, 1966), 89–97.

LALANDE, ANDRÉ, *Vocabulaire technique et critique de la philosophie* (1926, 2 vols. 16th edn. Presses Universitaires de France, 1988; repr. Quadrige/Presses Universitaires de France, 1993).

LAPLANCHE, JEAN, and J.-B. PONTALIS, *Vocabulaire de la psychanalyse* (12th edn. Presses Universitaires de France, 1994).

LARGE, DUNCAN, 'Proust on Nietzsche: The Question of Friendship', *The Modern Language Review*, 88 (1993), 612–24.

LEIBNIZ, *Essais de Théodicée sur la bonté de Dieu, la liberté de l'homme et l'origine du mal* (1710; Amsterdam: Changuion, 1747).

LEJEUNE, PHILIPPE, 'Écriture et sexualité', *Europe* (numéro spécial Proust, Feb.–Mar. 1971), 113–43.

—— *Je est un autre: L'Autobiographie de la littérature aux médias* (Éditions du Seuil, 1980).

—— *Le Pacte autobiographique* (Éditions du Seuil, 1975).

—— 'Les Carafes de la Vivonne', in Gérard Genette and Tzvetan Todorov (eds.), *Recherche de Proust* (Éditions du Seuil, 1980), 163–96.

LÉVINAS, EMMANUEL, 'L'Autre dans Proust', *Deucalion*, 2 (1947), 117–23 (repr. in *Noms propres: Agnon, Buber, Celan, Delhomme, Derrida, Jabès, Kierkegaard, Lacroix, Laporte, Picard, Proust, Van Breda, Wahl* (Montpellier: Fata Morgana, 1976), 149–56).

LUCKHURST, NICOLA, *Science and Structure in Proust's* A la recherche du temps perdu (Oxford: Oxford University Press, 2000).

LUCRETIUS, *De rerum natura*, tr. W. H. D. Rouse (London: Heinemann, 1924; repr. 1966).

MCDONALD, CHRISTIE, *The Proustian Fabric: Associations of Memory* (Lincoln, Nebr., and London: University of Nebraska Press, 1991).

MALEBRANCHE, NICOLAS, *De la recherche de la vérité* (1674–5), 3 vols. (Vrin, 1962).

Mardrus, Joseph Charles Victor, *Le Livre des Mille Nuits et Une Nuit, traduction littérale et complète du texte arabe* (Éditions de la Revue Blanche, 1899–1904; repr. 18 vols. Charpentier, 1920–4).

MARKS, JONATHAN E., 'The Verdurins and their Cult', *YFS* 34 (1965), 73–80.

MILLY, JEAN, *La Phrase de Proust: Des phrases de Bergotte aux phrases de Vinteuil* (Larousse, 1975).

—— 'Le Pastiche Goncourt dans *Le Temps retrouvé*', *Revue d'histoire littéraire de la France,* 5–6 (1971), 815–35.

MONTAIGNE, MICHEL DE, *Essais,* in *Œuvres complètes* (Gallimard, 1962).

MOORJANI, ANGELA, 'A Cryptanalysis of Proust's "Les Intermittences du cœur" ', *MLN* 105 (1990), 875–88.

MULLER, MARCEL, 'Charlus dans le métro ou pastiche et cruauté chez Proust', *Cahiers Marcel Proust, 9, nouvelle série, Études Proustiennes III* (Gallimard, 1979), 9–25.

—— *Les Voix narratives dans 'la recherche du temps perdu'* (Geneva: Droz, 1965; repr. 1983).

MURPHY, JONATHAN, 'Sight or Cite? Aspects of the Visual in Proust' (unpublished doctoral thesis, University of Cambridge, 1996; Peter Lang, forthcoming).

MUSSET, ALFRED DE, *Œuvres complètes,* ed. Philippe van Tieghem (Éditions du Seuil, 1963).

NIETZSCHE, FRIEDRICH, *The Birth of Tragedy* (1872), tr. Shaun Whiteside, ed. Michael Tanner (Harmondsworth: Penguin, 1993).

NUSSBAUM, MARTHA C., *Love's Knowledge: Essays on Philosophy and Literature* (Oxford: Oxford University Press, 1990).

OVID, *Metamorphoses,* tr. Mary M. Innes (Harmondsworth: Penguin, 1955).

PAINTER, GEORGE D., *Marcel Proust* (London: Chatto & Windus, i (1959); ii (1965); publ. as one vol. Harmondsworth: Penguin, 1983; repr. 1990).

PARKES, COLIN MURRAY, *Bereavement: Studies of Grief in Adult Life* (3rd edn. London: Routledge, 1996).

PATMORE, COVENTRY, 'The Point of Rest in Art', *Principle in Art etc.* (London: Bell, 1898), 12–17.

POE, EDGAR ALLAN, *The Imp of the Perverse* (1845; Harmondsworth: Penguin, 1982), 281–2.

POULET, GEORGES, *L'Espace proustien* (2nd edn. Gallimard, 1982).

PROUST, MARCEL, *A la recherche du temps perdu,* 3 vols. (Gallimard, 1954), Online, FRANTEXT Base de données textuelles du français (http://www.ciril.fr/~mastina/FRANTEXT), Internet, 5 June 1997.

PUGH, ANTHONY, *The Birth of 'A la recherche du temps perdu'* (Lexington, Ky.: French Forum, 1987).

Quine, W. V., 'On Simple Theories of a Complex World', *The Ways of Paradox and Other Essays* (New York: Random House, 1966), 242–5 (1st publ. in *Synthese*, 15 (1963)).

QUINTILIAN, *Institutio Oratoria*, tr. H. E. Butler, 4 vols. (London: Heineman, 1921; repr. 1977).

RABELAIS, *Pantagruel; Gargantua; Tiers Livre de Pantagruel; Quart Livre*, in *Œuvres complètes* (Gallimard, 1994).

RAIMOND, MICHEL, *Le Signe des temps* (SEDES, 1976).

—— 'Les Scènes mondaines dans *A la recherche du temps perdu*', in John D. Erickson and Irène Pagès (eds.), *Proust et le texte producteur* (Guelph: University of Guelph, 1980), 71–7.

—— *Proust romancier* (SEDES, 1984).

RIBOT, THÉODULE, *La Logique des sentiments* (1906; 5th edn. Alcan, 1920).

RICHARD, JEAN-PIERRE, *Proust et le monde sensible* (Éditions du Seuil, 1974).

RICKS, CHRISTOPHER, *Keats and Embarrassment* (Oxford: Clarendon Press, 1974).

RIFFATERRE, MICHAEL, 'Compelling Reader Responses', in Andrew Bennet (ed.), *Reading Reading* (Tampere English Studies, 3; Tampere, Finland: University of Tampere, 1993), 85–106.

RIVERS, J. E., *Proust and the Art of Love: The Aesthetics of Sexuality in the Life, Times, and Art of Marcel Proust* (New York: Columbia University Press, 1980).

ROBBE-GRILLET, ALAIN, *La Jalousie* (Éditions de Minuit, 1957).

RORTY, RICHARD, *Contingency, Irony, and Solidarity* (Cambridge: Cambridge University Press, 1989).

ROUSSEAU, JEAN-JACQUES, *Œuvres complètes*, ed. B. Gagnebin, R. Osmont, and M. Raymond, 4 vols. (Gallimard, 1959–69), *Les Confessions, dialogues, Les Rêveries du promeneur solitaire, fragments autobiographiques* (1959).

SABRY, RANDA, *Stratégies discursives: Digression, transition, suspens* (Éditions de l'École des Hautes Études en Sciences Sociales, 1992).

SAID, EDWARD W., *Orientalism: Western Conceptions of the Orient* (London: Routledge & Kegan Paul, 1978; repr. Harmondsworth: Penguin, 1995).

SARTRE, JEAN-PAUL, *L'Être et le néant: Essai d'ontologie phénoménologique* (Gallimard, 1943).

SHAKESPEARE, WILLIAM, *The Complete Oxford Shakespeare*, ed. Stanley Wells and Gary Taylor, 4 vols. (Oxford: Oxford University Press, 1987).

SHATTUCK, ROGER, *Proust's Binoculars* (New York: Random House, 1963; repr. London: Chatto & Windus, 1964).

SHERINGHAM, MICHAEL, *French Autobiography: Devices and Desires: Rousseau to Perec* (Oxford: Clarendon Press, 1993).

SHKLAR, JUDITH N., *The Faces of Injustice* (New Haven: Yale University Press, 1990).

SILVERMAN, KAJA, *Male Subjectivity at the Margins* (New York and London: Routledge, 1992).

SPITZER, LEO, *Études de style* (Gallimard, 1970; repr. 1988; 1st publ. as *Stilstudien* (Munich: Hueber, 1928).

SPRINKER, MICHAEL, *History and Ideology in Proust: 'A la recherche du temps perdu' and the Third French Republic* (Cambridge: Cambridge University Press, 1994).

STAROBINSKI, JEAN, *Les Mots sous les mots: Les Anagrammes de Ferdinand de Saussure* (Gallimard, 1971).

STENDHAL, *Le Rouge et le Noir*, 1831, ed. H. Martineau (Garnier, 1960).

STERNE, LAURENCE, *The Life and Opinions of Tristram Shandy* (1759–67; Harmondsworth: Penguin, 1967; repr. 1988).

STURROCK, JOHN, *The Language of Autobiography: Studies in the First Person Singular* (Cambridge: Cambridge University Press, 1993).

TADIÉ, JEAN-YVES, *Proust* (Belfond, 1983).

TERDIMAN, RICHARD, *The Dialectics of Isolation: Self and Society in the French Novel from the Realists to Proust* (New Haven: Yale University Press, 1976).

THEOPHRASTUS, *The Characters* (Harmondsworth: Penguin, 1967).

WIESEL, ELIE, *La Nuit* (Éditions de Minuit, 1958).

WILSON, EDMUND, *Axel's Castle: A Study in the Imaginative Literature of 1870–1930* (New York: Scribner, 1931; repr. New York: Norton, 1984).

WILSON, EMMA, *Sexuality and the Reading Encounter: Identity and Desire in Proust, Duras, Tournier, and Cixous* (Oxford: Clarendon Press, 1996).

WILSON, STEPHEN, *Ideology and Experience: Anti-Semitism in France at the Time of the Dreyfus Affair* (London: Associated University Presses, 1982).

WINTON, ALISON, *Proust's Additions: The Making of 'A la recherche du temps perdu'*, 2 vols. (Cambridge: Cambridge University Press, 1977).

WITTGENSTEIN, LUDWIG, *Philosophical Investigations*, tr. G. E. M. Anscombe (1953; 3rd edn. English text with index, Oxford: Blackwell, 1968; repr. 1992).

YOSHIKAWA, K., 'Marcel Proust en 1908: Comment a-t-il commencé à écrire *A la recherche du temps perdu*', *Études de langue et littérature françaises*, 22 (1973), 135–52.

ZELDIN, THEODORE, *A History of French Passions 1848–1945*, 2 vols. (Oxford: Clarendon Press, 1973, 1977), ii. *Intellect, Taste and Anxiety* (1977).

ZOLA, ÉMILE, *La Bête humaine* (1890, Garnier-Flammarion, 1972).

SELECTED WORKS ON PROUST

BARDÈCHE, MAURICE, *Marcel Proust romancier*, 2 vols. (Les Sept Couleurs, 1971).

BARTHES, ROLAND, 'Une idée de recherche', in Gérard Genette and Tzvetan Todorov (eds.), *Recherche de Proust* (Éditions du Seuil, 1980), 34–9.

BATAILLE, GEORGES, 'Proust', *La Littérature et le mal* (Gallimard, 1957), 97–108.

BELL, WILLIAM STEWART, *Proust's Nocturnal Muse* (New York: Columbia University Press, 1962).

BELLEMIN-NOËL, JEAN, 'Psychanalyser le rêve de Swann?', *Poétique*, 2/8 (1971), 447–69.

BLONDEL, C., *La Psychographie de Marcel Proust* (Vrin, 1932).

BOUILLAGUET, ANNICK, *Marcel Proust: Bilan critique* (Nathan, 1994).

BOWIE, MALCOLM, *The Morality of Proust*, Inaugural Lecture Delivered before the University of Oxford (Oxford: Clarendon Press, 1994).

BRUN, BERNARD, '*Le Temps retrouvé* dans les avant-textes de "Combray"', *Bulletin d'informations proustiennes*, 12 (1981), 7–23.

—— 'Notes sur la genèse du *Temps retrouvé*', *Bulletin d'informations proustiennes*, 11 (1980), 49–51.

BUCKNALL, BARBARA, *Critical Essays on Marcel Proust* (Boston, Mass.: Hall, 1987).

CAIRNS, LUCILLE, 'Homosexuality and Lesbianism in Proust's *Sodome et Gomorrhe*', *French Studies*, 51 (1997), 43–57.

CAMPION, PIERRE, 'Le "Je" proustien: Invention et exploitation de la formule', *Poétique*, 23 (1992), 3–29.

CAWS, MARY ANN, and EUGÈNE NICOLE (eds.), *Reading Proust Now* (New York: Peter Lang, 1990).

COCTEAU, JEAN, *Poésie critique* (Éditions des quatre vents, 1946), 197–200.

COMPAGNON, ANTOINE, 'Disproportion de Proust: Les Carnets de la *Recherche*', in Louis Hay (ed.), *Carnets d'écrivains, i. Hugo, Flaubert, Proust, Valéry, Gide, du Bouchet, Perec*, (coll. 'Textes et manuscrits', Éditions du CNRS, 1990), 151–76.

—— 'La Dernière victime du narrateur', *Critique*, 598 (1997), 131–46.

—— 'Proust 1, contre la lecture', *La Troisième République des lettres, de Flaubert à Proust* (Éditions du Seuil, 1983), 221–52.

CZONICZER, ELISABETH, *Quelques antécédents de 'A la recherche du temps perdu': Tendances qui peuvent avoir contribué à la cristallisation du roman proustien* (Geneva: Droz, 1957).

DANDIEU, A., *Marcel Proust: Sa révélation psychologique* (Firmin-Didot, 1930).

ERMAN, MICHEL, *L'Œil de Proust: Écriture et voyeurisme dans 'A la recherche du temps perdu'* (Nizet, 1988).

EVANS, CHRISTINE ANN, 'The Fate of Speaking: Realist Dialogue in the Anti-Realist Narrative of *A la recherche du temps perdu*', *Modern Language Studies*, 19 (1989), 75–81.

FLORIVAL, GHISLAINE, *Le Désir chez Proust* (Louvain and Paris: Nauwelaerts, 1971).

FRASER, ROBERT, *Proust and the Victorians: The Lamp of Memory* (Basingstoke: Macmillan, 1994).

GANDELMAN, CLAUDE, 'The Artist as "Traumarbeiter" ', *YFS* 84 (1994), 118–35.

GAUBERT, SERGE, 'La Conversation et l'écriture', *Europe*, 496–7 ('Centenaire de Marcel Proust', 1970), 171–92.

GENETTE, GÉRARD, ' "One of My Favourite Writers" ', *YFS* 89 (1996), 208–22.

—— *Palimpsestes: La Littérature au second degré* (Éditions du Seuil, 1982).

GIDE, ANDRÉ, *Corydon* (1911; Gallimard, 1924).

—— *Journal I 1887–1925*, ed. Éric Marty (Gallimard, 1996).

GODEAU, FLORENCE, *Les Désarrois du moi: 'A la recherche du temps perdu' de M. Proust et 'Der Mann ohne Eigenschaften' de R. Musil* (Tübingen: Max Niemeyer, 1995).

GOODKIN, RICHARD E., *Around Proust* (Princeton: Princeton University Press, 1991).

—— 'Proust and Home(r): An Avuncular Intertext', *MLN* 104 (1989), 993–1014.

—— 'T(r)yptext: Proust, Mallarmé, Racine', *YFS* 76 (1989), 284–314.

GRAHAM, VICTOR E., *The Imagery of Proust* (Oxford: Oxford University Press, 1966).

GRAY, MARGARET E., 'Skipping Love Scenes: The Repression of Literature in Proust', *MLN* 104 (1989), 1020–33.

GRAY-MCDONALD, MARGARET, 'Marcel's "Écriture Féminine" ', *Modern Fiction Studies*, 34 (1988), 337–52.

GREENE, ROBERT W., 'Quotation, Repetition and Ethical Competence in *Un Amour de Swann*', *Contemporary Literature*, 25 (1984), 136–55: repr. in Robert W. Greene, *Just Words: Moralism and Metalanguage in Twentieth-Century French Fiction* (University Park, Pa.: Pennsylvania State University Press, 1993).

GRIMALDI, NICOLAS, *La Jalousie: Étude sur l'imaginaire proustien* (Arles: Actes Sud, 1993).

GUNN, DANIEL, *Psychoanalysis and Fiction: An Exploration of Literary and Psychoanalytic Borders* (Cambridge: Cambridge University Press, 1988; repr. 1990).

HENROT, GENEVIÈVE, *Délits/Délivrance: Thématique de la mémoire proustienne* (Padua: CLEUP, 1991).

HENRY, ANNE, *Marcel Proust: Théories pour une esthétique* (Klincksieck, 1981).

HENRY, ANNE, *Proust* (Balland, 1986).

—— *Proust romancier: Le Tombeau égyptien* (Flammarion, 1983).

HERSCHBERG PIERROT, ANNE, 'Les Notes de Proust', *Genesis*, 6 (1994), 61–78.

HUAS, JEANINE, *Les Femmes chez Proust* (Hachette, 1971).

HUGHES, EDWARD, *Marcel Proust: A Study in the Quality of Awareness* (Cambridge: Cambridge University Press, 1983).

HUMPHRIES, JEFFERSON, *The Otherness Within: Gnostic Readings in Marcel Proust, Flannery O'Connor and Françoise Villon* (Baton Rouge, La.: Louisiana State University Press, 1983).

JACKSON, M. J., 'Proust's Churches in *A la recherche du temps perdu*', *Journal of Literature and Theology*, 5 (1991), 296–310.

JAUSS, HANS ROBERT, *Zeit und Erinnerung in Marcel Prousts 'A la recherche du temps perdu': Ein Beitrag zur Theorie des Romans* (Heidelberg: Winter, 1955).

JOHNSON, J. THEODORE, 'Marcel Proust et l'architecture III: La Conception du roman-cathédrale', *Bulletin de la société des amis de Marcel Proust et des amis de Combray*, 26 (1976), 247–66.

JULLIEN, DOMINIQUE, *Proust et ses modèles* (Corti, 1989).

KAMBER, G., and R. MACKSEY, ' "Negative Metaphor" and Proust's Rhetoric of Absence', *MLN* 85 (1970), 858–83.

KASELL, WALTER, *Marcel Proust and the Strategy of Reading* (Amsterdam: Benjamins, 1980).

KAUFMAN, VINCENT, *Post-Scripts: The Writer's Workshop*, tr. Deborah Treisman (Cambridge, Mass.: Harvard University Press, 1994).

KILMARTIN, TERENCE, *A Guide to Proust* (Harmondsworth: Penguin, 1985).

KUBERSKI, PHILIP, 'Proust's Brain', *The Yale Review*, 78 (1989), 97–112.

LAPORTE, ROGER, *Marcel Proust: Le Narrateur et l'écrivain* (Fata Morgana, 1994).

LEONARD, DIANE R., 'Proust et Ruskin: Réincarnations intertextuelles', *Bulletin d'informations proustiennes*, 24 (1993), 67–82.

LOWERY, BRUCE, *Marcel Proust et Henry James: Une confrontation* (Plon, 1964).

MABIN, DOMINIQUE, *Le Sommeil de Marcel Proust* (Presses Universitaires de France, 1992).

MACKENSIE, ROBIN, 'Proust's "Livre intérieur" ', in Peter Collier and Judy Davies (eds.), *Modernism and the European Unconscious* (Oxford: Polity Press and Basil Blackwell, 1990), 149–64.

MASSIS, HENRI, *Le Drame de Marcel Proust* (Grasset, 1937).

MAURIAC, FRANÇOIS, *Du côté de chez Proust* (La Table ronde, 1947).

MEHLMAN, JEFFREY, *A Structural Study of Autobiography: Proust, Leiris, Sartre, Lévi-Strauss* (Ithaca, NY: Cornell University Press, 1974).

MIGUET-OLLAGNIER, MARIE, *La Mythologie de Marcel Proust* (Belles Lettres, 1982).

MILLER, MILTON L., *Nostalgia: A Psychoanalytic Study of Marcel Proust* (London: Victor Gollancz, 1957).

MILLY, JEAN (ed.), *Les Pastiches de Proust* (Colin, 1970).

MINGELGRÜN, ALBERT, *Thèmes et structures bibliques dans l'œuvre de Marcel Proust: Étude stylistique de quelques interférences* (Lausanne: Éditions de l'Âge d'Homme, 1978).

NABOKOV, VLADIMIR, *Lectures on Literature*, ed. Fredson Bowers (London: Weidenfeld & Nicholson, 1980).

NATHAN, J., *Citations, références et allusions de Marcel Proust dans 'A la recherche'* (Nizet, 1969).

—— *La Morale de Proust* (Nizet, 1953; repr. 1969).

NATTIEZ, JEAN-JACQUES, *Proust musicien* (Christian Bourgeois, 1984).

NEMEROV, HOWARD, *The Oak in the Acorn: On 'Remembrance of Things Past' and on Teaching Proust, Who Will Never Learn* (Baton Rouge, La.: Louisiana State University Press, 1987).

NEWMARK, KEVIN, 'Ingesting the Mummy: Proust's Allegories of Memory', *YFS* 79 (1991), 150–77.

OLSEN, ROBERT, 'The Semantic Complexity of Novelistic Fiction: The Expansion and Collapsing of Proust's Fictional Universe', *Style*, 25 (1991), 177–95.

PHILIP, MICHEL, 'The Hidden Onlooker', *YFS* 34 (1965), 37–42.

PINTER, HAROLD, *The Proust Screenplay* (London: Methuen, 1978).

QUÉMAR, CLAUDINE, 'L'Église de Combray, son curé et le narrateur', *Cahiers Marcel Proust, Études Proustiennes*, 1 (1973), 277–346.

RECANATI, JEAN, *Profils juifs de Marcel Proust* (Buchet Chastel, 1979).

RICŒUR, PAUL, *Temps et récit*, 2 vols. (Éditions du Seuil, 1984), ii. *La Configuration dans le récit de fiction*, 194–225.

RIFFATERRE, MICHAEL, 'On Narrative Subtexts: Proust's Magic Lantern', *Style*, 22 (1988), 450–66.

—— 'The Intertextual Unconscious', *Critical Inquiry*, 13 (1987), 371–85.

RIVERS, J. E., 'The Myth and Science of Homosexuality in *A la recherche du temps perdu*', in George Stambolian and Elaine Marks (eds.), *Homosexualities and French Literature* (Ithaca, NY: Cornell University Press, 1979), 262–78.

ROBINSON, CHRISTOPHER, *Scandal in the Ink: Male and Female Homosexuality in Twentieth-Century French Literature* (London: Cassell, 1995).

ROUSSET, JEAN, *Forme et signification: Essais sur les structures littéraires de Corneille à Claudel* (Corti, 1962).

ROY, ALAIN, 'Bref, peut-on digresser?', *Critique*, 598 (1997), 156–63.

SARTRE, JEAN-PAUL, *Situations*, 10 vols. (Gallimard, 1947), i, ii.

SAYLOR, DOUGLAS B., *The Sadomasochistic Homotext: Readings in Sade, Balzac and Proust* (New York: Peter Lang, 1993).

SCHMID, MARION A., 'Teleology and Textual Misrepresentation: The New Pléiade Proust', *French Studies Bulletin*, 56 (1995), 15–17.

SHATTUCK, ROGER, 'Proust's Stilts', *YFS* 34 (1965), 91–8.

SIDORSKY, DAVID, 'Modernism and the Emancipation of Literature from Morality: Teleology and Vocation in Joyce, Ford and Proust', *New Literary History*, 15 (1983), 137–53.

SOURIS, STEPHEN, 'The Status of the Self in *Du Côté de Chez Swann* and *Le Temps retrouvé*: A Deconstructive Analysis', *Dalhousie French Studies*, 24 (1993), 99–110.

TADIÉ, JEAN-YVES, *Marcel Proust* (Gallimard, 1996).

—— *Proust et le roman* (Gallimard, 1971).

TAYLOR, ELIZABETH RUSSELL, *Marcel Proust and his Contexts: A Critical Biography of English Language Scholarship* (London: Garland, 1981).

THOMAS, FRANCIS-NOËL, 'Marcel Proust: Psychological Explanation', *The Writer Writing: Philosophic Acts in Literature* (Princeton: Princeton University Press, 1992), 104–32.

TOUTTAVOULT, FABRICE, *Confessions: Marx, Engels, Proust, Mallarmé, Cézanne* (Belin, 1988).

VALDMAN, BERNARD, 'Langage parlé et communication dans *A la recherche*', *Constructions* (1986), 41–52.

VOGELY, MAXINE ARNOLD, *A Proust Dictionary* (New York: Whitston, 1981).

WARREN, JONATHAN, 'The Lessons of the Living Dead: Marcel's Journey from Balbec to Douville-Féterne in Proust's *Cities of the Plain: Part Two*', *Studies in Twentieth-Century Literature*, 19 (1995), 257–68.

WINZ, BURGUNDE HŒNIG, *The World of Suffering in 'A la recherche du temps perdu'* (New York: Peter Lang, 1989).

ZURBRUGG, NICHOLAS, *Beckett and Proust* (Totowa, NJ: Barnes & Noble, 1988).

SELECTED SPECIAL REFERENCE MATERIAL ON PROUST

L'Arc, 47 (numéro spécial 'Proust', 1971).

Bulletin de la société des amis de Marcel Proust et des amis de Combray, 46 vols. (1950–96).

Bulletin d'informations proustiennes, 24 vols. (Presses de l'École Normale Supérieure, 1975–93).

Cahiers Marcel Proust (includes *Études proustiennes*), 14 vols. (Gallimard, 1970–87).

Europe (numéro spécial Proust, Feb.–Mar. 1971).

Exposition: Bibliothèque Nationale Marcel Proust, Paris, 1965.

Exposition: 'Le monde de Proust: photographie de Paul Nadar', 1977.

Exposition: 'Marcel Proust en son temps', 1971, Musée Jacquemart-André, catalogue, Jacques Suffel.
Yale French Studies, 34 (1965).

GENERAL WORKS CONSULTED

ANZIEU, DIDIER, *L'Auto-analyse: Son rôle dans la découverte de la psych-analyse par Freud* (Presses Universitaires de France, 1959).
ARIÈS, PHILIPPE, *Essais sur l'histoire de la mort en Occident: Du moyen âge à nos jours* (Éditions du Seuil, 1975).
ARISTOTLE, *The Art of Rhetoric*, tr. H. C. Lawson-Tancred (Harmondsworth: Penguin, 1991).
BAKHTIN, M. M., *Problems of Dostoyevsky's Poetics*, ed. and tr. Caryl Emerson (Manchester: Manchester University Press, 1984).
BARTHES, ROLAND, *Fragments d'un discours amoureux* (Éditions du Seuil, 1977).
BELSEY, CATHERINE, 'Literature, History, Politics', in David Lodge (ed.), *Modern Criticism and Theory: A Reader* (Harlow: Longman, 1988).
BENVENISTE, ÉMILE, *Problèmes de linguistique générale* (Gallimard, 1966).
BHABHA, HOMI K., 'Of Mimicry and Men: The Ambivalence of Colonial Discourse', *October*, 28 (1984), 125–33.
BOOTH, WAYNE C., *A Rhetoric of Irony* (Chicago: University of Chicago Press, 1974).
BOWIE, MALCOLM, *Lacan* (London: Fontana, 1991).
BRUSS, ELIZABETH W., *Autobiographical Acts: The Changing Situation of a Literary Genre* (Baltimore: Johns Hopkins University Press, 1976).
BUCHANAN, JAMES, *The Doctrine of Justification* (1867; Edinburgh: Banner of Truth Trust, 1984).
COE, RICHARD N., *When the Grass was Taller: Autobiography and the Experience of Childhood* (New Haven: Yale University Press, 1984).
CONSTANT, BENJAMIN, *Adolphe* (1816; Flammarion, 1989).
CULLER, JONATHAN, *Flaubert: The Uses of Uncertainty* (London: Elek Books, 1974).
—— *On Deconstruction: Theory and Criticism after Structuralism* (Ithaca, NY: Cornell University Press, 1982; repr. London: Routledge, 1994).
DE MAN, PAUL, 'The Epistemology of Metaphor', *Critical Inquiry*, 5 (1978), 13–30: repr. in Sheldon Sacks (ed.), *On Metaphor* (Chicago: University of Chicago Press, 1979).
—— 'The Resistance to Theory', *YFS* 63 (1972), 3–20.
DERRIDA, JACQUES, *La Carte postale de Socrate à Freud et au-delà* (Flammarion, 1980).
—— 'La Différance', in *Tel Quel: Théorie d'ensemble (choix)* (Éditions du Seuil, 1968), 43–68.

DERRIDA, JACQUES, *Marges de la philosophie* (Éditions de Minuit, 1972).

—— 'Télépathie', *Psyché: Inventions de l'autre* (Galilée, 1987), 237–70.

—— 'Ulysses Gramophone: Hear Say Yes in Joyce', in *Jacques Derrida: Acts of Literature*, ed. Derek Attridge (New York: Routledge, 1992), 253–309.

DOSTOYEVSKY, FYODOR, *Crime and Punishment* (1865–6), tr. David McDuff (Harmondsworth: Penguin, 1991).

—— *Notes from Underground* (1864), tr. Jessie Coulson (Harmondsworth: Penguin, 1972).

DRUMONT, ÉDOUARD, *La France Juive devant opinion* (48th edn. 2 vols. Marpon et Flammarion, 1886; repr. La Librairie Française, 1986).

ECO, UMBERTO, *Interpretation and Overinterpretation*, ed. Stefan Collini (Cambridge: Cambridge University Press, 1992).

ELBAZ, ROBERT, *The Changing Nature of the Self: A Critical Study of the Autobiographic Discourse* (London: Croom Helm, 1988).

ELLENBERGER, HENRI F., *The Discovery of the Unconscious: The History and Evolution of Dynamic Psychiatry* (London: Allen Lane, 1970).

EMPSON, WILLIAM, *Seven Types of Ambiguity* (1930; 3rd edn. London: Chatto & Windus, 1953; repr. Harmondsworth: Penguin, 1995).

FLETCHER, ANGUS, *Allegory: The Theory of a Symbolic Mode* (Ithaca, NY: Cornell University Press, 1964).

FONTANIER, PIERRE, *Les Figures du discours* (Flammarion, 1968).

FORÊTS, LOUIS-RENÉ DES, *Le Bavard* (Gallimard, 1946; repr. 1978).

FORRESTER, JOHN, ' "Mille e tre": Freud and Collecting', in John Elsner and Roger Cardinal (eds.), *The Cultures of Collecting* (London: Reaktion Books, 1994), 224–51.

FOUCAULT, MICHEL, *Surveiller et punir: Naissance de la prison* (Gallimard, 1975).

FREUD, SIGMUND, *The Standard Edition of the Complete Psychological Works of Sigmund Freud*, tr. under the general editorship of James Strachey, 24 vols. (London: The Hogarth Press and the Institute of Psycho-Analysis, 1953–74). Below are works by Freud not already listed in the 'Works cited' section.

—— with Josef Breuer, *Studies on Hysteria*, SE, ii (1895).

—— *Jokes and their Relation to the Unconscious*, SE, viii (1905).

—— 'Fragment of an Analysis of a Case of Hysteria', *SE*, vii. 3–122 ('Dora': 1905 [1901]).

—— 'Analysis of a Phobia in a Five-Year-Old Boy', *SE*, x. 3–149 ('Little Hans': 1909).

—— 'The Theme of the Three Caskets', *SE*, xii. 291–301 (1913).

—— 'The Moses of Michelangelo', *SE*, xiii. 211–38 (1914).

—— 'On Narcissism: An Introduction', *SE*, xiv. 69–102 (1914).

—— ' "A Child is Being Beaten" ', *SE*, xvii. 177–204 (1919).

—— 'The "Uncanny" ', *SE*, xvii. 219–56 (1919).

—— 'Dreams and Telepathy', *SE*, xviii. 197–220 (1922).

—— 'The Infantile Genital Organization, *SE*, xix. 141–45 (1923).

—— 'Neurosis and Psychosis', *SE*, xix. 149–53 (1924 [1923]).

—— 'The Economic Problem of Masochism', *SE*, xix. 157–70 (1924).

—— *An Autobiographical Study*, *SE*, xx. 3–74 (1925).

—— 'Dostoyevsky and Parricide', *SE*, xxi. 175–96 (1928).

—— *Civilization and its Discontents*, *SE*, xxi. 59–145 (1930).

—— 'A Disturbance of Memory on the Acropolis', *SE*, xxii. 239–48 (1936).

—— 'Analysis Terminable and Interminable', *SE*, xxiii. 211–53 (1937).

—— 'Medusa's Head', *SE*, xviii. 273–4 (1940 [1922]).

—— 'Psycho-Analysis and Telepathy', *SE*, xviii. 177–93 (1941 [1921]).

FUMAROLI, MARC, *Le Genre des genres littéraires français: La Conversation*, Zaharoff Lecture for 1990 (Oxford: Clarendon Press, 1992).

GILBERT, SANDRA M., and SUSAN GUBAR, *The Madwoman in the Attic: The Woman Writer and the Nineteenth-Century Literary Imagination* (New Haven: Yale University Press, 1979).

GILLIGAN, CAROL, *In a Different Voice: Psychological Theory and Women's Development* (Cambridge, Mass.: Harvard University Press, 1982).

GOFFMAN, ERVING, *Stigma: Notes on the Management of Spoiled Identity* (Harmondsworth: Penguin, 1990).

GROSZ, ELIZABETH, *Sexual Subversions* (Sydney: Allen & Unwin, 1989).

HAND, SÉAN (ed.), *The Levinas Reader* (Oxford: Blackwell, 1989).

HAWES, CLEMENT, *Mania and Literary Style: The Rhetoric of Enthusiasm from the Ranters to Christopher Smart* (Cambridge: Cambridge University Press, 1996).

HAY, LOUIS, 'History or Genesis?', *YFS* 89 (1996), 191–207.

HOBBES, THOMAS, *Leviathan* (1651; Harmondsworth: Penguin, 1985).

HOBSBAWM, E. J., *Nations and Nationalism since 1780* (2nd edn. Cambridge: Cambridge University Press, 1992).

HOLLAND, NORMAN N., *The I* (New Haven: Yale University Press, 1985).

HOWELLS, CHRISTINA, *Sartre: The Necessity of Freedom* (Cambridge: Cambridge University Press, 1988).

IRIGARAY, LUCE, *Éthique de la différence sexuelle* (Éditions de Minuit, 1984).

—— *Spéculum de l'autre femme* (Éditions de Minuit, 1974).

JAMESON, FREDRIC, *The Political Unconscious: Narrative as a Socially Symbolic Act* (London: Routledge, 1989).

LA ROCHEFOUCAULD, *Maximes suivies des Réflexions diverses, du Portrait de La Rochefoucauld par lui-même et des Remarques de Christine de Suède sur les Maximes* (Garnier Frères, 1967).

LE DŒUFF, MICHÈLE, 'Women and Philosophy', *Radical Philosophy*, 17

(1977), 2–11: rev. in Toril Moi (ed.), *French Feminist Thought: A Reader* (Oxford: Basil Blackwell, 1986), 181–209.

LELEU, MICHÈLE, *Les Journaux intimes* (Presses Universitaires de France, 1952).

LÉVINAS, EMMANUEL, *Autrement qu'être ou au-delà de l'essence* (The Hague: Martinus Nijhoff, 1974; repr. Kluwer Academic, Livre de Poche, 1990).

—— *Éthique et Infini: Dialogues avec Philippe Nemo* (Fayard/Radio-France, Livre de Poche, 1982).

—— *Totalité et Infini: Essai sur l'extériorité* (The Hague: Martinus Nijhoff, 1961; repr. Kluwer Academic, Livre de Poche, 1992).

LEWIS, C. S., *The Allegory of Love: A Study in Medieval Tradition* (Oxford: Clarendon Press, 1936; repr. 1995).

LUKÁCS, GEORG, *The Historical Novel*, tr. Hannah and Stanley Mitchell (London: Merlin, 1962).

—— *The Meaning of Contemporary Realism*, tr. John and Necke Mander (London: Merlin, 1963; repr. 1972).

—— *Studies in European Realism*, tr. Edith Bone (London: Merlin, 1950; repr. 1978).

LYCAN, WILLIAM G., *Judgement and Justification* (Cambridge: Cambridge University Press, 1988).

LYONS, W., *Emotion* (Cambridge: Cambridge University Press, 1980).

LYOTARD, JEAN-FRANÇOIS (ed.), *La Faculté de juger* (Éditions de Minuit, Colloque de Cerisy, 1985).

—— *Le Différend* (Éditions de Minuit, 1983).

MCELHONE, JOHN, *Glossary of Photographic Media* (Ottawa: National Gallery of Canada, 1995).

MACHEREY, PIERRE, *Pour une théorie de la production littéraire* (Maspero, 1966).

MÂLE, ÉMILE, *L'Art religieux du XIIIe siècle en France* (8th edn. Colin, 1948; repr. Livre de Poche, 1993).

MARKS, ELAINE, and ISABELLE DE COURTIVRON (eds.), *New French Feminisms: An Anthology* (New York: Harvester, 1981).

MARX, KARL, *The Eighteenth Brumaire of Louis Napoleon*, in *Karl Marx: Selected Writings*, ed. David McLellan (Oxford: Oxford University Press, 1977), 300–25.

MERLEAU-PONTY, MAURICE, *Phénoménologie de la perception* (Gallimard, 1945), tr. Colin Smith as *Phenomenology of Perception* (London: Routledge & Kegan Paul, repr. Routledge, 1996).

MILLER, J. HILLIS, *The Ethics of Reading: Kant, de Man, Eliot, Trollope, James, and Benjamin* (New York: Columbia University Press, 1987).

MILLETT, KATE, *Sexual Politics* (New York: Doubleday, 1970; repr. London: Virago, 1977).

MOI, TORIL (ed.), *French Feminist Thought: A Reader* (Oxford: Blackwell, 1986).

—— (ed.), *The Kristeva Reader* (Oxford: Blackwell, 1986).

NIETZSCHE, FRIEDRICH, *Ecce Homo: How One Becomes What One Is*, tr. R. J. Hollingdale (1908; Harmondsworth: Penguin, 1979; repr. with new introduction, 1992).

NORRIS, CHRISTOPHER, *What's Wrong with Postmodernism: Critical Theory and the Ends of Philosophy* (New York: Harvester Wheatsheaf, 1990).

OLNEY, JAMES (ed.), *Autobiography: Essays Theoretical and Critical* (Princeton: Princeton University Press, 1980).

—— *Metaphors of Self: The Meaning of Autobiography* (Princeton: Princeton University Press, 1972).

PASCAL, ROY, *Design and Truth in Autobiography* (Cambridge, Mass.: Harvard University Press, 1960).

PLATO, *The Republic*, tr. Paul Shorey, 2 vols. (London: Heinemann, 1969).

—— *The Symposium*, tr. W. R. M. Lamb (London: Heinemann, 1967).

PLUTARCH, *Comment écouter*, tr. Pierre Maréchaux (Payot & Rivages, 1995).

—— 'On Praising Oneself Inoffensively', *Moralia*, tr. Phillip H. de Lacy (London: Heinemann, 1959), vii. 110–69.

PRENDERGAST, CHRISTOPHER, *The Order of Mimesis* (Cambridge: Cambridge University Press, 1986).

RACINE, *Phèdre* (Larousse, 1990).

RAYMOND, F., and PIERRE JANET, *Les Obsessions et la psychasthénie*, 2 vols. (Alcan, 1903).

RIBOT, THÉODULE, *Les Maladies de la volonté* (Germer Baillière, 1883).

RICHARD, JEAN-PIERRE, *Littérature et sensation* (Éditions du Seuil, 1954).

RICHARDS, I. A., *Principles of Literary Criticism* (1924; 2nd edn. London: Routledge & Kegan Paul, 1967; repr. Routledge, 1995).

RICŒUR, PAUL, *De l'interprétation: Essai sur Freud* (Éditions du Seuil, 1965).

ROBBE-GRILLET, ALAIN, *Pour un nouveau roman* (Éditions de Minuit, 1963).

ROUSSEAU, JEAN-JACQUES, *Du Contrat social* (1762); *Discours sur l'origine et les fondements de l'inégalité parmi les hommes* (1755), in *Œuvres complètes*, ed. B. Gagnebin, R. Osmont, and M. Raymond, 4 vols. (Gallimard, 1959–69).

RUSSELL, BERTRAND, *A History of Western Philosophy* (3rd edn. London: Unwin Hyman, 1984).

SERRES, MICHEL, *Hermès*, 5 vols. (Éditions de Minuit, 1968–80), ii. *L'Interférence* (1972).

SHKLOVSKY, VICTOR, 'Art as Technique', in David Lodge (ed.), *Modern Criticism and Theory: A Reader* (Harlow: Longman, 1988), 15–30.

SPENGEMANN, WILLIAM, 'The Study of Autobiography: A Bibliographical Essay', in *The Forms of Autobiography: Episodes in the History of a literary Genre* (New Haven: Yale University Press, 1980), 170–245.

STAROBINSKI, JEAN, *L'Œil vivant* (Gallimard, 1961).

SULEIMAN, SUSAN RUBIN, *Risking Who One Is: Encounters with Contemporary Art and Literature* (Cambridge, Mass.: Harvard University Press, 1994).

TAMBLING, JEREMY, *Confession: Sexuality, Sin, the Subject* (Manchester and New York: Manchester University Press, 1990).

TAYLOR, GABRIELE, *Pride, Shame and Guilt: Emotions of Self-Assessment* (Oxford: Clarendon Press, 1985).

WAGNER, RICHARD, 'Le Judaïsme dans la musique', *Œuvres en prose*, tr. J. G. Prod'homme and F. Caillé (2nd edn. Delagrave, 1928), vii. 94–123.

WEBER, SAMUEL, *Return to Freud: Jacques Lacan's Dislocation of Psychoanalysis*, tr. Michael Levine (Cambridge: Cambridge University Press, 1991).

WHITE, HAYDEN, *Metahistory: The Historical Imagination in Nineteenth-Century Europe* (Baltimore and London: Johns Hopkins University Press, 1973; repr. 1993).

WHYTE, LANCELOT LAW, *The Unconscious before Freud* (New York: Basic Books, 1960).

WORTON, MICHAEL, and JUDITH STILL (eds.), *Intertextuality: Theories and Practices* (Manchester: Manchester University Press, 1990).

Index

Dreyfus Affair 4, 27, 36–9, 41, 44, 45,
	70–2, 119, 161 n., 221, 230, 232
Dumas, Alexandre 63 n.

Eliot, George 138
Ellison, David R. 109 n.
Elstir 4, 84, 149, 152, 219, 220, 228, 234
Empiricus, Sextus 82 n.
Eumenides 2

Faces of Injustice, The 2
Fauré, Gabriel 234
feminism 6
Finn, Michael R. 141 n.
Flaubert, Gustave 62, 138, 140 n.
Forrester, John 136 n.
'Fort-da' game 50
Foster, Dennis 11
Foucault, Michel 11 n., 80
Fraisse, Luc 101
FRANTEXT 28 n.
Frazer, James 194
Freud, Sigmund 15, 48 n., 50, 97, 102,
	117, 119, 124 n., 126 n., 128, 136, 166
	n., 205, 228
Fromentin, Eugène 10

Galland, Antoine 78, 81
Gallimard, Gaston 217 n.
Gaubert, Serge 34 n., 120 n.
Gaudí y Cornet, Antoni 95
genetic criticism 16
Genette, Gérard 3 n., 10, 85 n., 98 n.,
	120 n., 217 n.
Gide, André 10
Giotto 1–2, 14, 98 n., 210
Girard, René 34 n., 37 n., 58, 135 n.
Goethe, Johann Wolfgang von 79,
	141 n.
Golo 39
Gosse, Philip Henry 58 n.
Grasset, Bernard 217 n., 220
Griffiths, Eric 138 n.

Hahn, Reynaldo 13
Halévy, Fromental 162
Hegel, G. W. F. 79–80
Hodson, Leighton 15 n.
Hughes, Edward 37 n.
Hugo, Victor 63 n.
Huxley, Thomas Henry 89 n.

Indifférent, L' 12 n.
intermittence 24, 51, 66, 123 n.

Jacques le Fataliste 79
Jakobson, Roman 217 n.
James, Henry 181 n.
Jay, Paul 11 n.
Jean Santeuil 12, 13, 41
Jefferson, Ann 186 n.

Kant, Immanuel 25
Keats, John 156
Kierkegaard, Søren 138
Kolb, Philip 12–13 n.
Krailsheimer, A. J. 136 n.
Kristeva, Julia 13, 26 n., 53 n., 121 n.,
	132, 161–2

La Bruyère, Jean de 134, 167
La Rochefoucauld, François, duc de
	167
Lacan, Jacques 97, 102, 108 n., 126 n.
Lalande, André 17
Landru 86
Laplanche, Jean 128 n.
Leconte de Lisle, Charles-Marie-René
	162
Lejeune, Philippe 11 n., 12, 98–9 n.,
	121 n.
Lévinas, Emmanuel 176–7
Life and Opinions of Tristram Shandy, The
	79
Lohengrin 62
Louis XIV 59
Lucretius 67 n.

McDonald, Christie 174 n.
Maeterlinck, Maurice 50 n.
magic lantern 39
Malebranche, Nicolas 18–23, 24,
	26
Mardrus, Joseph 78
Mauriac, N. 176 n.
mémoire involontaire 4, 88 n., 103,
	123 n.
Mille et Une Nuits, Les 78, 80–1
Mille Nuits et Une Nuit, Les 78
Milly, Jean 76, 120 n.
Montaigne, Michel Eyquem de 78,
	167
Mourey, Gabriel 101
Mozart, Wolfgang Amadeus 63
Muller, Marcel 8–9, 147 n.
Musset, Alfred de 64
mutuelle conservation of passions 21